Praise for *Exponential Groups*

"Wouldn't it be great to have all of your people connected to groups in which they can do life together, learn about God, and encourage each other? The problem is that we might be standing in the way of that happening without even knowing it.

If you want to learn how to empower your people to step up and serve, and effectively reach those outside of the church, pick up a copy of *Exponential Groups* by Allen White. Your people have the power to impact the lives of others for God in the long-term, and you can help them discover it."

Greg Surratt, Founding Pastor Seacoast Church, President, Association of Related Churches, author of *Ir-Rev-Rend*

Allen White eats, sleeps, and breathes small groups and the strategies that help churches engage and connect their people. His experience is rich, broad, and deep. Not only will his stories of success inspire you, but his stories of what hasn't worked will give you confidence in his advice. If you are serious about groups this book will give you plenty to chew on and encouragement for the journey.

Rick Rusaw, Lead Pastor, LifeBridge Christian Church, Longmont, CO, Author of *The Neighboring Church* and *The Externally Focused Church*

"What you'll find in the pages of this book is time-tested strategy to exponentially multiply your small group ministry. Allen has the heart of a pastor, the wit of a standup comedian, and the experience of a professional football coach. If you are a senior pastor or a small group champion and want to take your ministry to the next level, I would order this book for yourself and your entire leadership team."

Brett Eastman, Founder and President, Lifetogether Ministries, Author of the *Doing Life Together* curriculum series.

"Allen has written a terrific book from the seat of a practitioner. Having helped countless churches start and maintain small groups ministries, Allen's voice is one to be trusted. But beware: only read this book if you're ready for your small groups to grow!"

Steve Gladen, Saddleback Church, Small Groups Pastor Author, *Small Groups with Purpose* and *LEADING Small Groups with Purpose*

"All of us learn from others. Allen has had the opportunity not just to learn from the best, but to be with and work alongside the best. No other small group book that I have read in my lifetime has captured the principles and practices of generations of group gurus as has *Exponential Groups*."

Rick Howerton, Church Consultant for the Kentucky Baptist Convention, Author of *A Different Kind of Tribe: Embracing the New Small Group Dynamic*

"Pastors know Christ-centered groups make thriving disciples. The hard part is developing a clear, workable strategy that empowers leaders, launches groups and connects people. Allen's book just made the hard part a whole lot simpler! A true gift."

Dr. Bill Donahue, best-selling small groups author and leadership coach.

"I'm thankful Allen White has leveraged two decades of leading, launching, coaching, studying and unleashing the power of small groups. Every church leader who would like to take their small groups ministry to the next level will benefit from his insights and experience."

Gene Appel, Senior Pastor, Eastside Christian Church, Anaheim, CA

"If you're ready to take your small group ministry to the next level, Allen White's *Exponential Groups* is a perfect playbook. Very few people have Allen's deep experience in helping small group ministries grow exponentially."

Mark Howell, Pastor of Communities, Canyon Ridge Christian Church

"I don't know anyone who has worked with more churches on maximizing their small groups than Allen White. In *Exponential Groups: Unleashing Your Church's Potential,* Allen takes that wealth of experience and breaks it down for every church to easily digest and implement immediately. If your goal is to connect a lot of people into community in a short amount of time, then this book is for you."

Chris Surratt, Discipleship and Small Group Specialist, LifeWay Christian Resources, Author of *Small Groups for The Rest Of Us*

"This book, *Exponential Groups*, is one of the most practical, applicable books on small groups that I have ever read. As a Lead Pastor, I have believed in small group ministry as a key competent of effective local church ministry for over twenty-five years. Small groups, however, are always more messy and challenging to manage. Allen White's thinking on this subject is clear, compelling, and effective. At Allison Park Church, we are using the plans laid out in *Exponential Groups* as a manual for how to execute on a higher level than ever before."

Jeff Leake, Lead Pastor, Allison Park Church,
Author of *Praying with Confidence*

"Allen White is one of the world's leading thinkers in Small Group Ministry. The practical tools he presents in *Exponential Groups* coupled with his easy-to-read writing style will keep your attention and equip you for better small group ministry. If you want your small group ministry to achieve greater things faster, then this book is for you!"

Alan Danielson, CEO at Triple Threat Solutions,
a ministry consulting firm.

"Allen is a groups genius and *Exponential Groups* is a gift to churches serious about building meaningful community."

Caleb Anderson, author of *Favor with Kings*,
Lead Pastor of Mariners Church Huntington Beach

"True to Allen's conversational writing style, *Exponential Groups* is full of practical small group resources that come from real life experience in an enjoyable, easy to read book."

Naki Theo, Small Groups Spanish Pastor, Lakewood Church

"*Exponential Groups* is a powerful, biblical resource that puts Allen White's decades of experience leading group life into your hand. No matter the size of your congregation, Allen's mindset and hard-won strategies will open a new chapter in the life and growth of small groups in your church community."

Herbert Cooper, Senior Pastor of People's Church,
Author of *But God Changes Everything*

"*Exponential Groups* brings to light a plethora of ideas and practices for the Small Group Point Person. You will walk away with new approaches to your Small Group system as Allen shares transparently from his ministry's successes and failures. Allen communicates the foundational structure of Small Group Ministry in the three sections: Strategy, Launch, and Structure has the added guidance of statements such as "This is not your work," which is a bolstering statement that clarifies for readers the need to share the load of small group ministry."

**Eddie Mosley, Small Group Pastor, LifePoint Church, Smyrna, TN,
Author of *Connecting in Communities:
Understanding the Dynamics of Small Groups***

"Every ministry leader I know who is involved in group life wants to see more leaders developed who can lead more healthy groups that are making more disciples and living out Christ's mission. But how? Allen White knows how from his wide experience, and I love how he shows rather than just tells leaders how to develop a practical strategy—one that is not overly programmatic, but is organic and relational. Allen shows the leader step-by-step how to implement this strategy, and even includes what to avoid as well as roadblocks and obstacles to watch for."

**Michael C. Mack, Owner, Small Group Leadership
(www.smallgroupleadership.com),**

"Allen is the real deal, bringing insightful, strategic, and practical help for an area of ministry he is passionate and experienced in. Timely resource!"

Doug Slaybaugh, Partner and Lead Trainer, the Paterson Center

"Allen is a respected and diverse practitioner, who cuts through the rabbit trails of unrehearsed theory, and offers his hard-earned wisdom with disarming wit and piercing clarity. *Exponential Groups* captures his balance of being a can-do strategist that is realistic and honest about what works and what doesn't. By standing on his shoulders, you will be empowered to grow healthy group life and reach more people with the Gospel."

**Reid Smith, Director of Discipleship—
Christ Fellowship Church, West Palm Beach, FL**

"Allen White was instrumental in helping our church move to a whole new level of effectiveness in our small group ministry. This book provides a practical and positive game plan for helping your church take transformational next steps in your groups. If you're ready to develop disciples, build community, and grow your church, this book is for you!"

**Matthew Hartsfield, Lead Pastor of Van
Dyke Church, Tampa, Florida.**

"What I love about this book is that it's not gimmicks and empty promises. It's real life, and it challenges you to think deeply and creatively about connecting people into meaningful relationships. It's what I love about Allen White too! He isn't just giving you a research paper, and it isn't "what studies have shown." Allen has spent most of his ministry creatively and courageously helping churches and leaders create life together. I've watched him do it up close and personal . . . and it works."

**David Larson, Senior Pastor, New Life
Christian Center, Turlock, CA**

"Clear, practical, and doable direction from an experienced and wise guide who has hiked the small group path. His words will show you what to avoid and point you the way forward. Read and discover how the Spirit can use these words to shape your groups in new ways."

M. Scott Boren, author of *Missional Small Groups*

EXPONENTIAL GROUPS

EXPONENTIAL GROUPS
UNLEASHING YOUR CHURCH'S POTENTIAL

ALLEN WHITE

HENDRICKSON PUBLISHERS

Exponential Groups: Unleashing Your Church's Potential

Copyright © 2017 Allen White
Hendrickson Publishers Marketing, LLC
P. O. Box 3473
Peabody, Massachusetts 01961-3473
www.hendrickson.com

ISBN 978-1-61970-841-9

Printed in the United States of America

First Printing—February 2017

Library of Congress Cataloging-in-Publication Data

A catalog record for this title is available from the Library of Congress
Hendrickson Publishers Marketing, LLC ISBN 978-1-61970-841-9

To all of the Doug Howards, who will discover they
are the leaders they never knew they were.

TABLE OF CONTENTS

ACKNOWLEDGMENTS

I am grateful to so many people who have invested in me over the years: my parents, Rudy and Alice White; my pastors Clare Rose, Paul Sandgren, and Richard Peterson; and too many friends to name.

I am thankful to the two pastors I served: Dave Larson from New Life Christian Center in Turlock, California; and Perry Duggar from Brookwood Church in Simpsonville, South Carolina. Thank you for letting me experiment with small groups and for supporting the success we discovered.

Thank you to so many churches across North America who allowed me to play in their small group sandboxes. You have been an amazing laboratory to try new things. You have taught me so much.

I am especially grateful to my wife, Tiffany, who endured two moves, many trips, and my long hours to support the ministry. Thank you to my children: Sam, Timothy, Julia, and Jesse. I love being in your small group.

Then there's Brett Eastman, my creative genius friend, who changed my thinking about groups and opened up so many doors. I am forever grateful.

Special thanks to so many small group friends in the world: Carl George, Joseph Myers, Steve Gladen, Bill Donahue, Eddie Mosley, Mark Howell, and Michael Mack. You are all gurus, but only Carl will be "Yoda."

FOREWORD

Small groups are a big part of what we do at Venture Church in Los Gatos, California, and at Living on the Edge, where we've witnessed hundreds of thousands of people start groups all over the world. Over the years I've seen a lot of small group strategies and big ideas come and go. I've seen some pastors practically wreck their churches to start small groups. I have also seen big group launches start with a bang and end with a whimper.

But small groups are far more than a church program or ministry methodology. As I wrote in my book, *True Spirituality*,

> Small groups are a means, authentic community is the goal. Authentic community is powerful. Authentic community is something we all long for. Authentic community goes way beyond simply being on a team or being a part of a club. Authentic community occurs when the real you shows up and meets real needs for the right reason in the right way. It's when the love of Christ is shared and exchanged with vulnerability, sacrifice, and devotion. It's a place where you can be just who you are and be loved in spite of your struggles, hang-ups, and idiosyncrasies.'"

And small groups are the container in which authentic community is formed.

None of us want to create something new for the sake of something new. We want effective strategies which will grow our people and expand the kingdom of God, a place where people experience life on life and have the freedom to grow their gifts. Our people don't need more hoops to jump through. They need a place where they can connect in community in such a way that their faith grows, a place where grace is extended to others and real disciples are made.

A little while back, I met Allen White. He has served churches and groups for over twenty-five years both as a small group pastor and as a coach to well over one thousand churches across North America. One of those churches was mine. We started four hundred new small groups in a single church-wide campaign, then saw many of those groups continue on.

In this book, you will find a balance between new strategies and respect for what is already working in your church. You will see how you can build something new alongside something old and live to tell about it. Above all else, you will see how your people can become an army of leaders to create authentic community in your church to impact your city or town.

Allen offers practical insights and proven steps to start new groups in your church, whether you've been at groups for a long time or are just getting started. These are principles from the trenches, not unproven theories. What Allen has done in his own churches and in our church will work for your church as well. This isn't a cookie-cutter strategy that treats every church exactly the same. No two churches are really the same. The variety and flexibility you will discover in this book will help you make a custom fit for your congregation.

The end result isn't bragging rights about statistics related to how many people were connected into groups. No, the end result is far more important than that. Your people will experience community, mature in their faith, and become difference-makers in their world, for the glory of God.

Chip Ingram
Senior Pastor—Venture Christian Church
Teaching Pastor—Living on the Edge

INTRODUCTION

Everyone is already in a group.

When I say "group," something from years of church Bible studies comes to mind. You might protest that there are plenty of people who aren't in groups like this. But it's true. Everyone is already in a group, it's just not the group you have in mind. People are in groups called families, friends, coworkers, neighbors, soccer moms, and many others. If your question is *how are these church groups?* I want to suggest you change your question to *what can these groups do intentionally about their spiritual growth?*

When Pastor Troy Jones from New Life Church in Renton, Washington, stood up and invited his 2,500 adults to gather their friends for a six-week study, three hundred adults volunteered to lead a group. At first glance, hundreds and hundreds of people immediately "joined groups." But the truth is, they were already in these groups. The additions were a sermon-aligned curriculum, on-the-job training, and a support structure to help them, but, overall, these groups weren't strangers who became friends. They were friends becoming closer to each other and closer to God.

I've seen this happen in churches of fifty members and churches of over twenty thousand, but I didn't start out thinking about groups this way.

Over twenty years ago, when we first launched groups at New Life Christian Center in Turlock, California, I believed all of our "sheep" were lost without a "shepherd," and there is definitely some truth to that. I looked out at our congregation of 250 or so adults and felt we needed to do something to get our people connected, since our church had rapidly grown from eighty-five to 250. As

Rick Warren says, "Our church must always be growing larger and smaller at the same time. . . . there must be a balance between the large group celebrations and the small group cells."[1]

My senior pastor and I handpicked nine mature couples to join me and start groups. We invited our congregation to sign up for one of these groups for twelve months. Every group chose their own curriculum. I led a monthly huddle and, for the most part, was the sole coach. The groups went strong for twelve months, then all ten of them quit, including mine.

Not only was my method not multiplying groups, it wasn't even adding. It was time to get serious about groups if they were ever going to work at our church.

I spent the summer of 1997 on sabbatical and studied churches and their groups. I attended fifteen different church services and interviewed a dozen pastors. I read about a dozen books. At the end of that research effort, our church set out to start groups in a different way from our previous attempt. We decided to start groups using the findings Carl George presents in *Prepare Your Church for the Future*, which were popularized by the small group model at Willow Creek Community Church. I recruited two mature leaders to coach and ten more leaders to lead, and we started a turbo group—a temporary group designed to give leaders a crash course in group life, then help them launch groups of their own. In the six weeks of the turbo group, we covered all of the basics of group life. (Well, at least as many basics as you can cover in six weeks.) Then we launched groups.

People filled out sign-up cards to join groups, and all of the groups started on the same study about building community. This time all of the groups were starting from the same DNA. All of our leaders were expected to identify apprentice leaders who would be trained, then eventually released to start their own groups. This time we were going to move from a group method that produced no new groups to a system that would give us new groups hand over fist. Our total number of groups would grow by double or better every year. We dreamed that in just five years all of our adults would be connected into groups.

But none of my leaders could find an apprentice.

I plugged along with a new turbo group every year. I would handpick the new recruits. Some years we launched ten new groups. Other years, we launched only two. A couple of years we launched none. After seven years of pounding this nail, we had 30 percent of our eight hundred adults in groups, but we were stuck.

The thought of connecting everybody in a group was my dream, but we weren't growing past 30 percent. We were slugging it out the old-fashioned way—raise up an apprentice, birth a group, and deal with the aftermath—but we were headed nowhere.

I thought my senior pastor was in favor of small groups, but not enough. My small group leaders were stifled by the whole apprenticing-multiplication process. None of them could find an apprentice in their group. Some of them had started greeting me on Sunday morning with "I'm working on my apprentice." I thought, "Whatever happened to 'Hello'?" (I didn't consider how often, when I handpicked my new recruits, I was plucking potential apprentices from under the noses of my group leaders.) Only one guy, named Carlos, ever trained an apprentice and launched a new group in our church. It seemed that connecting everyone was only a pipe dream.

Then, a few months later, at a gathering of church leaders, I listened as Brett Eastman, from Lifetogether, and Kent Odor, from Canyon Ridge Christian Church in Las Vegas, shared how they had connected large numbers in their congregations in a relatively short period of time. I heard how groups could multiply without dividing. I learned how people overlooked in recruiting would actually start some of the best new groups.

I was intrigued, but unconvinced.

There were some decisions to make. On the 350-mile drive home, I began to think about what my senior pastor, David Larson, was the most passionate about. At the time, it was the approaching release of *The Passion of the Christ*, the Mel Gibson movie everyone was buzzing about. Dave had planned a message series and ordered a banner for our church sign on the highway. He was passionate about *The Passion*.

The light suddenly came on: Why not launch small groups based on *The Passion*?

And that's exactly what we did. I asked Dave to invite anyone willing to open their hearts and their homes to a group of people for a six-week study to host a group. In one day, our church of eight hundred adults doubled the number of groups! After Easter, we added 50 percent more new groups in another campaign. Things were getting out of control in a very good way!

When fall hit, we started recruiting for the biggest launch of the year. Pastor Dave aligned his weekly messages with a video-based curriculum we had produced ourselves. We took fifty verses from the Bible and asked fifty members of the church to write a one-page devotional, which we then compiled into a book. When it was all said and done, we had enough groups for 125 percent of our average adult attendance and had given out 1,088 study guides. Well over 100 percent of our average adult attendance was plugged into a group!

We were all in awe. The pipe dream was suddenly a reality.

I realized the only reason the church had been stuck on that plateau was because of a mental block. It was like back in the 1950s when everyone said no man could ever run a four-minute mile. It was just a dream. Then, on May 6, 1954, Roger Bannister ran the mile in 3:59.4 minutes. After that, many runners broke that barrier. Four minutes wasn't a physical barrier. It was a mental block.

Our church had just broken the four-minute mile. Churches could actually start groups that would involve the majority of the congregation and then reach their communities through community!

This wasn't about numbers, though. One man named Ken invited his coworkers to join him for a study on *The Passion*. Two of them accepted Christ.

When one guy named David was asked, "What motivates you to continue your group?" he replied, "My dad showed up." Because of a painful experience years before, David's dad had turned his back on church. But though he refused to walk through the church doors, he was willing to attend a small group meeting at his son's house. That was his first step back toward God.

Our small groups began to reach out beyond the congregation. Groups served hot meals to the homeless every Friday night. One lady took the study to a local women's shelter.

Groups met in coffee shops, restaurants, bookstores, community rooms at apartment complexes, homes, and even on a commuter train. Once we gave our people the freedom to form groups in more flexible ways, they became very creative about the groups they would lead.

Connecting 100 percent of a congregation in groups is far more than a sales pitch. Connecting 100 percent is the first step in reaching beyond the walls of your church and connecting your community. In the pages that follow, you will read about principles that have unlocked amazing growth and community outreach for church after church. It can happen in your church too, if you are willing!

Allen White
Simpsonville, SC
October 2015

THE STRATEGY

CHAPTER 1

LAUNCHING GROUPS AND LIVING TO TELL ABOUT IT

Why groups?

The easy answer, from a pastor's perspective, is because people are already in groups.

When a woman approached the small group table one Sunday at our church in California and said to me, "I meet with three friends every Thursday morning at Starbucks. Could we do the study together?" I knew we were on to something.

Alfred, another group leader, came to me asking for a second set of curriculum materials. My response was, "Dude, you didn't lose your materials, did you? That's like seventy bucks!"

He said, "No, no. Vicki and I are doing our couples' group, but I need another set for the guys I work with at the shop." Alfred was a mechanic at a local GM dealership.

Groups work because people are already in them. I didn't have to tell the lady to hang out at Starbucks, meet three random strangers, and do a study with them. She and her friends were already a group and were already meeting. They just needed to do something intentional to grow spiritually.

Alfred didn't need another group. He was already in two, simply by virtue of being himself. Now, as the small group pastor, I immediately embraced the trajectory of my percentages if every group leader led two groups. Alfred's reason was more pure. He wasn't thinking about this group as a professional goal. He believed his coworkers would enjoy and benefit from our church's study. Of course, he was right.

From both ministry and personal perspectives, there are plenty of good reasons people are drawn to groups.

GROUPS TAKE YOU BEYOND FOUR WALLS

The church I served in California had a 25,000-square-foot facility, which the members built themselves over a three-and-a-half-year period with ongoing construction and repairs for the next twenty or so years. We learned that a church could create their own facility and stay out of debt, which was tremendous. Money could be used for ministry and not interest payments. We also learned that roofing should be left to the professionals. We did the best we could, but on the roof, we lacked some expertise.

On a weekly basis, we used up every square foot of that building with classes and Bible studies. From the original midweek service to elective classes to support groups and Awana, we used the facility well. We expanded a little for children's and student ministry, but we hit a limit. As our church continued to grow, we could no longer accommodate adults, children, and students in the building. Something had to give.

So, for the most part, we kicked the adults out. We made space for Celebrate Recovery and a few other support groups, but adult groups needed new space. We found the new space in property we already owned and places we shared with others. When we changed our mind-set, we realized our church had hundreds of millions of dollars of property in the homes of our members spread across four counties along the Highway 99 corridor.

In my last few years at the church, we averaged about eight hundred adults on the weekend. As we cast vision for groups, we discovered 105 places where groups could meet outside of the church building. Most of those meeting places were homes. Some of the groups met in a third place like Starbucks or the breakroom at a GM dealer. We didn't need to build another square foot of education space for adults. We already had it.

The discipleship of your adults and the growth of your groups is only limited to available space. If that space is on campus during certain hours of the week like Sunday morning and Wednesday night, then you have a great limitation on how much more you can do. But, if you add that space and the places they frequent, there is no limit to who you can reach.

GROUPS WILL MULTIPLY (BUT NOT THE WAY YOU THINK)

In my early attempts at multiplying groups, I personally re-cruited each leader, trained them, launched them (or attempted to), and then coached each one. I encouraged/required/threatened each group leader to develop an apprentice leader who would eventually step out of the group to start another group. My five-year plan was to increase the number of groups so that everyone in my church would be connected into a group. Things didn't go as planned.

Seven years into my five-year plan only 30 percent of our adults were in groups. I pushed the leaders harder to find apprentices. The leaders worked harder to avoid me. Only one group leader ever trained an apprentice and launched a new group. (Some have de-bated with me that the apprentice model works well in "educated" congregations—thanks for the insult. I do think culture is a factor. I have come to believe the apprentice model works really well outside of North America. More on this as we go!)

I joined a coaching group with about forty other pastors led by Brett Eastman. If you know Brett, then you understand his purpose in life is to disrupt your thinking and stretch your elastic well beyond its reasonable capacity. He wasn't content with any church connecting 100 percent of their average adult attendance into groups. Brett wanted to connect 100 percent of a church's Easter attendance. My system wasn't designed to go there.

I wrestled with these ideas. I pleaded with God, "God, I can't re-lease leadership to just anyone. I need to know and trust the people. I need to train them and keep a close relationship with them. We need more small groups, but we've got to have quality control."

God talked back, "Allen, when you say 'quality control,' quality is your excuse." God tends to play rough with me. He was right. To paraphrase Rick Warren, "You can structure for control or for growth, but you can't structure for both."[2] My groups system was structured for control.

Over the next six months, I experimented with the structure of groups. Many very qualified people who successfully gather groups simply didn't regard themselves as group leaders, so we decided to make a change at that point of confusion. We started our new structure with HOST homes, which changed the perception of the role from "leader" to "host." In this approach, HOST is an acronym which stands for:

H—have a heart for people.

O—open your place (meet in a home, coffeehouse, restaurant, or workplace).

S—serve a snack.

T—turn on the DVD.[3]

The first time we implemented the HOST strategy with a self-produced video curriculum based on our pastor's teaching, we doubled our groups in one day. I had worked for seven years, remember, to get 30 percent of our adults into groups. Now, in one day, we had groups for 60 percent of our adults. It was a stunning success. For a while.

We discovered the HOST home strategy worked to get us to the two-thirds point in group connection, but then stalled. It wouldn't get us completely to 100 percent of our members in groups.

On a coaching call with Brett Eastman and Mark Howell, someone suggested we put curriculum in gift bags and offer them to anyone who wanted to do the study with friends. It just so happened that I had overbought curriculum for our second group launch by thirty-one group packs, so we decided to give it a try.

My senior pastor challenged our congregation: if they weren't in a HOST home, then they could pick up one of these bags and do the study on their own with their friends. The curriculum bags went fast. By the end of the second service, we had run out. I pulled our pastor aside and told him not to pitch the idea in the third service.

The next week on our coaching call, I remember Mark Howell asking if anyone had any exciting updates from the past weekend.

I told the coaching group how we had offered the gift bags and started thirty-one "groups" on the fly. Mark responded, "Dude, that's awesome! You're the first one to do that."

The "Gather and Go" strategy was born.

In coaching and training leaders, we treated everyone the same whether they started a traditional small group in the first seven years, a HOST home group, a "Gather and Go" group, or some other variation on one of those strategies. More options gave us more opportunity to connect people into groups. One size did not fit all.

One Sunday morning I was standing at the small group table when a very confused man walked up. He waved a postcard I had sent him about leadership training. (Remember postcards? They were printed on the copy machine, addressed, stamped, and sent through the mail. We email now. It's cheaper.) The man waving the card said, "I don't understand why I keep getting these postcards in the mail. I am doing the study with my friends, but we are not a small group and I'm not the leader, so I don't understand why I'm getting these postcards for leadership training."

I just smiled at him and said, "Don't worry about it." In that moment I began to imagine what it would be like if what this man just described to me became the normal experience of every believer—a group of friends gathered together in community to study God's word and do something about it. I can't wait for that day.

Another change in my thinking came when I was sitting at dinner with my small group team and Carlos spoke up. (You remember Carlos? He's the only group leader who ever developed an apprentice.) He said, "I was talking to Rick the other day. Rick is so excited about his group. He says this is the best thing he'd ever done."

I looked at Carlos and said, "Who's Rick?" This was a big step in my thinking. We had reached a point where not only was I not recruiting, training, launching, and coaching each leader personally, now I didn't even know all of the leaders. But I knew Carlos, and Carlos was getting to know Rick.

Then I thought, "What if I was still doing this the old way? I didn't know Rick. I hadn't met Rick. Rick never would have been invited to lead a group in my old system. What if my fear of turning people loose to lead groups had prevented Rick from discovering 'the best thing he'd ever done'? Then, shame on me." There were many, many more Ricks to come.

Fast-forward to a church of 6,500 I served in South Carolina. I didn't even attempt to get to know everyone who volunteered to lead. But, each member of the small group team oversaw coaches who connected with the leaders. Every leader needed to be in relationship with someone, but they couldn't all be in relationship with me. And, they didn't need to be in relationship with me.

In a structure designed for control, I saw 30 percent of our adults connected into groups. When I changed the approach to a structure designed for growth, 125 percent of our average adult attendance was connected into groups within six months of changing the structure. (Now, 125 percent is not funny pastor math. Not everyone attends every Sunday, but they go to their group.) My elastic had stretched beyond our weekend attendance and was now pushing toward our Easter attendance. And, of course, not everyone in groups even attended our church.

A few years ago, I worked with Van Dyke Church in the Tampa area. If you've spent much time in Tampa, you know that traffic is a big deal. Van Dyke is located in Lutz, which is in the north suburbs of Tampa. People working in downtown Tampa had trouble getting home in time for a small group. So, they didn't. An engineer started a group in his engineering firm in downtown Tampa during lunch. Many people from the office joined the study, and even the company's insurance agent joined the group.

When the group was invited into a second study, the insurance agent asked if he could have a copy of the study to start a group with his coworkers back at the insurance agency. No one from the insurance agency had ever been to Van Dyke Church, but they became a Van Dyke group. It's amazing what will happen when we allow it.

GROUPS WILL GROW YOUR CHURCH

At New Life Christian Center when we launched that initial wave of HOST homes back in 2004, we encountered a dynamic we didn't count on. As I mentioned before, my pastor was already planning a sermon series based on the movie *The Passion of the Christ.* We created our own small group curriculum based on the themes of the movie and the questions it would raise.

Please understand, my motivation was not to create curriculum. It was a lot of hard work. I used my personal video camera, edited the video on my laptop, and drove the master tapes every week to a duplicator in Modesto. We shot the videos one week ahead of when our groups needed the content, so every week I had a VHS tape exchange upstairs by my office. The hosts would turn in last week's tape and collect this week's tape. Then I took the used tapes to the duplicator to become the following week's tape. Whew!

But here's the result we didn't plan on.

We wanted to launch groups to get our members connected into community. We hadn't yet embraced the idea that they were already connected. That would come later. Our belief was that believers gathered together studying God's word and applying it through the influence of the Holy Spirit and each other would produce amazing things. And it did. In fact, it produced some things we didn't plan for.

As our hosts invited their friends, neighbors, coworkers, relatives, and others to join them for the study, we had quite a number of people in groups who had never darkened the doors of our church. When the host invited the group to attend a service together, the group members felt like they already knew our pastor because they had spent several weeks watching his teaching on those good ol' VHS tapes in their friend's living room.

Our groups started out to fulfill the purposes of fellowship and discipleship, but soon became evangelistic without ever calling it "evangelism." Many believers fear evangelism. But going to a movie with their friends seemed natural, even though it was a Christian film. The movie raised questions, so friends were invited to the group. The group started in a comfortable place for them—their friend's living room. This led to an invitation to church, which challenged them, but they went with their friend to hear teaching from our pastor, whom they already liked from the videos.

Our intent wasn't to start a side-door strategy for evangelism or church growth, but that's exactly what happened. Of course, over the years we had many different evangelistic emphases. All of them worked to some extent. But, for most people, evangelism felt unnatural. They felt required to memorize a bunch of stuff, put themselves in an uncomfortable position with a friend, and then make a sales pitch hoping they would succeed, but most of all hoping they wouldn't lose a friend in the process.

I remember my friend Carl George sharing a group leader's complaint, "My group members won't attend our group because they keep going out to the movies with their friends."

Carl replied, "Well, thank God that your group members have friends." Their relationships with unchurched friends provided the potential for growth through evangelism and invitations to church. If they had spent their Friday nights in small group meetings, these relationships could suffer. Now the moral of the story is not to cancel all of our groups and go to the movies, but bringing people into a group context by leveraging existing relationships, then inviting those folks to church when they're ready to consider that, is certainly a pretty awesome by-product of group life.

WHAT ABOUT EXISTING GROUPS?

A while back I watched a webcast of a pastor announcing a new small group model at his church. Their current model had connected roughly half of their members into groups, but it wasn't attracting the other half. He felt the solution was to scrap their current model and move to a new model. I actually screamed at my computer, "No! Why are you wrecking what works for half of your people? It's working for them!"

The pastor went on to explain that now about 120 of his previous 200 groups were embracing the new model. I chose to withhold my applause. Why? Because he already had those folks in groups! If only a little more than half of the people already in groups were signing onto the new thing, isn't that actually going backward?

IF IT AIN'T BROKE . . .

There is a reason you have the groups you currently do. They are working for somebody. Whether they are connected in Adult Bible Fellowships, inductive Bible studies, Sunday school (*Gasp!* More on this later), or women-addicted-to-Beth-Moore groups, it's working for them. As long as the groups aren't worshipping the devil or talking bad about the pastor, leave them alone.

At Brookwood Church in Simpsonville, South Carolina, we had a very large women's group, more than two hundred members, who met every Wednesday morning and called themselves WOW. They would meet in a large group setting to view teaching by Beth Moore, Priscilla Shirer, Kay Arthur, and others, and then they broke into seventeen different groups that met in the adjacent rooms. When it came time for a church-wide "campaign" with the group curriculum aligned with the weekend messages, I didn't even ask the WOW women to participate. Why?

First, I didn't need to enter into a fight that I wasn't going to win. You can call me a wimp. I call it wise. Why volunteer for unnecessary trouble?

Next, I knew if the WOW women did the church-wide study on Wednesday morning, I was giving their husbands an out. If the ladies were already doing the study, then more than likely, the men weren't going to join a men's group, and they weren't going to do the same study on the same week in a couples' group.

By encouraging WOW to continue on their path of study, the ladies and their husbands also participated together in a couples' group for the church-wide study. Not only were the men involved in groups, I got to count the women twice! Okay, not really, but you understand what I'm saying.

A day will come when membership in a failing initiative will decrease. That is the time to consider a hard conversation about ending the group, class, or ministry. But as long as it's helping someone, it's worth keeping around. If you attempt to transition a ministry too quickly, you will upset its constituency, which could come back in many ways from reduced giving to personal "political" fallout. Don't fight battles that you can't win or that will greatly injure you. Be patient.

WHY DO PASTORS LONG FOR A MAGIC BULLET?

Pastor, there is no one strategy or model that will appeal to your entire congregation. It doesn't exist. At our church in California, we connected 125 percent of our average adult attendance into groups by using five different strategies simultaneously. Some groups were already established through our metachurch strategy. Others started groups as a HOST home. Some took a small group vacation and left their existing groups to start new groups with the option of returning to their existing groups. (They did not return.) For some, none of those strategies worked, so they just got together with friends and did the study on their own. No one was the "leader," and they didn't call themselves a "group." There were workplace groups and hobby groups and even a few adult classes that embraced the study in their on-campus setting. If they didn't say "Yes" to one strategy, we kept offering new ones until they had something to say "Yes" to.

People have asked me, "Wasn't that confusing to the groups?" Actually, it wasn't. Each group only used one strategy. Was it confusing to me? That actually doesn't matter, does it?

If one strategy could connect every member in our church, if one model could work for everyone, it would be a pastor's dream come true. Why? Because it's efficient, or, dare I say, convenient. For busy pastors, it's easier to manage one system, not three, four, or five.

But on that score, merely forming small groups in the first place could contribute to more problems. Rather than individuals leaving the church, now they might leave linking arms. (Keep reading. It's okay.) If groups offer care, encouragement, fellowship, Bible study, and leadership development, can that only happen in an off-campus group? What if a Sunday school class was accomplishing those things? What if your existing groups were already doing that? Isn't this meeting your goal? Isn't this building people up?

Your members are looking for variety, not uniformity. Look at how many car models were made last year. Look at how many new books appear on the shelves of Barnes & Noble. Look at how many ways you can drink coffee at Starbucks. The blue-plate special died fifty years ago.

DO NEW THINGS WITH NEW PEOPLE

Men don't join groups for the same reasons as women. Younger generations are motivated differently than older generations. Some folks will join because they ought to. Others will see what's in it for them. Still others will see a chance to make a difference together. And, some will think the whole thing is lame. That's okay.

When new freshmen enter college, they are given a college catalog. The catalog delineates all of the requirements to graduate with a chosen degree. If the college chooses to change any of the requirements along the way, they do so with the incoming freshmen. They can't make the changes with the upperclassmen. Their contract, if you will, was established during their freshman year.

Your existing groups are like the upperclassmen. They came in while you were doing groups, classes, or Bible studies a certain way. If a model is reaching the end of its effectiveness, try something new with the new groups. Don't force them into the existing model. Discover what will work for them. Similarly, while you can always invite existing groups to try something new, you should refrain from making the change mandatory. Again, if you lose what you have for the sake of something new, you're just being stupid. (Some take offense when I say this. "Are you calling me stupid?" I tell them, "No, because you're not going to do that.")

When we launched our groups for *The Passion of the Christ* at New Life years ago, we didn't even tell our existing groups what we were doing. Partly because we were in a bit of a rush, having decided to launch the groups only three weeks before the series started, but also because we already had the existing groups. We just needed to build on that.

My leaders came to me and asked, "Can our group do *The Passion* study or is it only for new groups?"

Being the kind, compassionate pastor I am, I said, "What's it worth to you?" Nearly all of our existing groups participated in the study. They didn't have to, but they wanted to. You attract more flies with honey.

ONE SIZE DOES NOT FIT ALL

When I arrived at Brookwood Church in Simpsonville, South Carolina, about 30 percent of the adults were in groups. It was a solid foundation. We had on-campus groups, off-campus groups, Beth Moore Bible study groups, and the Holy Smokers, who focused on Bible and barbecue. We launched lots of new groups through church-wide campaigns. We connected hundreds of new folks to groups. We gained another 30 percent in groups. Sixty percent ain't bad.

But, as I became better acquainted with the congregation, I discovered that some in the Bible Belt really were intimidated by the Bible. They resisted small groups because they were afraid they would have nothing to contribute to the discussion. Whoa. (In California, we just asked folks to do a study with their friends. They did it. But this was a whole other deal.)

We created large groups for men, women, young couples, businesspeople, law enforcement, and senior adults. These are what Carl George calls "fishing ponds."[4] In these large groups people could move from the crowd of a 2,500 seat auditorium to a living room of a few friends, old or new, with a temporary stop in a mid-sized group.

We offered a solid recreation ministry for adults and children. We created a system of classes called BrookwoodU where people could get to know each other while they learned cooking, digital photography, leadership, Microsoft Word, sign language, and even hermeneutics. (Many friendships were forged in their hermeneutical fox holes.)

I didn't join the staff of a megachurch to start classes or to send seniors to Branson, Missouri. But, those not connected into groups didn't necessarily care about what I wanted. What did they need?

After four years, we reached 78 percent of our then five thousand adults connected in small groups, large groups, and BrookwoodU. We didn't get to 100 percent, but maybe someone else can take them there in the future.

You wouldn't transition small groups to a Sunday school model, would you? Start with what's working as a foundation, then figure out what you can add to that.

WHAT ABOUT SUNDAY SCHOOL?

My friend Mike Womble has served for more than a decade in a legacy church in North Carolina, but he admitted in a conversation that small groups are just frustrating to him. Their congregation has weathered many ups and downs over the decades. They are a traditional church whose adult Sunday school attendance rivals their adult worship attendance. He loves the idea of small groups, but how do you do it? I suggested maybe he shouldn't.

I've met a lot of pastors who want to shutter their old school Sunday school to get everyone into home groups. In fact, after seminars, pastors have come up to me and said as much. I would tell them, "I know what your spiritual gift is." Now, I had their attention. "You have the gift of martyrdom." Of course, as Rick Warren says, the problem is you can only use that gift one time.

Again, we need to think about the goal. If we want people to connect with other believers, why can't they connect in Sunday school? Now, there is limited time and most people are sitting in rows, but could you change the seating arrangement to round tables and offer time for interaction and prayer around the tables?

If the reason for wanting small groups over Sunday school is that we want people to serve, well, at my friend Mike's church Sunday school adults serve through missions both local and worldwide. As we get to the core of what we believe is essential to healthy spiritual growth, the form could and should vary greatly. To be pro small groups doesn't require us to be anti Sunday school.

If Sunday school works for some of your people, run Sunday school. Don't expect everyone to go to Sunday school, even though the old song says they "ought" to. If one type of group works for most, but not for all, then let those groups work for most. Do something else with the rest.

When a church introduces small groups into an established ministry, care should be taken to bring existing educational ministries like Sunday schools, Adult Bible Fellowships, and others up to speed. After all, people are down on what they're not up on. They should be reassured that the introduction of a new method for care, Bible application, and serving called "small groups" isn't going to upset their class, fellowship, or large group. My line is that they can continue just as they have, while they are always welcome to join in a church-wide initiative at any time.

As Michael Mack writes in *The Synergy Church*,

> Small groups are often seen as an element of change. A better way of looking at it is to see small groups as agents of change in the congregation. The real change that is desired is spiritual, not physical or structural. Small groups can help make disciples, build relationships that encourage and support, grow people in maturity and service, and build leadership. Most Christians see these as good things. When leadership emphasizes the spiritual transformation desired and that small groups—along with other current forms available in the church—can help bring that transformation about, difficulties such as those discussed here can be lessened in intensity.[5]

A few years back, when I was working with a traditional United Methodist church in South Carolina, the small group director faced exactly this issue. They had a well-established Sunday school, but a very low percentage of their adults participated. The church created their own video-based curriculum with the senior pastor's teaching. They reassured their Sunday school classes that this was not an evil plot for their destruction.

One week on a coaching call, the small group director said an eighty-five-year-old woman confided in her, "Oh we're still doing our Sunday school class." Then, she whispered, "But, some of us girls are getting together during the week for the small group study." Over one thousand of the church's 1,400 adults participated in the church-wide study. No Sunday school class was harmed in the process.

Everyone is already in a group. Some of those groups are called "Sunday school" classes.

STAFF AND CARE OF THE CONGREGATION

No church can afford all of the staff they need or will need in the future. I've worked with churches as small as forty-two members and as large as more than twenty thousand. No church has the budget to hire a shepherd for every sheep, nor should they.

In Jethro's advice to Moses, he says that personal involvement in meeting the needs of a large number of people by one individual is unhealthy for the individual, his or her family, and the people.[6] Jethro advised Moses to select capable people who feared God, were trustworthy, and were not greedy[7] to lead Israel. Some of these leaders would serve small groups of ten people, while others would develop a support structure to serve the leaders in groups of fifty, one hundred, and one thousand.[8]

Scholars estimate the total population of Israel in Moses's day at around two and a half to three and a half million.[9] Most pastors try to manage congregations of dozens, hundreds, or even thousands of people. Moses had millions of people. And yet, many pastors attempt to serve all of the people themselves or hire staff who are soon overwhelmed and burned out. This is not good!

If we applied Jethro's advice to the church, a group leader of "ten" would be cared for by a coach of "fifty" or "one hundred" people. Coaches are in relationship with a leader of "one thousand." This is either the pastor, a staff member, or a community leader (a volunteer leader of leaders of leaders on a small group team). It all depends on the size of the church.

Once Moses embraced this strategy, his load was lighter, the people's satisfaction was higher, and Moses's family was reconciled—indicated by the departure of his father-in-law.[10]

This ministry strategy has existed for thousands of years, yet many pastors ignore its effectiveness out of fear or a need for control. I was once one of those pastors. Yet, my fears limited what

God intended in the churches I've served and the hundreds of churches I've coached.

A BABY OR A LOAF OF BREAD?

I hear a lot of pastors who debate the need for a quality experience at the expense of connecting and growing the vast majority of their congregations and their communities. I also hear the reverse of this, that in order to embrace a large quantity of groups, quality must somehow be sacrificed.

We approach ministry as if we have all of the time in the world. Somehow we think our people will live forever, and so will the people our people need to reach for Christ. But, let's be honest, we don't have the luxury of time.

The apostle Paul didn't have the luxury of time either. Paul never spent more than eighteen months in any one location, yet in his quest to spread the gospel throughout the known world and to reach Spain, he put leaders in place everywhere he planted a church, then gave them the crash course on ministry. We would call this "quick and dirty" before we would call it "quality." Paul gave them their marching orders, then basically instructed them, "Do the best you can. The Holy Spirit will guide you. If you run into trouble, then send me a letter." Then, Paul was off to the next place.

In living with the tension between the quality and quantity of ministry, I want you to consider these words from Peter Drucker:

> . . . there are two different kinds of compromise. One is expressed in an old proverb, "Half a loaf of bread is better than no bread." The other, in the story of the judgment of Solomon, is clearly based on the realization that "half a baby is worse than no baby at all." In the first instance, the boundary conditions are still being satisfied. The purpose of bread is to provide food, and half a loaf is still food. Half a baby, however, does not satisfy the boundary conditions. For half a baby is not half of a living and growing child.

It is a waste of time to worry about what will be acceptable and what a decision maker should or should not say so as not to evoke resistance. . . . In other words, the decision maker gains nothing by starting out with the question, "What is acceptable?" For in the process of answering it, he or she usually gives away the important things and loses any chance to come up with an effective—let alone the right—answer.[11]

In retelling this story, my friend and mentor Carl George once asked this question, which changed the course of my thinking about small group ministry: "Are your groups more like a baby or a loaf of bread? Because if it's like a baby, then half a baby won't do. You want a perfect baby. But, if it's more like a loaf of bread and you're starving, any amount of bread will help to alleviate the hunger."[12]

In managing the tension between quality and quantity, we must figure out a way to embrace the "Genius of the *And*," as coined by Jim Collins.[13] This isn't an either/or circumstance, in that, if there is no quantity, then quality doesn't actually matter. The question is whether the limitation on the quantity is a matter of necessity or a personal need for control.

Everyone is already in a group. Now, how are you willing to help these groups grow?

CHAPTER 2

WHY AN ALIGNMENT?

When Bill Hybels and Willow Creek Community Church dove into reviving their small groups a few years ago, our team helped them develop a new series called *Wiser Together* based on the book of Proverbs. While Bill has certainly published a wide variety of small group curriculum, Willow had never used one to align with the weekend services. After a few weeks of promoting groups, Willow had responses from around 2,100 people to lead a group. Yes, that's *lead* a group. Groups were revived, indeed.

I met Pastor Guillermo Velazquez from House of Faith in Miami, Florida in one of our coaching groups nearly a decade ago. Their church of two hundred adults decided to launch the *40 Days of Purpose* campaign. They "downgraded" the invitation from "leader" to "host" and let their congregation get creative in forming groups. Upon the launch of the series, Pastor Guillermo discovered their groups had connected 350 people from the church and the community. Their church is no longer two hundred people.

To celebrate twenty-five years of ministry, Greg Surratt and Josh Surratt at Seacoast Church in Mt. Pleasant, South Carolina, chose to create a curriculum called *I See a Church* to cast vision for the next twenty-five years. While Seacoast connected a large majority of their members into groups just a couple years before with a self-produced series called *Make Room*, the appeal for the new series helped them to connect 94 percent of their twelve thousand people into groups.

From my personal experience as well as my observations of hundreds of churches that my team has had the privilege to coach over the last decade, I can say with conviction that an aligned series produces leaders, connects members, and catalyzes spiritual growth unlike any other model I have ever seen or attempted. There are other strategies to launch many groups in a church, and we will explore those going forward, but first let's deconstruct an alignment and see how it works.

The key to these successful launches was the involvement of the senior pastor. Whether pastors align their sermons with a purchased "campaign" or create their own, their leadership is significant in recruiting and connecting people into groups.

Let's face it, senior pastors, if your congregation is not connected to each other, the only reason (other than Jesus Christ) they attend your church is you. Now, don't tell your worship pastor. It will break his heart. People attend because they like your teaching. They laugh at your jokes. They connect with your personality.

When you stand up and say, "We've developed this series with my teaching," you are just giving them more of what they already like. When you lead them by saying, "I want everybody in a group for this series," they will follow your leadership. When you invite them to not just join any group, but say, "I want you to get together with your friends and do this study," you have made a new experience comfortable for them and they are much more likely to participate. Your teaching plus your leadership plus an appealing invitation is a win, win, win!

WHAT IS AN ALIGNMENT?

By alignment, I mean a six-week group study which aligns with the weekend sermon series. This goes by several names like church-wide campaign, emphasis, initiative, experience, spiritual growth campaign, and a few others. Now, let me start by saying I do understand some churches have *been there, done that* with an alignment or a church-wide campaign. Maybe your church is one of those. It's okay. While you will gain from the ideas about an alignment, at the end of this chapter I will give you other ideas of how to involve your senior pastor in a group launch without an alignment.

The length of an alignment goes back to some sage advice from Lyman Coleman, who said six weeks is short enough for a man to commit to, yet long enough for a man to sense community. (The operative word there is "man." No offense to the ladies: most don't need six weeks to see this happen!) If your series is a week shorter or a week longer, it's not the end of the world. Anything longer than six or seven weeks becomes too long for a man to commit to. I know some churches have an established system that uses twelve-week semesters for groups. We will address this more later on.

The idea of an alignment series started with David Mains and the Chapel of the Air, at least according to one version of the story. He introduced the "50 Day Spiritual Adventure," with the study aligned to the weekly topics of his radio program. The most popular alignment series were those produced first by Rick Warren and Saddleback Church. An early campaign called "The Millennial Member" was delivered to groups through a study guide and cassette tape. The group would listen to Pastor Rick's teaching via audio only, then discuss the weekly topic, which took the congregation back to the five biblical purposes. The church-wide campaign was born.

The campaign of all campaigns was certainly the *40 Days of Purpose* based on Rick Warren's *The Purpose Driven Life*. Over thirty thousand churches have done this campaign since 2002. Those of us that worked with the material saw some remarkable things.

My church in California was still stuck in my seven years of small group tribulation when the *40 Days of Purpose* came out. This was back when I recruited, trained, coached, and controlled all of our groups. We were excited about the *40 Days of Purpose*, but we saw it as a spiritual growth campaign, not a platform to launch groups. We certainly missed the boat. I think we had three groups form for the campaign, and then all three ended when it was over. If I only knew then what I know now.

A lot was at stake even for Saddleback back then. They have always been innovative with small group strategies such as the Small Group Connection, in which prospective group members were gathered in a room with no designated leaders. By the end of the evening, Steve Gladen and Brett Eastman led them through an exercise where they not only formed groups, but the groups also recruited their leader on the spot. I remember listening to the tapes about Saddleback's connection process back in the early 2000s. It scared me to death. I put the materials in my bottom desk drawer and didn't look at them again for three years. (I've come a long way in my thinking.)

The HOST home strategy emerged with *40 Days of Purpose*. As mentioned in the previous chapter, the bar was lowered on leadership. Anyone could lead a group. Here is Brett Eastman's account of what happened:

> On the eve of the first *40 Days of Purpose* campaign at Saddleback, we had another idea: What if we invited people to host, rather than lead, a group? It seems like such a small change in terminology, but it proved to be a phenomenal factor in rapidly growing our groups.
>
> With the new video curriculum we told our people: "If you have a VCR, you can be a star." Anybody can host a group. More than 3,000 people opened their homes for 6 to 8 weeks. I was overjoyed and overwhelmed. Who were these people, and where did they come from?
>
> The elders and I thought these people must be living in their cars. How long had those people been Christians? Were they Christians? Had they been in a small group? Had they even attended our church?
>
> Glen Kruen, Saddleback's executive pastor, and Tom Holladay, our teaching pastor, helped me create a survey. It showed us that something amazing had happened. The new hosts had, on average, been Christians for 14 or more years. They had attended Saddleback for 10 or more years, and many had attended small groups before. On average they had heard more than 500 of Pastor Rick's messages. They were definitely capable of hosting a video-led study and asking a few questions.
>
> When the dust settled, our team had trained more than 2,000 new hosts and launched another 2,300 groups. Well over 20,000 people joined in a six-week study of *The Purpose Driven Life*, taught by Pastor Rick. Virtually every Christian in our church family was aligned in reading the book and participating in the Forty-Days study.[14]

Many other alignment series have since come from Saddleback and other churches, including *50 Days of Faith* by Rick Warren, *My Near Death Experiment* by Caleb Anderson (Mariners Church in Huntington Beach, California), the *Christian Life Trilogy* by Rev. Charlie Holt (St. Peter's Episcopal Church in Lake Mary, Florida), and many others. Maybe your church has participated in one or more of these.

The synergy of alignment reinforced the teaching in the weekend service and helped principles to stick better in participants' minds as they discussed what the pastor spoke on the weekend before. The church I grew up in offered Sunday school, morning worship, a Sunday night service, and a midweek Bible study. The problem with this model is people received four different messages per week. We couldn't remember all of these, let alone apply them to our lives!

The strength of an alignment lies in helping people take their weekend into their week. They hear the message in the weekend service, then they revisit the same topic in their group. I've participated in groups like this for years. While the weekend service is strong on worship and teaching, the group experience is strong on care, discussion, and application. The message sinks in a lot further.

WHAT TO ALIGN

An alignment can take a couple of different directions. If the goal is to reach the community, then the topic of the series should be heavily felt needs like *40 Days of Purpose* or *One Month to Live* by Kerry Shook at Woodlands Church in The Woodlands, Texas. When we launched *One Month to Live* at Brookwood Church, we sent a postcard out to the community announcing the series. On the first Sunday of the series, our attendance jumped from six thousand to seven thousand people. One thousand new people from the community responded to a compelling topic.

Both of those series have been around for a while, so if you've already done them, there are other clear directions to go, like a series on relationships, marriage, parenting, hope, stress, or other things people face every day. When I was at New Life in California, we did a marriage and family series called *Home Improvement*. (The title was relevant back then.) I challenged our hosts to invite anyone they overheard complaining about their marriage or children. Just that idea filled groups pretty quickly.

The other direction to take is a series focused on the church body. This is good to rally the core and get everybody on the same page. Topics could include the church's mission, vision, and values, or vision casting for the future of the church.

Money management would definitely be more of an insider series, since unchurched people already assume the church just wants their money. But, "mature" believers who don't give can't be considered "mature." This suggestion comes with a caution: because people are so close to their money, this is not a great series to use when *starting* groups. It's not even a great follow-up series. If you want to change behavior toward group life, then focus on that change. To change attitudes and behaviors toward both money and group life simultaneously is too much change to ask for all at once.

The only thing worse than launching groups with a financial series is launching groups with a financial series during a capital campaign. It will brand groups as a fund-raising strategy rather than all of the good things groups really are. A few years ago I worked with a church who was writing a group curriculum for their capital campaign. The topics were money, money, money, and more money. It was pretty clear it wouldn't fly. I asked them why they were raising money. They told me they needed funds for children's ministry, campus expansion, and evangelism. I encouraged them to create a curriculum about that. They could cast vision through the curriculum, and the pastor could do the heavy lifting on fund-raising on the weekend. It wasn't perfect, but it was better.

If you want to reach the community, choose a topic the community will care about. If you want to focus on your members, then choose a topic for them. Members will relate to the "community" series, but the reverse is not always true.

WHAT IF MY PASTOR DOESN'T SPEAK IN SERIES?

Every pastor has a different process for sermon prep. I've worked with a pastor who took a study break every summer and planned fifty-two weeks of sermons and series. I've worked with a pastor who planned a series at a time. And, I've worked with a pastor who started his sermon prep on Saturday. Every pastor is different, and you're probably not going to change their processes. That said, sometimes a pastor who doesn't preach in series will do a series to create an alignment to launch groups. Not always, but sometimes.

Beyond the mechanics of a church-wide campaign or alignment series, the secret to success is the senior pastor's involvement and interest. Without the senior pastor leading the charge, you will end up with a lot of activity, but very little effectiveness. When all is said and done, your senior pastor will seem to have confirmation that church-wide campaigns just don't work at your church. Let's try to avoid that.

If your pastor plans ahead or teaches in series, get ahead of where they are going. Either find a curriculum you can purchase which will align well with their series or create your own curriculum based on the series. Make this as easy as possible for your pastor. If you create your own curriculum, you only need six ten-minute talks from your pastor, then you do the rest. Most pastors will love to see their teaching extend beyond the weekend service and become a group curriculum. Some pastors have even seen their curriculum used by other churches.

If the pastor doesn't speak in series, it's not the end of the world. Think about a topic your pastor is interested in or is a common theme in his or her preaching over the years. It's possible to create a small group curriculum based on your pastor's teaching, then launch it with one sermon on one weekend. The group curriculum doesn't have to align with the weekend message for six weeks in a row, even though alignment makes this stronger. The fact that your pastor has invested time in creating the curriculum will create enough interest in the congregation, and, more importantly, from your pastor, to cause the series to succeed.

If your church wants to purchase a church-wide series, but your pastor does not want to do the weekly message, more than likely, this will not work. The power of the purchased church-wide series is the tie to the pastor's weekend messages. If your pastor does not want to present the series, it won't be an effective tool for a group launch.

STATE UP FRONT WHAT THE CURRICULUM IS AND WHAT IT ISN'T

Church-wide campaigns are a powerful vehicle for connecting congregations into community and impacting spiritual growth. A number of church-wide experiences prove the catalytic impact of a small group study aligned with a sermon series. Churches and their members will never be the same.

One size never fits all, especially in a church-wide campaign. When you invite all of your groups to do the same study that aligns to the weekend service, you might have just set yourself up for trouble. Your groups are made up of new Christians and non-Christians, "mature" Christians and critical ones. How do you meet the needs of all of your different groups with one curriculum?

Over-Promising + Under-Delivering = Great Frustration.

Managing expectations is key to focusing your groups on the right track. If your curriculum is designed for the broadest appeal, you will soon be hearing from your "mature" folks that the study is "lightweight." For the critics I know well, my line usually is, "I can see how you could think that, if you were only talking about the material. . ."

Recently in helping a church full of nuclear engineers and rocket scientists develop a curriculum on the "One Anothers of Scripture," we concluded that if the group members simple memorized all of the One Anothers, then we had failed. Practicing the One Anothers was the key, and it isn't rocket science.

Let your groups know up front how the curriculum is designed and why. "We have created this curriculum for any person to use in doing this study with their friends." It's not that you avoided creating a "deeper" study—boy, that's a loaded word—but, you have intentionally designed or chosen a study to include as many people as possible. After six weeks, groups can choose something that's maybe more to their liking.

DESIGN YOUR CURRICULUM TO MEET A VARIETY OF NEEDS

In designing your own curriculum, you can meet a variety of needs with one study. As my friend Brett Eastman says, "You need to double-clutch the study." At the beginning of the study offer two different icebreaker questions. For new groups and new believers, maybe the question is lighthearted and offers a way for folks to get to know each other. This is something that everyone will feel comfortable talking about. "Who is your favorite superhero and why?" "What was the source of warmth in your home?" "If you were a tree, what kind of tree would you be?" (That last one's a joke.) For more mature believers, the question should go something like, "How did you apply what you learned in last week's study?" Deeper involves doing.

For the rest of the study, you can offer a variety of questions at different levels. For newer folks, you want to start with questions that are easy to answer right out of Scripture. For more mature members, it's good to include a "Deeper in the Word" section that offers more personal questions as well as Scripture cross-references to the core text. The aim in the "Deeper" section is to meet a need for knowledge along with a greater need for application.

The point here is to create different questions for different types of people, and then articulate the study design to the group members. Some groups will use the first half of the study only. Other groups will skip the first section and dive into the deeper questions. Giving group members the full picture of the design will help them to understand and appreciate what you have developed.

You can't please everybody all of the time, but by taking the time to develop your own study with different group members in mind, you go a long way in meeting a variety of needs. Hearing and addressing their expectations up front will go a long way in leading a unified campaign.

WHY SHOULD OUR CHURCH PRODUCE OUR OWN VIDEO CURRICULUM?

Video-based small group curriculum has been with us for a while now. Early innovators like Rick Warren and the team at

Saddleback Church brought the local pastor into the living room. Brett Eastman went on to found Lifetogether, which has sold about four million units of their branded curriculum to date. Many other video-based studies have followed and have succeeded.

With all of the professionally produced video curriculum out there, why would a church want to create their own? While well-known pastors have produced some excellent studies, your pastor's face on the screen presents some strong advantages for your congregation.

A GROUP STUDY ALIGNED WITH THE SERMON HELPS PEOPLE TAKE THEIR WEEKEND EXPERIENCE INTO THE WEEK

The hustle and bustle of life tends to edge out the Sunday morning sermon after a day or so. While some sermons are remembered better than others, most are long forgotten by midweek. By providing small groups with studies based on the weekend message, the points made on Sunday can take deeper root.

By creating space in the small group to review the weekend message via a short video (no more than ten minutes), the group has a chance to review the points, ask questions, discuss issues, and make a specific application to their lives. Giving groups the opportunity to think about the message and what it means to them causes the group members to retain more. In groups, they can involve more of themselves in the teaching. Rather than simply listening and maybe taking notes, group members can wrestle with hard questions and get the encouragement and accountability they need to live out the message.

PRODUCING YOUR OWN CURRICULUM ENGAGES THE SENIOR PASTOR'S TEACHING GIFT

A senior pastor without a teaching gift is not a senior pastor for long. This is the most public and most personal role of any senior pastor. Speaking is hard work. Even the most gifted teachers spend hours gathering material, studying, collecting illustrations, and polishing their messages. Once Sunday is finished, for most pastors, the countdown clock to next week's sermon begins. The one they worked so hard on for this week is now a thing of the past. But it doesn't have to be.

What if the pastor could sit down in a living room with his church members and teach them the part he couldn't get to on Sunday morning? What if in that circle the pastor could share his heart about what the Bible passage means and what it would mean if people started obeying it? A video-based curriculum can breathe new life into a message destined for the archives. Not only will the congregation learn more, but the message will go farther through the group.

THE SENIOR PASTOR'S INVOLVEMENT ELEVATES THE ROLE OF GROUPS

As I said earlier in the chapter, for most churchgoers the initial draw to a church is the pastor's teaching and the music. As hard as the other church staff work in their roles, this is the simple truth. Senior pastors play a highly significant role in the spiritual lives of their congregations.

By connecting the small group study to the weekend message, you can leverage the influence of senior pastors in leading the people to connect in small groups. Once pastors have created a video curriculum, the next question will be, "How do we use this? How do we recruit more leaders? How do we get people into groups?" Don't you want your senior pastor asking those questions?

What's important to the senior pastor will be what's important to the congregation. Bulletins, video announcements, websites—none of these come close to having the number-one influencer in the church direct the congregation. When the pastor asks for people to host groups, people will host groups. When the pastor invites members to join groups, members will join groups.

I learned this lesson over a decade ago. I had spent seven years recruiting and training leaders to find only 30 percent of our congregation in groups. The first time our senior pastor stood up and asked for HOST homes, we doubled our groups in one day. I never looked back. He did all of the recruiting and leading from that point forward. I have not recruited a group leader myself since 2004, even though I have served in another church since then.

THE PASTOR'S TEACHING ON VIDEO CURRICULUM MOVES THE WEEKEND MESSAGE BEYOND THE CHURCH WALLS

When church members invite their friends, neighbors, coworkers, relatives, and others to join them for a church-produced Bible study, the senior pastor is introduced to many more people than actually attend the church on Sunday. In homes, workplaces, Starbucks, and even commuter trains, the pastor's teaching goes out to many new people.

Often new people will meet the pastor via video before they meet him or her in person. But, the transition from the living room to the church sanctuary now is not quite as daunting. New folks feel they've already met the pastor through the weekly group studies. And, don't tell the group hosts and leaders, but they're actually doing evangelism. Shhh.

A SIMPLE TEACHING TOOL PUTS GROUP MULTIPLICATION ON STEROIDS

A video curriculum is easy to use. In fact, someone who has never led before simply needs to follow the instructions. The teaching on the video provides the wisdom and expertise. The questions in the book provide the pathway for a great discussion. Pushing play and reading questions is not so hard.

Think about this: every person in your church has friends. The people who are less involved in the church will actually have far more friends outside of the church. What if your church members each gathered a group of eight to ten people for a video-based study featuring your senior pastor? Could a church of one hundred members reach one thousand people? What about a church of one thousand going after ten thousand? What about a church of thirteen thousand reaching over one hundred thousand? Is it possible? The Bible says all things are possible with God.[15]

WHEN TO ALIGN

An aligned series is a considerable investment. Whether you create your own curriculum or purchase a church-wide campaign, it requires a great deal of effort. Now, don't get scared by this. The payoff is huge. But, considering what you will put into this, you definitely want to choose the right season of the year. There are three key seasons of the year that tend to work better than others: the fall, the new year, and after Easter.

Think about when your church members become reengaged with church. We know the weak times of year: summer and Christmas. Now, obviously, someone is coming to church, otherwise you'd cancel all of your services. But these are seasons when people are not open to adding anything else to their lives. They've got enough going on.

The best season of the year to align groups is the fall. As summer comes to a close, and kids are back in school, people are open to starting something new. The actual dates will depend on the culture of your church and your community. I've had churches launch a fall series as early as the third week in August and as late as the second week in October.

The key in choosing a start date is to allow at least three weeks to recruit group leaders prior to the launch of your alignment series. Most senior pastors will want to jump into a series right after Labor Day. This is a mistake. If your members are not reengaged until after Labor Day, it will be very difficult to form groups prior to Labor Day for a post-Labor Day launch.

Please understand, when it comes to making suggestions for the pastor's preaching schedule, I approach the topic with much fear and trembling. It's usually best to casually mention something you read about in a book by this crazy guy, Allen White. . . . (Let me take the heat. That's what I'm here for.)

One solution is to skip the sermon series right after Labor Day and align a group study with the October sermon series. As long as you have a strong six-week run that ends by Thanksgiving in the U.S. (or starts after Thanksgiving in Canada), you're in great shape. Use the time in September to form groups during the

September-October series, then launch groups with the aligned series in October.

That said, in 2013, Dr. Tony Evans, the senior pastor of Oak Cliff Bible Fellowship in Dallas, Texas, launched his series *Destiny*, based on his book by the same title. He preached a message about community on Labor Day weekend. Now, he didn't ask me if that was a good time to recruit leaders, but who am I to tell Dr. Evans what to do? After the message, he asked those interested in gathering groups to fill out a commitment card. Over two hundred and fifty people responded to lead a group. It's a good thing he didn't ask me. By the end of three weeks of recruiting, around five hundred people agreed to start a group.

The next-best season to launch an alignment series is the new year. People are ready to try something new. They want to lose weight, exercise more, get out of debt, and grow spiritually. The time is right for an alignment series.

The timing for the launch is significant here as well. I've seen series start as early as the third week in January and as late as the second Sunday in February. Again, keep your church's culture in mind. You want to allow three weeks prior to the start of the series to recruit leaders (again). And, again, many senior pastors want to kick off the new year with a series.

A couple of years ago, we were talking to the church about a coaching partnership. They wanted to launch groups and kick off an alignment series on the first Sunday of the year, which was January 1. The situation seemed so impossible that I actually discouraged the partnership. I've tried to recruit group leaders in December for an early January launch before. The result was spending several weeks standing in an empty room wondering if I'd missed the call of God on my life. I hadn't. We just chose the wrong timing.

The church with the January 1 start date reconsidered. They moved their January series to February and chose to do the alignment between the Christian holidays of Super Bowl Sunday and Easter. This schedule took us from a potential punt to first and goal. We had plenty of time to recruit leaders, form groups, and recruit coaches in January, then launch the alignment series in a big way in February.

The third-best season for an alignment is after Easter. Now, there are some big reasons to not launch groups in the spring, but Easter Sunday is the one day when everyone who calls your church home is in attendance. Sure, there are plenty of visitors who saw your ad in the local paper or were invited by a friend, but the majority of the crowd is your people.

Now, if Easter is the largest Sunday of the year, then the Sunday after Easter is among the lowest attended of the year. Everyone came on Easter. The folks who only attend once every four to six weeks were at Easter. Don't worry. You'll see them again before Memorial Day. There is a way to get them back sooner.

By launching an alignment series off of Easter Sunday, not only will a high percentage of your members start or join a group, but they will want to participate in the weekend services as well as their small group study since they are connected. Attendance after Easter will not see as significant a drop.

A couple years ago, we created a series with Gene Appel at Eastside Christian Church in Anaheim, California. Prior to Eastside, Gene had served as senior pastor at both Central Christian Church in Las Vegas, Nevada, and Willow Creek Community Church in South Barrington, Illinois. (He has the distinction of being the only senior pastor of three megachurches.) Eastside was growing rapidly, but was lagging behind in connecting their people into groups.

Gene decided to launch an alignment series starting at Easter based on his message, *Hope Rising*. He partnered with Lifetogether Ministries to create a video-based six-week curriculum which groups would begin using the week after Easter. Gene gave a copy of the study guide to everyone who attended on Easter. They handed out about seven thousand books. When the dust had settled, 460 groups started for *Hope Rising*. They got caught up with getting people into groups in a hurry.

ROADBLOCKS AND OBSTACLES TO AN ALIGNMENT SERIES

Sometimes it's difficult to find six weeks in a row available on the church calendar. The fall or new year can be especially competitive seasons of the year, and there are some things you might not be able to move. Guest speakers, missions conventions, city-wide serving events and other large-scale events are often planned for months in advance. They are big rocks with no way of getting around them. Some events are even an annual church tradition and certainly are not the hill to die on. So, do you just call off the alignment series?

Absolutely not. You innovate. If a guest speaker is on the church calendar, then if it's appropriate you can invite the guest to take that week's topic in the series. If it's not, then the groups can continue to meet as planned, but the sermon for that week won't align and it's not the end of the world.

The main thing to keep in mind is to start the alignment series at least two weeks before the "obstacle" or to wait until after. You will need at least three weekends to gather groups, so you don't want the timing to get too goofy. You also want the series to get off to a good start. At least two weeks of the series will allow for the alignment to build some momentum before the interruption.

Let's say you have a guest speaker or major event scheduled for the first weekend in October. If you start the alignment series the third weekend in September, then you will need to start gathering groups either the last weekend in August or Labor Day weekend. When are your people back in church after the summer?

The other alternative is to give the groups a week off. If your church has an event like a missions conference which will not only involve the weekend, but will also have events throughout the week, then just skip that week. Again, timing is key. Do your best to have the week off occur somewhere around the third or fourth week of the series. Now your six-week series has become seven, but as long as the series ends before Thanksgiving in the fall, before Easter in the new year, or before Memorial Day in the spring, it will work out just fine.

Invite the groups to participate together in the conference, serving project, or event. Groups are more than meetings. A different setting or serving together is a great way for group members to see their group in a different light. They can focus on group life and not just group meetings.

Sometimes the obstacle is beyond your church. If you live in the Washington, D.C., area and Congress is in recess, it's probably not a great time for an alignment. If you live in Boston and you're expecting a winter with over one hundred inches of snow, again, probably not the best season of the year for you. If you live in Florida, you need to be aware of when the snowbirds will migrate north or south. They will certainly have an impact. These are very specific examples, but every community has something. Don't fight this. Embrace it.

And, of course, there are holidays on every calendar that may impede your launch regardless of where you live. To launch an alignment series or even try to gather groups between Thanksgiving and New Year's Day in the U.S. is futile. I know, because I have stood in a briefing room the second week of December listening to the crickets and feeling like a failure. The series was right. The briefing was right. The timing was wrong.

When are your schools on spring break? When are graduation ceremonies? What's the date for Super Bowl Sunday? When do most people in your church head to the lake or go on vacation? You can rail against them and even accuse them of being uncommitted, but you are fighting a losing battle, and you're the loser.

There are ways to schedule an alignment series with enough time to gather groups. Once you identify the obstacles, decide how and when to launch your series. I've coached churches in every region of the U.S., Canada, and a few other places. They have all launched alignment series. It can be done.

LAUNCHING GROUPS WITHOUT A SERMON ALIGNMENT

As promised, let's address a few ways of establishing groups without an alignment.

1. *Create your own curriculum without aligning with a sermon series.* In the early days of church-wide campaigns like *40 Days of Purpose* by Rick Warren, alignment was necessary to achieve the maximum involvement from the congregation. While there is great synergy in connecting the small group study with the sermon series, the secret to success in creating groups for the *40 Days of Purpose*

was the senior pastor's involvement by preaching the topics in the weekend service that aligned with the group curriculum and the readings from *The Purpose Driven Life*. By involving the senior pastor, it became "our thing" and not just using "Saddleback's thing." And, of course, as I stated before, the senior pastor's involvement creates interest and enthusiasm. Without the senior pastor, groups would certainly benefit from Rick Warren's teaching and from reading the second-best-selling nonfiction book in history, but with the senior pastor the church-wide campaign turned into something very powerful for a church.

But, let's up the ante here, if you will. If a church produces its own video-based group curriculum featuring the senior pastor's teaching, then the pastor is already involved. He or she is on the video. You have the senior pastor's contribution, so do you need a sermon alignment?

While the sermon alignment is key to using a purchased curriculum, if a church offers the congregation their pastor's teaching on video, then groups can be launched without aligning the sermon series. This is great news for churches whose senior pastor doesn't teach in series or if the church has many guest speakers. Maybe the pastor could preach one sermon to kick off the series. Then the weekend service could go back to the normal pattern, while the groups receive the pastor's teaching via video in their group. This is a solid alternative to an alignment.

2. *Purchase a curriculum that aligns with the church's vision or current theme.* For some churches, the idea of producing their own video-based curriculum is a bit daunting. I don't have time to elaborate here, but I have coached a church of fifty people to successfully create their own curriculum with an all-volunteer team. It can be done!

If your church is not in a place to create your own curriculum (or think you can't), then purchasing video-based curriculum that goes along with the pastor's sermon series is a good alternative. Many churches are producing alignment series which are being used by other churches. Once they put in the hard work of creating a video curriculum, they want to see the end result go beyond the six-week use in their church.

When a church purchases a curriculum, this does take us back to the scenario where aligning the weekend service with the purchased curriculum is more important in making the group launch feel like it's "ours" rather than something that is being imposed from somewhere else.

3. *Add a video component to your current sermon discussion guide.* Many churches already produce discussion questions based on the pastor's sermons. While this is an effective strategy for helping your members take their weekend into their week and enhance personal application, this is even stronger with a video component.

A short video teaching by the senior pastor or that week's speaker will help to introduce the topic to the group, and then they can go into the discussion from there. This is especially helpful for new leaders or people who gather their friends for discussion. The Bible expert is on the video, so they only need to facilitate the discussion.

Recently in coaching C4 Church in Ajax, Ontario, we faced a tension between the workload of the church's production team and adding a new weekly responsibility. We came up with a low-cost, effective solution which didn't involve the production team at all. Every week after the pastor has prepared his sermon, the small group pastor does a five-minute interview with the pastor as an introduction to the group discussion. They shoot the interview on an iPhone in one take and stream it online. The audio and video quality is remarkable. And, their groups are very enthusiastically using the video along with the discussion guide.

4. *The senior pastor is onboard to promote the series.* If your senior pastor is willing to promote the series from the platform on the weekend, you are greatly blessed. The senior pastor will recruit three times more new leaders than a small group pastor would ever dream of recruiting. If your pastor is willing to give exclusive promotion to groups for a three-week period prior to a group launch or the start of a semester, then you are well on your way in becoming a church of small groups. Don't grumble about not getting an alignment series or self-produced curriculum. Thank God your senior pastor is interested, and run with it!

I believe there is a good, better, best scenario here. A good launch is having the senior pastor involved in promoting groups in any way. A better launch is producing your own curriculum with your senior pastor's teaching and promotion. The best launch is self-produced curriculum that aligns with the sermon series and of course, your senior pastor promoting and recruiting for the series.

CHAPTER 3

FINDING YOUR ACCEPTABLE LEVEL OF RISK

Trying anything new involves a certain amount of risk. Some people jump into things haphazardly and take foolish risks. Others hold back and risk little or nothing. Sometimes no risk is riskier than the other options.

The bottom line is change causes a sense of loss. You're saying goodbye to the way things used to be and welcoming something new, sometimes unproven. It's risky business for sure.

If we risk too much on the wrong things, we ended up bankrupting the leadership credit we had in the bank. But, if we don't risk any change, we are just burying our leadership "talents" in the ground, which really doesn't help anyone.

The fear of every pastor is that change will alienate the church's core members. If the stakeholders become upset, they might leave. If the change alienates the base, reduces giving, and ultimately costs the pastor his job, then why would anyone want to take a risk?

It's possible to take risks that aren't so risky. There's a big difference between a strategic risk and reckless abandon.

EVALUATE WHAT'S WORKING

As I mentioned in chapter one in the "If It Ain't Broke" section, if embracing groups is merely a matter of chasing the elusive "silver bullet" that will get every person in your church connected and growing, you are heading into a world of trouble. There are some things your members have already said "Yes" to that are working.

While Sunday school certainly may seem old school, some of your people are old school. They might not drive at night, so Sunday morning is the ideal time for them to meet for connection and discipleship. Don't throw this out because it doesn't work for everybody. But, on the other hand, don't force Sunday school on everybody either. If they've said "No" to Sunday school, then give them something to say "Yes" to.

What else is working? Women's Bible Studies? Midweek Prayer Meetings? An early morning Men's Breakfast? Let these things work for those they are working for, but don't expect any of these things to work for everybody.

Groups can offer a new option for those not connected to Sunday school or a midweek study. A couple of years ago, we were working with a church of 4,500 adults in the Chicago suburbs. They had a thriving adult Sunday school as well as a strong midweek experience, which included an on-campus restaurant. They feared small groups might upset the good things they already had going.

However, once we added up the attendance, we discovered only about 1,500 adults participated in Sunday school and midweek Bible study. I told the pastors, "What I see here is you are basically killing yourselves for a third of your adults, while the other two-thirds have nothing for their spiritual growth outside of the weekend service." The pastors agreed, and we launched groups for the other three thousand ASAP. Both Sunday school and the midweek service held steady.

I'VE HEARD SMALL GROUPS CAN CAUSE PROBLEMS . . .

This is true. Some small groups can cause problems. But, as my friend Mark Howell says, "There is no such thing as Problem-Free." My challenge to you is this: Do you want to have problems for a good reason or problems for no reason at all?

There may be a few folks with wrong motives who want a small group to establish a platform for themselves. In some churches, if a person gets twenty people together, then they may think suddenly they have their own "ministry." While groups are definitely a ministry, these folks see it as an opportunity to grab a microphone and take up a collection. The simple way to avoid this is, as we say back in Kansas, to "nip it in the bud."

In an orientation ask the pastor to state up front, "If you see starting a small group as a means to launching your own ministry, you are seeing this wrong. I will tell you right now that this is not the pathway. God will not bless you in this. If we need to have a conversation about this, then let's talk." End of story.

Most problems generated by a small group are actually not generated by the small group. Small groups don't create problems as much as they reveal the problems you already have. The question is whether you want your people to get closer and go deeper with each other or live in denial of what's going on in their lives.

FROM RISK AVERSE TO RISK TAKER

I've already told my story, so I won't repeat it in detail here. When I started off in small group ministry, I was risk averse. I wanted no more problems. No, thank you. My method of preventing problems was recruiting only people I knew personally to lead groups, and then personally training and coaching them. This worked great until we reached thirty groups. Then it got stuck. Everyone has limits. Thirty groups was mine.

Our church was growing, but our groups weren't. Our newcomers were not assimilating well, and our other discipleship offerings like elective classes and other Bible studies weren't meeting the need. Something had to change. That something was actually me.

The HOST home strategy was a stretch for me. We were now inviting people who I didn't know to lead groups. It immediately pushed matters out of my control.

A survey of our congregation helped to allay my fears and move forward. In surveying our members, we discovered our people, on average, had been Christians for over eighteen years and had been a part of the church for six years. Rather than assuming we were casting a broad net to a bunch of people who didn't have a clue, we were actually inviting people who had plenty of Bible under their belt and who had heard at least three hundred of our pastor's sermons. They weren't new.

Sure enough, we had some fine upstanding citizens offer to host a group in their home. Following the lead of Brett Eastman and Saddleback Church, we asked the hosts to fill out a brief information sheet. We asked about their relationship with Christ and how long they had been at the church. Then, we asked them if there was anything going on in their lives that would be considered harmful to the church or the cause of Christ. More often than not, people who would have answered "Yes" to the last question simply didn't turn in their sheet. But, a few did.

Jim, one of my coaches, ran up to me one Sunday morning, excited that Chris and Lisa had decided to lead a group. In fact, they were so excited about the group, they had already started inviting people. I had to break the news to Jim, "Chris and Lisa are living together, but they're not married." In our church, this was a no-go to be a group host. They had filled out the information sheet, but didn't feel their relationship was a "Yes" on the last question about harming the church or the cause of Christ.

Jim was flabbergasted, and asked, "What should I do?"

I told him, "We're going to take Chris and Lisa to dinner to work this out. And, you're going to pay because you got us into this." He agreed.

The four of us went to dinner. After we'd ordered, I said, "Well, we all started out with good intentions, but we ended up at a place that is not so good. Unfortunately, we can't do what was originally planned, but let's consider some options:

"First, you could go ahead and get married before your group starts." They said they couldn't because they had big wedding plans for the next spring.

"Second, you could delay your group until after your wedding." They had already invited people who were really excited about the study. I asked them who they had invited. So far, they had some neighbors, family members, a couple friends, and a guy from church who had needle tracks on his arms.

"Third, one of you could move out." They wouldn't consider this option. There were financial and other reasons.

50   EXPONENTIAL GROUPS

"Fourth, considering you've invited people who already know you and your situation, you could go ahead and do the group. But, we won't make the group official until you're official." They agreed to this. Then, I said, "But here's the thing. You have chosen to honor God in your relationship by getting married next year. Rather than waiting to honor God six months from now, I want to challenge you to honor God in your relationship now by refraining from sex outside of marriage until your wedding day." They agreed. I added that I would check up with them. They agreed to that too.

Their group started. When I saw them on Sunday mornings, I would ask them, "How's it going?" I didn't mean just a casual "How's it going?" I meant "How's it going with your abstinence?" And, they would tell me they were doing great or if there was a struggle. Several months later I performed their wedding. I also changed the information sheet to be more specific about what might harm the cause of Christ.

Now, I ask folks who are hosting groups the same question, but I qualify the question with two categories:

1. Current habitual struggles or moral issues (an addiction, co-habitation, a sexual relationship outside of marriage, homosexuality, or similar) that would bring shame on the name of Jesus Christ or the church.

2. Current marital struggles (infidelity, separation, divorce in process, or similar).

While we would never expect people to be perfect to host (that would disqualify everybody), we also wouldn't want to put people out there to represent the church who are dealing with deeper issues. As a pastor, I don't want people to ever think we are more interested in how they can serve the church than we are in how we can serve them. If people are going through a major crisis, they need care. It's not the best time to lead a group.

At first I dreaded these conversations. Again, more problems. But, over time I found these to be great pastoral opportunities to talk about things in people's lives that we might not have been aware of before or wouldn't otherwise have the opportunity to discuss with them.

After one host briefing, a guy came up to me with his sheet. I said, "Oh, you decided to do a group, great!"

He said, "Look at the last question." He had indicated on his form that he was struggling with a drug addiction.

I asked him, "Where are you in your recovery?" He said he had been drug free for about six months and was participating in Celebrate Recovery. (I learned later that neither statement was true.)

Then, I asked him, "By stepping out to host a group, the enemy isn't going to like this. There's going to be added stress and pressure in your life. When the pressure's on, where do you tend to go?"

He admitted, "I'd better wait." He made the right decision.

If you are going to present people as group hosts on the church's website, in the bulletin, or during a Small Group Connection event, there is an implied endorsement that the church supports the leaders and is behind each group. While only about 2 percent of my applicants ever presented a problem, you have to know what's going on with them, especially if you're going to list them on the church website or send people to their group.

The HOST home strategy helped us connect two-thirds of our congregation into groups, and then we got a little stuck again. It was time to try something new: Grab and Go.

I told the story earlier of how I became the inadvertent pioneer of this strategy. It was the next logical step in giving our people something they could say "Yes" to. If they had rejected my personal recruiting or the HOST home strategy, they need another option. But, the "Grab and Go" strategy is not where I started. In fact, as I mentioned, years before just a glimpse at a similar strategy terrified me. But, after a successful launch that doubled our groups with the HOST home strategy, I was ready for a new challenge.

The "Grab and Go" strategy, which was later refined to the "Gather and Grow" strategy (some folks objected to the grabbing), allowed anyone who chose to gather a group of their friends to do the study together. Now, these groups were completely "off the record." The church did not send people to their groups. We did not advertise these groups in any way, shape, or form. It was on the person who started the group to invite everyone to the group.

While this may appear riskier than the other strategies, it actually presents less risk to the church. Consider that if the church promotes a HOST home that turns out to be bad, then it's kind of on the church, since the church vetted the host and promoted the group. But, in the Gather and Grow strategy, since everyone is invited by a friend, if the group turns out bad, well, it's on them. It's their friend. I didn't send them there.

I did, however, start a group of lesbians once. At first, I was a bit horrified. A group like this was out of character for our church at the time. My pastor asked me one day, "Do we have a lesbian small group?"

I wanted to say, "I don't know how they got the materials. They must have stolen them." I didn't say that, but I got over myself. A member of our church, who happened to be a lesbian, took us up on the Gather and Grow offer and invited her friends to do the study just like every other Gather and Grow group at our church.

Now, after a couple of weeks the lady who started the group brought the materials back and said, "This isn't going to work for us." The study didn't quite fit with where the group was spiritually. I thanked her for trying.

If, in my first attempt at launching groups, I had ended up with Chris and Lisa or the lesbian group, I probably would have gone back to my onesie-twosie approach to recruiting leaders. It would have scared me off. But, after launching 105 groups in a church of eight hundred adults and only having two "problems," I had 103 reasons to celebrate overcoming my fear and moving beyond my high-control approach, which had only netted thirty groups after seven years of hard work.

FEAR LEADS TO FAILURE. START WHERE IT'S SAFE FOR YOU.

People typically don't find a lot of success in promoting something they fear. They can actually be relieved when they have a poor result. There is less to be afraid of.

One pastor admitted to me, "What if I put myself out there and no one responds? I would be embarrassed." That is definitely true.

The answer is: don't invite people to something you don't believe in. But, what do you and your church believe in?

First, if you're a small group pastor or director, ask yourself, "where does my pastor want to start?" If your pastor is more risk averse, like I used to be, then ask for your pastor's help to hand-pick solid citizens who could lead groups, and then promote those groups. You won't get as far as you would if you threw down the gauntlet to everyone, but you will get much farther than if you went beyond where your pastor wants to go. Start where your pastor wants to start, then see where it goes from there. Once you have the first success under your belt, then your pastor will be open to try other things.

I've also seen the reverse. Sometimes the pastor wants to go full bore, but the small group pastor or director is more risk averse. While you definitely don't want to squander the opportunity, you also have to reach a place where your fear doesn't impede your success.

A few years ago, we were working with a very large church. This is a great church with a great history of biblical teaching and a solid group ministry, but their groups needed to catch up with their attendance.

In one teleconference, the small group team reported back that their existing group leaders were fearful of the Gather and Grow strategy. They perceived many problems from letting the uninitiated lead a group. Part of their concern related to the fact the experienced leaders had paid their dues in the leadership process, and now we were telling them "you're going to let anybody in."

I said a quick prayer during the teleconference, "God, what do I say to them? This could be dead in the water."

After I finished listening to the concerns, these words came out of my mouth, "This isn't a call to leadership. This is a call to obedience, because we are all called to go and make disciples." The room was quiet. I wasn't sure what would happen next. Maybe I killed it.

Then someone spoke up and said, "Could you repeat that?"

Suddenly, the light came on for them (and for me). The Gather and Grow strategy was the way to go. The senior pastor was already there, but it took his team a little more time. When it was all said and done, hundreds of people offered to gather their friends and grow together using video curriculum based on their senior pastor's teaching.

I've had staff members freak out when their senior pastors have suddenly taken initiative in their area of ministry. They've said things like, "Why couldn't we plan ahead on this? We could be better prepared for the response. We could do this in a better way." Some folks have become downright angry over their pastors meddling in their area of ministry.

If your senior pastor takes an interest in small groups out of the blue, first, thank God your pastor is interested in groups. Then, do whatever you have to do to make it work. After all, you don't know when this opportunity may come again. Some pastors are strategic and lead with a road map. Some pastors are more intuitive. Their leadership appears more like a lightning strike. Learn to organize yourself around those lightning strikes and make the most of it.

IF YOU WANT TO WALK ON WATER, YOU'VE GOT TO GET OUT OF THE BOAT

John Ortberg wrote a book with this title a few years back based on Jesus's invitation to his disciples on the Sea of Galilee and Peter's response to jump in.[16] While Peter became intimidated by the wind and waves and started to sink, he deserves the credit for giving it a try. While the other disciples remained somewhat safely in the boat during the storm, Peter took the risk and experienced something other humans have not . . . walking on water in its liquid form.

While some of us don't want to rock the boat, let's face it, as culture changes and our people abandon traditional means of discipleship, the boat is not as safe as it seems. In fact, the boat is actually sinking. As my friend Jeff B. Baker told me one day, "Sometimes to walk on water, God has to sink the boat."

Which seems scarier: to have people who have partial biblical knowledge attempting to live for Christ and wondering why things aren't working so well, or to have people sit in the rows week after week, not growing enough to influence one another, and not given an opportunity to walk in obedience by discipling others? Leaders may not be Bible scholars, but they can certainly give what they have. Of course, with a video-based curriculum, the teaching is readily available.

What's going to cause you to jump out of the boat? Newcomers need to be assimilated. Believers need to be discipled. Everyone needs to serve others in a meaningful way. Groups can meet all of these needs.

Whether you start with handpicking leaders or having your senior pastor invite anyone who is breathing, it's time to jump out of the boat. As your Sunday school and midweek attendance continue to decline, there will come a point in time where your cruise ship will become the Titanic. While you need to have due respect for established ministries, you cannot afford to allow the growing percentage of your congregation to remain undiscipled. Do something.

WHO BELIEVED IN YOU?

Looking back at my own journey from risk averse to risk taker, I had to ask myself a hard question in that journey: Who believed in me? Once upon a time, I was a seventeen-year-old high school student who felt God's call on my life to ministry. The fulfillment of that call didn't happen by itself. My pastor, Paul Sandgren, saw my potential and sensed my calling. He let me preach my first sermon in children's church. Eleven kids gave their lives to Christ that day. After that, there were other opportunities.

When I would come home from Bible college, I learned to have a sermon prepared, because inevitably I would get a call on Saturday night. Sure enough the phone would ring, it was Pastor Sandgren, and he would say, "Allen, how would you like to speak at the 8:00 service tomorrow morning?" I always agreed. Now, the 8:00 service at our church was about one hundred people, so if I flubbed, not much damage was done. But, if I did well, then I received another invitation to speak at the 10:45 service. I was called up from the minor leagues. In baseball terms, I was going to the show!

I have a file with those sermons. Honestly, they're not that great. But a pastor who believed in me and a congregation who knew me since I was four years old loved me. That is great. I am forever grateful for the opportunity to grow my gifts.

Someone believed in me, and I followed my calling in ministry. Now, as a pastor my dilemma had to do with who I believed in. Not a few handpicked people, but believing enough in our congregation that anyone could gather a group of friends and grow. At New Life, I started out believing in ten people to lead. Then, that led to thirty leaders. Then, we launched the HOST strategy, which stretched my thinking to sixty leaders. Then, we offered Gather and Grow, and saw 103 leaders in our first campaign with this strategy. We lost thirty groups, and then we were at 105 leaders for our next campaign. Did I mention this was in a church of eight hundred adults?

If I hadn't believed this could happen, it wouldn't have happened. In fact, for seven years I didn't believe in it, so I only had 30 percent of our adults in groups. Once we embraced the risk and jumped out of the boat, things happened.

STOP LYING TO YOURSELF

Your present is not nearly as rosy as you think it is. You'd like it to be, but let's face it, traditional methods of discipleship are slipping or have completely collapsed. Now, don't get out your wrecking ball just yet. If Sunday school, midweek Bible study, Adult Bible Fellowships, Sunday evening services, and other well-seasoned means of growing people are working for some, then let them work for those folks. But those numbers are not increasing in most churches.

As more and more of the older generations graduate to Glory, fewer people are served by these means. Younger people simply do not feel they have four hours every Sunday morning to devote to church. They also won't usually come back during the week. How do you disciple people you don't have access to?

Growth is one issue, but connection is also a major issue. As your church continues to grow, people tend to have fewer connections in the church and more connections outside of the church. This is not a bad thing. In fact, it has huge evangelistic potential.

But, when these members have trouble, where do they go? Who do they know?

A smaller, portable, well-equipped means of discipleship is necessary. Now, I know you are expecting me to say that groups are the answer and the best thing since sliced bread. (What was the best thing before sliced bread anyway?) But, here is what I would say.

Groups are one of the ways to disciple and care for increasingly mobile and increasingly distracted believers. But, we must look to other means. What could be done with scalable websites, apps, blogs, or video? The future of discipleship involves content that is portable, mobile, and pushed out to church members. The more pastors can influence their people on the devices they look at constantly, the more they will be influenced by the church.

Decentralizing discipleship is the future. Providing great content and effective coaching is the challenge.

While your present situation is not as rosy as you might think, your future is not as scary as you think. If the church thrived in Roman oppression, the church can thrive in your community. You just have to be careful what you call "church."

When I was a child, I learned a little rhyme with a pantomime: "Here is the church. Here is the steeple. Open the doors and see all the people." It was completely heretical. It's a good thing I left that cult. (Okay, I dearly love my home church and the people who invested in me.) It would be more accurate to say: "Here is a building. Here is a pointy thing our building may or may not have on the roof. Go inside and see the Church."

If the building is irrelevant, then we can have "Church" anywhere we go. Whether at Starbucks, in a living room, during lunch at work, or on a commuter train, the Church can meet, connect, and grow.

I don't know where we pastors got the idea that groups and classes were more under our control when they met in our building. Think about it. We can control the room temperature and the hours of operation, but we can't be present in every group that meets on campus. Just because it's in the building doesn't make it any better.

A couple approached me one Sunday morning saying the teacher of their class was teaching some things that just didn't seem right. The teacher called it "British-Israelism" or "Anglo-Israelism." To be honest, I had to go find out what it was.

> The basic premise of the Anglo-Israelite theory is that ten tribes were lost (Israelites) when the Jews were captured by the Assyrians under King Sargon and that these so-called "lost" tribes are, in reality, the Saxae, or Scythians, who surged westward through Northern Europe and eventually became the ancestors of the Saxons, who later invaded England. The theory maintains that the Anglo-Saxons are the "lost" ten tribes of Israel and are substituted, in Anglo-Israel interpretation and exegesis, for the Israel of the Bible.[17]

In short, the teaching wasn't harmless. It was racist. It was a "doctrinal" justification of white supremacy. I shut that down very quickly. Please note, this did not happen in a home group. It happened in a Sunday school class on the church campus.

We don't have nearly as much control as we might imagine. Several years ago, I worked with a great church in New Hampshire. They were a church plant with about four hundred adults on average. When we started coaching them, they had about a dozen semester-based groups. All of the leaders were carefully handpicked. Group members would sign up for a group every semester, and at the end of the semester, they would practice what we called in elementary school "Fruit Basket Upset," with everyone joining a different group for the next semester. Their small group system was on the higher control side of things.

When I proposed removing the requirements and inviting "those among the breathing" to host a group, the pastors were a little quiet on the phone. The senior pastor pointed to the executive pastor and said, "You just blew his mind."

The executive pastor and small group director proceeded with creating curriculum, which we would offer to "the breathing" with the chance to host groups. As we talked further about what the training and coaching would look like, they began to feel better about what they were about to introduce in their church.

When we arrived at game day and their senior pastor began to recruit hosts, we ended up with some decent folks. In fact, we started fifty new groups in that church of four hundred people. Everything went really well. Until, one day on our weekly call, they had some unusual news.

We joined our regular teleconference, but the look on the executive pastor and small group director's faces told me things were not okay. I asked what was going on. They were hesitant to respond, but eventually divulged the bad news.

Apparently, two couples who were group leaders had gone out the weekend before and done quite a bit of drinking. The drinking led to skinny-dipping. The skinny-dipping led to swinging.

My first fear was that in lowering the standards for group leaders in their church, we had made a real mess of things. This was not the behavior any pastor would expect from their group leaders.

Very hesitantly and very quietly, I asked, "Were these some of the new hosts?"

They said, "No, these were some of our handpicked, established group leaders."

My dread immediately turned to relief. While obviously this was an uncomfortable situation, the irony was thick. They had feared letting anyone lead a group, because they didn't know how mature the hosts would be or what kind of trouble the groups would find themselves in. They had vetted their handpicked leaders thoroughly, and now this.

The initial fear was that new, unproven leaders would be the source of problems, when in this case, the seasoned leaders had behaved worse than the new leaders. The high-control system they started with did not prevent this behavior from happening. None of us have as much control as we think we do.

The end result with the two couples was several pastoral conversations and a step away from leadership. It didn't dampen the church's enthusiasm for groups. This situation reminded us all that just because we are careful, it doesn't mean we will avoid problems.

The present is not as rosy as it seems. The future is not so scary.

GREAT REASONS TO INVEST IN GROUPS AND OVERCOME OUR FEARS

People deepen their spirituality with the help and encouragement of other believers. Regular interaction and application of God's word in the context of a group produces spiritual growth like little else, except for maybe painful circumstances. This is not to say that individuals are unaffected by large group meetings or private quiet times; rather, the relationship and interaction of those participating in a small group has been shown to have a significant influence on a person's spiritual growth.

1. GROUPS WILL INCREASE YOUR WEEKEND ATTENDANCE

I have seen over the last decade of working with churches across North America that when a church offers an aligned series, people will not only participate in groups, but will more regularly attend the weekend services. Capital Area Christian Church in Mechanicsburg, Pennsylvania, is a great example of this.

In their first two back-to-back, aligned series, they saw attendance not just hold steady, but increase. Nate Graella, Spiritual Formation & Shepherding Pastor at the church, reported that, compared to the first six months of the previous year, church attendance had increased by 7.5 percent. The only difference in their ministry strategy was launching small groups in an alignment series.

But, these aren't merely anecdotal findings. Princeton sociologist Robert Wuthnow discovered people in a group take a much more active part in other programs in the church (61 percent), including the weekend service.[18]

2. PEOPLE IN GROUPS FEEL MORE CARED FOR

This just makes sense. The span of care is much better in a group than in a large weekend service. Even megachurches with staff dedicated to pastoral care cannot possibly keep up with all of the needs. Remember Jethro's advice to Moses: thinking staff are the only ones qualified or willing to help is "not good."

According to Wuthnow's research,[19] people who participated in groups felt better about themselves (84 percent). They were more open and honest in their communication (79 percent), and they were more open and honest with themselves (78 percent). In a secure, loving environment, group members can find a little shelter from the world and find love and acceptance in a more meaningful way.

3. PEOPLE IN GROUPS WHO FEEL CARED FOR TEND TO GIVE MORE

When people feel loved and cared for, they are more open to giving financially than people who are not having this group experience. Wuthnow reports that 50 percent of group members increased the amount of money they gave to the church.[20] They were already giving, but now they were eager to give more.

In *Transformational Groups*, Ed Stetzer and Eric Geiger confirm this finding from their research, which shows people in groups contribute 10.34 percent of their total annual income (before taxes) compared to people not in groups, who contribute only 6.07 percent. If the average salary in your community is $35,000, that's a difference of $1,494.50 per household annually. Now, multiply that number by fifty, one hundred, or one thousand households, and you've just solved a lot of the financial problems at your church.[21]

Our friends at Capital Area Christian Church discovered that in addition to increased attendance, their giving had increased by 7 percent in the same time frame Nate studied above. If your church has a one million dollar annual budget, then you would have a $70,000 increase just from starting groups. That could provide for a new staff member or a raise!

4. PEOPLE IN GROUPS SERVE MORE THAN OTHERS

Going back to the research, Wuthnow reports 69 percent of group members say the group "has helped me serve people outside the group."[22] Forty-three percent of group members also became involved in volunteer work in their communities.[23]

Stetzer and Geiger found something similar in that comparing group members with non-group members, 47 percent of group members were involved in community service compared to 26 percent of non-group members. What's more, they also discovered 63 percent of group members had other responsibilities in their churches compared to only 25 percent of non-group members.[24]

Groups are also a great place for people to serve together. At New Life Christian Center where I served in California, we challenged our groups to prepare and serve a hot meal every Friday night at an emergency homeless shelter which ran five months of the year. We asked for groups to volunteer together instead of as individuals, because the group dynamics would guarantee ten out of ten group members participated, whereas individual recruitment might have netted four or five out of ten.

Our groups took this project to heart. Even on the year when both Christmas Eve and New Year's Eve were on a Friday, the sign-up sheet was completely filled up by our groups within an hour of placing it at our information center. My group didn't even get a chance to sign up!

One group member told me he was very reluctant to participate. His attitude toward the homeless had always been, "I started with nothing and pulled myself up by the bootstraps and built a successful construction company. Why couldn't the homeless work hard and do the same?"

He went with his group to serve the meal at the shelter. He later admitted that as he stood in line serving those men and looking them in the eye, he realized if circumstances had been different in his life, then he might be standing on the other side of that line receiving the meal.

Six months later, he was sending his construction crews over to San Francisco every Friday to renovate a building which would be used as a homeless shelter in the Tenderloin. Talk about a change of heart. Not only did he see the homeless differently, he was compelled to do something about it. Instead of his crews building multimillion dollar homes on Fridays, they were renovating a homeless shelter. The positive peer pressure of a small group serving together made a difference not only in his life, but in the lives of many homeless people he might never meet.

5. PEOPLE IN GROUPS GROW MORE

Groups allow for learning which could never take place in a weekend service or a Sunday school class. Now, don't get me wrong. People receive plenty of solid teaching and inspiration in both, but learning in a group is a much different dynamic.

Adult learners tend to be more distracted than younger people. Often we hear people talk about how ADD or ADHD children are and how they have such short attention spans. Adults are actually worse. Adult brains are kind of like a Google search. You get one piece of information, which leads to another thought, which leads to an additional search, and before we know it, we're wondering where the last hour went.

When people are rearranged from rows to circles, and from church facilities to homes or another comfortable place, the dynamic changes. They are no longer just spoken to. Now they have the opportunity to speak and work through the ideas which were presented.

Adults are not blank slates where new content has sole dominance. New ideas must compete with the things adults have already learned both formally and in life. Let's face it, most believers are discipled by television and the internet. With such a strong influence from the entertainment world and news commentators, adults must see how the Bible study jibes with everything else they've encountered. It takes some processing.

By allowing a place to interact with God's word as well as the experiences of other believers, group members are allowed to "try on" new ideas and concepts in a safe and loving environment. Anyone who has ever made a New Year's resolution or tried to break a bad habit knows both accountability and support are necessary to make the change. The accountability doesn't need to be heavy-handed, but just knowing someone will ask about your progress and pray for your success is certainly a key to success.

Wuthnow's research shows growth produced in significant ways in those participating in groups. Group members shared "a deeper love toward other people" (73 percent), "a better ability to forgive others" (71 percent), "feeling closer to God" (66 percent), and "the Bible becoming more meaningful to [them]" (57 percent).[25]

Now, if everyone is already in a group, then why don't these results appear spontaneously in our churches? Why do groups need any kind of organization, curriculum, or direction? For most churches and their members, these results just don't organically appear. This is exactly why we need organization, curriculum, and direction.

The group's focus will determine the goals it reaches. If the group is focused on making the best barbecue on the planet, which living in South Carolina means "pork" (everything else is considered "grillin' out"), then smoked meat with wonderful sauce (or dry) will be the result. Yet in one church I served, a group called the "Holy Smokers" made amazing barbecue, grew close to God, met for regular Bible study, and served the homeless as well as many others. Some of what they did was by the spontaneous urging of the Holy Spirit. Other results they saw in the change in attitudes and behavior came from a community intentionally committed to encouraging each other to grow spiritually. Iron was truly sharpening iron.

Community is significant. Otherwise, why write or read a book about it? But, community with purpose is far more significant. As Steve Gladen writes in *Small Groups with Purpose*,

> Even though fellowship may be the most frequently cited benefit of a small group, it is a mistake to allow groups to stay in the comfort zone of this benefit. True Christian community goes deeper than spending social time together. It dives below the surface into the heart and enables us to speak into each other's lives. It provides the strong foundation for living out all the purposes in a safe environment and is the glue that holds your group together when times get tough. This type of community will not happen, however, without direction and focused leadership.[26]

As Andy Stanley says in *The Principle of the Path*, "Direction, not intention, determines your destination."[27] This is where you come in. This is where leadership can unleash tremendous potential among groups of friends, coworkers, neighbors, relatives, and other groups who are already in your church.

I wish these "groups everyone is already in" could spontaneously serve, share, grow, care, and worship together. I wish the term "small group" would disappear. The new term would be "normal." It would be the normal practice of believers to encourage each other in their spiritual growth and influence the world for Christ. But we live among a distracted church. Leadership is necessary to give direction. You can see the results as mentioned above in both research and testimony. What's holding you back?

This is a start. Depending on how you choose to proceed, you could catch your groups up with your weekend attendance in a hurry or take your time, depending on your acceptable level of risk. In the churches I've served as well as those I've coached, we've created a few messes over the years that turned into something wonderful.

THE LAUNCH

CHAPTER 4

COACHING—BEGINNING WITH THE END IN MIND

While we have spent a decent amount of time casting vision for launching groups and giving some practicality to the church-wide campaign, up to this point, we haven't really addressed the actual work of the small group pastor. Here we go.

Some small group pastors get caught up in recruiting leaders. This is not your job. If the launch goes well, recruiting leaders is your senior pastor's job.

Other small group pastors brace themselves for a massive group sign-up and the need for placing hundreds to thousands of people into groups. This also is not your job. Once your pastor recruits the group leaders, the leaders will gather their groups. More on this later.

So what does the small group pastor do in a group launch? Now we are going to roll up our sleeves and get to the hard work of this. Your success both in a church-wide small group launch and your ability to sustain groups after the series hinges largely on coaching. It's not as difficult as you might think.

In my experience, the word "coaching" evokes more guilt in small group pastors than about anything else. Their coaching is broken. They don't know how to fix it. Maybe they don't even really understand the need for coaching—just like we don't understand the need to prepare for an emergency until there is an emergency. (You may understand it, but do you understand it enough to do something about it?)

So before we really get going, let's eliminate the guilt. If you have a lousy or nonexistent coaching structure, let's look at what is actually working. You have groups who have figured out how to function without the help of the coach. I'm not trying to give you a consolation prize here. I want you to see how you've felt guilty over something that for the most part wasn't seriously needed by your current group leaders up to this point. You might ask, "If groups can function and find their way without a coach, then why bother?" Well, your lack of coaching has greatly limited the size and health of your groups ministry. You are planning for what you can handle rather than preparing for what God can do with your groups. The lack of coaching has cost you groups over the years, but the fact you have groups despite the lack of coaching is a testament to our group leaders. You should still be ashamed. Okay, I'm kidding.

Experienced small group leaders who have figured out how to effectively lead without the benefit of a coach are prime candidates to coach other groups. So while your ineptitude at creating a coaching structure produced much guilt and exhaustion for you, it also produced some amazing candidates for your future coaching structure. See what a genius you are!

ISN'T THIS PUTTING THE CART BEFORE THE HORSE?

The reason we start with coaching instead of recruiting leaders or forming groups is that new leaders need the help of a coach. Anyone who starts anything for the first time has huge potential for discouragement and faces the temptation to quit. If anyone needs a coach, it's the person who just said "Yes" to leading a group for the first time. Start there. Don't inflict your established leaders with a coach just yet. More on this in chapter ten.

If you don't start a new leader with a coach, then it's harder to implement coaching later. While every leader needs coaching, they won't all be open to it. If a leader has led for a long time without a coach, they may actually become suspicious when a coach appears. "What have you heard about our group?" More on this later, but the point here is if the leader starts with a coach, it is "normal" for the new leader. But, coaching is not just new to a new leader.

Your new coach needs to start with "single Jeopardy" before they get to "Double Jeopardy." In the show, the Jeopardy round is made up of the "easy" questions. Then, Double Jeopardy ups the ante with harder questions with a higher dollar value. When leaders are new, for the most part, they have new leader questions. Their coaches are in single Jeopardy. They ask things like "How do we handle childcare?" or "Half my group didn't show up. Do I just stink as a leader or what?" New coaches are experts on newbie questions. They've got the answers.

Occasionally, more difficult questions will arise. These don't usually come up in the beginning, but I did have one of the most difficult questions come up in a new group a few years ago. I was working with a church in Hawaii, and the small group pastor told me a new leader called to say a man in his group asked him, "How do I tell my wife I used to be a woman before we were married?" After coaching over 1,500 churches, this was a first for me. Don't share this story with your coaches or leaders. They will run for the hills.

Before the questions get too difficult, let the coaching begin with the easy issues. As the groups get to know each other better and stuff begins to come out, then you've had time to prepare your coaches, and more importantly, the coaches have had time to build relationships with the group leaders.

MY OWN TRIAL AND ERROR WITH COACHING

Over the years, I have made many attempts at coaching and supporting group leaders. Coaching is something I am continuing to figure out, but I've made significant progress in my thinking over the years.

We made our first attempt with groups at New Life Christian Center in Turlock, California, back in 1994. The senior pastor and I handpicked the cream of the crop to lead groups. We chose nine couples and me. All ten groups started in January. All ten groups quit in December, including mine. This was not the plan.

We asked the leaders what happened. I mean, after all, if the leaders loved Jesus and wanted to go to heaven, then why weren't they continuing? The response came back, "I felt like a lone ranger out there."

Granted, at the time the church was only about three hundred people. We talked to the leaders all of the time, but we weren't coaching them. We weren't spending our time and attention specifically discussing their groups and what God was doing in them. There weren't really any big problems in any of the groups (except the one guy who would never leave my house after the meeting). Overall, the leaders just didn't feel the support and encouragement they needed to continue. Even though they could connect with our pastor or me at any point, the lack of intentional coaching cost us 100 percent of those group leaders in the end.

Lesson learned. Group leaders need coaches so they feel supported in ministry. They need the personal attention and "space" to talk about their groups with a coach.

Our second attempt at groups started in 1997. After studying group models, interviewing pastors, and reading every small group book I could get my hands on, we recruited two coaches first, then recruited the leaders, and then began Basic Training as well as monthly group leader huddle meetings. It was all by the book. Well, it was mostly by the book.

I didn't hear many complaints from the group leaders this time around. Mission accomplished. The new plan worked. But, I did hear complaints from the coaches.

"I feel like I'm your spy," Carol, one of my coaches, told me.

I said, "Well, it's because you are my spy." Then, I laughed. But Carol wasn't laughing.

The coaches visited groups, then turned in reports about what was going on with the groups. They were my eyes and ears. It's the only way I knew what was really going on in the groups. But, it made my coaches feel icky.

Lesson learned. In coaching, lead with the relationship, not the task. I didn't need to bug these living rooms to see what was going on. I needed the coach to develop a relationship with the group leader. Then, when they visited the group, they came in as a friend and not a supervisor with a clipboard. But, that was only the first complaint.

Carol stopped by my office another day and said, "Even though I enjoy working with the group leaders, I'm bored."

I thought, "Why is she bored? I'm busy." After all, I recruited the leaders, delivered the training, led the monthly group leader huddles, and tracked the groups. There was plenty to do. Why was she bored?

So, I fired her on the spot. After all, every time we met it was nothing but complaints. Okay, I didn't fire her.

Carol was bored because I was doing her job. While I had delegated the visits and most of the personal contact to my coaches, I was still doing most of the coaching and training.

Lesson learned. Recruit qualified people to coach group leaders, then get out of their way. Even though the small group team at the time included only two coaches and me, we were laying the groundwork for something much bigger.

While most of those groups continued, Carol dropped out of coaching. With the one remaining coach, we made our next attempt at coaching a few years later.

Even though I had learned a few lessons about staying out of the coaches' way, I hadn't learned the lessons completely. I remained at the center of our group ministry and coaching structure. Out of my own insecurity and need for control, I recruited, trained, and still coached almost everybody. My one remaining coach was an amiable guy that put up with me, but it wasn't good.

Lesson learned. Delegate all you can. Going back to Exodus 18, we only had leaders of tens and fifties, but the hundreds and thousands were coming. My actions were not only handicapping our present, they were also limiting our future. Similar to Moses in Exodus 18, I needed to get past my objections that I was the only one who could do it, and the leaders liked coming to me. I was getting in my own way and struggled to reach our small group goals.

In 2004, coaching changed dramatically in our church, not because of my well-laid plans, but because of the growing success of our groups. With no new coaches, and with me doing an inadequate job of coaching the leaders we had, we were completely unprepared when our groups doubled in a day. Now, we had a coaching crisis.

While the previous seven years hadn't required me to get my coaching act together, doubling our groups on a single Sunday quickly brought things into perspective. If I couldn't adequately coach the group leaders I had, how in the world could I help twice as many? Then, the lightbulb came on.

If we had doubled our groups, that meant half of our leaders had experience and the other half were brand-new and without a clue. I implemented the buddy system. This is how it went.

I sent all of the experienced leaders a letter, which basically said,

Dear group leader,

I am thrilled with the new leaders who have just volunteered to lead groups, and I'm totally overwhelmed. I need your help. I am assigning you to [INSERT NEW LEADER NAME] for the next six weeks of the series. Unless you absolutely can't do this, I am counting on you.

Sincerely,

Pastor Allen

Now, I had been at the church for twelve years at this point, so I actually got away with this. I probably spent every bit of leadership credit I had in the bank, but with the exception of one experienced leader who let me know she couldn't take this on, the rest helped the new leaders. It was quick and dirty, but we got it done.

Lesson learned. Experienced leaders will respond when they are truly needed, and they will do a much better job than I had originally given them credit for.

When the situation finally overwhelmed my ability to lead the small group ministry, it forced me to seek the help I needed. Without the luxury of time to ponder the wonders of coaching, I made a bold move and coaching took off like a rocket, even if it was temporary.

Around midyear that year, there was a definite need for a permanent, ongoing coaching structure. Not only had many of the groups continued, but we continued to add to that number. It was time to identify our leaders of hundreds.

I recruited five experienced leaders to form a small groups team. We had a lot of catching up to do. I called them "community leaders" because our hope was to create the small groups team with leaders of hundreds and eventually thousands, then add in coaches to lead fifties. Looking back, we probably should have started the other way, but this is what we did.

With my five community leaders, we needed to divide up our current groups among them and get started with our coaching. Rather than parceling all of these out along geographical lines, we conducted an NBA-style draft. I created a list of all of our current groups, then we started round one. Each community leader chose a name from the list whom they would be responsible for. Then, on to Round Two. This continued until every leader was selected by a community leader.

The point was to choose people they already had a relationship with rather than those who lived nearby or some other random criteria. As we whittled the list down, we reached a group of leaders none of the community leaders were familiar with. I had to sort of "sell" the leaders to them by giving my best description of who the leaders were and what their groups were like.

By the end of our "draft," all of the current group leaders had an assignment to one of these community leaders. The org chart was looking good. But I did make one mistake in the selection process.

I allowed a community leader to choose his son-in-law to coach. This put a strain on their relationship and certainly was not coaching at its best. I made as many apologies as I could to the son-in-law.

While we applied the lessons learned from the past to our coaching, we had merely caught up with the numerical growth of our groups. We hadn't planned for the future. After all, we had gone from 30 percent of our adults in groups to 60 percent in just a few weeks. How much more could we accomplish in a year? Turns out, we accomplished a lot more that year.

Our small group team met for about ninety minutes every Wednesday night for dinner. This was the place where we (including me) made all of the decisions for the small group ministry. I wasn't going to do the team's work for them anymore. I chose to work with them. I made two shifts in my approach. First, I invited this group of community leaders to figure out small groups with me. I didn't have it all figured out. This left me vulnerable, but as someone has said, "All of us is smarter than any one of us." Second, I committed to not making any decisions about small groups outside of that meeting. We were in this together. This was so much better. We brought any problems or issues that were coming up from leaders, then we discussed the solutions. We also made plans for future series, and what needed to happen during the recruitment and briefing process.

One night, I sat down at the table, and casually asked the community leaders how things were going. One quickly spoke up, "Well, it would be going a whole lot better if these group leaders would call us back." While we started our coaching based on each community leader's relationship with the group leaders, the next wave of new leaders came so fast that I just made assignments to the community leaders. Now, they had to follow up with leaders they had never met. I thought I certainly didn't want to spend the next ninety minutes talking about this.

I asked the group, "Whose calls do you return?"

They responded, "What do you mean?"

I said, "Well, you don't return every call. Who do you call back?"

We decided we returned calls to two categories of people. First, we called people who were important to us. Then, we called people about matters that were important to us. I challenged the team, "How do we become those people to our leaders?"

Lesson learned. Nobody likes cold calling. While we had made our best effort to match the community leaders up with group leaders they already knew, the new group leaders didn't know why these guys were calling, and in some cases, didn't know who they were. We made a quick change starting with our next group launch.

Instead of leading the new leader briefing alone (more on briefings later), the small group team was in the room with me. About midway through the briefing, I introduced the small group team by saying, "Let me introduce you to some *very important people* who are going to *help you get your group started.*" Now, the new leaders were receiving calls from someone who was (1) important to them, and (2) calling about a matter of significance. It wasn't 100 percent effective, but it was far more effective than what we were doing before.

In the following years, we continued to add new coaches as we added new leaders. In both churches I have served, we began to recruit new coaches on a trial basis. We would use a six-week series to give experienced leaders a test drive at coaching just like we were giving the folks in the pews a trial run at leading a group.

At Brookwood Church in Simpsonville, South Carolina, the sheer size of the church (about 6,500) forced the group model to expand rapidly. I inherited a well-formed groups system with a small group team (leaders of thousands), coaches (leaders of fifties and hundreds), and group leaders (leaders of tens). But, as we began to produce our own video-based curriculum and launch hundreds of new groups at a time, the coaching had to keep up.

Before we started recruiting new leaders, we held a Sneak Peek event for all of the established leaders. The leaders were honored by having the first look at the new series and group curriculum. It also took pressure off of our briefings for new leaders in the following three weeks by giving the experienced leaders all of the information in advance. In the past, I had situations where so many established leaders would crowd into the briefings that we couldn't get to the new ones.

The Sneak Peek was also our opportunity to recruit potential coaches for the new leaders we were expecting. As someone once said, "Never let a good crisis go to waste." At the end of the meeting, I would challenge the experienced leaders, "We are planning to be inundated with new leaders for this next series. Our current coaching team will be completely overwhelmed. Could you help us by walking alongside a new leader from when they say 'Yes' until the end of the series?"

The job description was pretty simple. I asked the experienced leaders to:

1. Call the new leaders once per week. This wasn't an email distribution list. After all, I could have done that. This was all

about the relationship and personal contact. Coaches need to pick up the phone.

2. Encourage them. Everybody needs encouragement, especially when they're doing something for the first time.

3. Answer their questions. Most of these were single Jeopardy questions, which the experienced leader could easily answer. If there were tougher issues, they just said, "I don't know, but I will find out for you."

4. Pray for the new leader whenever they thought about them.

Then, I passed around a clipboard to the experienced leaders at the Sneak Peek with the schedule for the new leader briefings. The experienced leaders didn't need to be at every briefing. They were only going to work with one new leader or maybe two (remember, they were getting a trial run at coaching). During the briefing, I would, once again, introduce these very important people who were going to help the new leaders get their groups started. We did our best to make sure every new leader left the briefing with a coach who would follow up with them later that week.

Even experienced, committed group leaders need to be motivated and held accountable for what they committed to. As the old saying goes, only the things that are supervised get done. This shouldn't be heavy-handed, but it is necessary for the success of both the new leaders and their "coaches."

If you're in a smaller church, then the pastor or small group director should call the coaches. If it's a larger church with a small group team, then the team should call the coaches. The call should go something like this.

"What are you learning from your new leaders?" The question is not "have you called them?" By asking what they are learning, you give the experienced leaders the benefit of the doubt. You are assuming the calls are being made just as they've committed to.

If the response is "I haven't had a chance to call them this week," then give them a deadline. "Why don't you go ahead and call your new leaders, then I'll give you a call on Friday to see what you found out."

People who are only accountable to themselves are not accountable. By offering some gentle accountability, small group pastors and their teams can both ensure new leaders are receiving the care and encouragement they need, and alleviate the guilt of experienced leaders who got a little behind or failed to follow through on their good intentions.

At the end of the series, I sent a survey to all of the experienced leaders who had helped a new leader. I asked only three questions:

1. On a scale of 1 to 5, how important do you feel you were to the success of your new leaders and their groups?

2. How difficult or easy was it for you to contact the new leaders (1 to 5)?

3. How many of your new groups plan to continue with the next series? The range is "All Continuing" to "None Continuing."

The results were uncanny. The answers either lined up one way or the other. Many experienced leaders said they felt their role was very important, it was easy to contact their leaders, and most of the groups were continuing. We invited these folks who were effective at helping other leaders into a larger coaching role. For the experienced leaders who responded with the opposite answers on the survey (unimportant, difficult to contact, and not continuing), we thanked them for fulfilling their commitment. They could go back to leading their group.

It's hard to tell who will be a good coach until you give them a trial run. Over the years, I've invited group leaders to lunch and presented them with a job description for coaching. They liked the idea of helping others. Some really liked the idea of having a title. The results were always mixed. The problem was I had to "fire" the coaches who weren't doing a good job (or were doing nothing other than polishing their title). Of course, firing a volunteer is always awkward. They don't even work for me! The trial run at coaching took a lot of pain out of this.

I've come to discover there is a *good, better, best* in coaches. A good coach has experience as a group leader. A better choice is an experienced group leader who is also mature in the faith. The best coaches I have ever found are the ones who actually care. They have a heart for group leaders. They care enough to pick up the phone and call. I would take a coach who cares over a coach with group experience or maturity who didn't care any day.

A few years back, one pastor had assigned all of his church staff to coach group leaders, but there still wasn't much coaching going on. He asked me how he could motivate his staff to coach. I said, "On Friday, ask them if they want their paycheck!" Even if you pay people to perform the task of coaching, you can't pay people to care. And, for people who actually care, they don't care about being paid.

Now you might ask why coaching matters so much at this point. After all, we haven't even recruited any leaders yet! Here's why.

During one season when I was on staff at New Life, we had challenged our groups to invite their members to step out of the group and start new groups. One couple took us up on it. I'll call them "Ray" and "Pam" . . . because those were their names. They stepped out of a group they loved to start a new group.

One Sunday morning, I bumped into Ray and Pam and asked them how their group was coming along. They said, "Not very well. We think we made a mistake leaving our group."

I asked what had happened. They replied, "We've invited twenty people to our group, and everyone turned us down. We don't understand it. We shower. Our house is clean. We just think this was a mistake."

I advised them, "Well, let's not give up yet. There's a reason you felt you should step out of your group to start a new group. You had an idea of who should be in your group. Now, let's pray and ask God about his idea for who should be in your group."

A week later they called me, "Pastor Allen, please stop sending people to our group. We have fourteen people who want to be in our group, and we don't really have room for more."

Now, how many people had I sent to their group? Zero. I hadn't sent one person to their group. But, we prayed, and God answered our prayer. After a while that group went on under new leadership and now has lasted for well over ten years. In fact, the new leader,

Alfred, who also started a group at the GM dealership, and his wife, Vicki, continued leading the couples' group.

What would have happened if I hadn't talked to Ray and Pam that day? It didn't have to be me checking in on them, but it needed to be somebody. New leaders can become easily discouraged and doubtful in starting a group. They need someone in their corner to encourage them.

After our third alignment series in a row at New Life, I surveyed the new leaders only to discover 30 percent were not going to continue their group. I needed to find out why. What I discovered is out of that 30 percent most had never started! This led me to a very wise conclusion: groups that don't start tend not to continue. Now that's worth the price of this book! We hadn't lost those groups. We never had them.

From that point forward, we had an experienced leader working with a new leader from when the new leader said "Yes" and attended a briefing until the end of the series. The weeks between the new leader's response to the pastor's invitation and the start of the series are mission critical.

The new leaders will get turned down by some of the people they invite to their groups and will become discouraged. If they get turned down enough, they won't continue to invite. Or, if they only have a couple of people in their group, they will join up with another group. Both of these choices need to be prevented.

Usually in the course of a series, groups will continue to add members. But, if a group of three people joins a group of eight people, then the growth of the group during the series will be limited. A new group of eleven might invite two or three more people, but a group of three could end up with six people, and a group of eight could end up with twelve people. What could have been two groups that totaled eighteen people ended up only being one group of twelve to fourteen people. At least four new people are missing out. Coaches can encourage groups to start on their own, even if they are starting small. Coaches see the bigger picture. More groups means more growth.

Every new leader is prone to both discouragement and spiritual attack. We have an enemy who wants to steal, kill, and destroy.[28]

Experienced leaders who are praying for new leaders and encouraging them will go a long way in helping the new leaders to continue forward with their group.

While it may seem odd to discuss the start of a coaching structure for new leaders before we've talked about recruiting leaders or forming groups, this coaching piece is crucial to the success of new leaders. Even though some of my approach feels a little "sink or swim" for new leaders, we can certainly give them a lifeguard to assist. There is not enough of any one small group pastor or director to manage dozens or hundreds of new leaders. By enlisting established leaders to coach new leaders, everyone's experience is improved. The established leaders get to share their knowledge and experience. The new leaders receive encouragement and support, and the new group members enjoy a better quality of group life from the start.

For those small group pastors and directors who dreamed of handpicking more leaders or assigning prospective members to groups, I am pleased to disappoint you. This is not your work. Your work is to establish the coaching structure to support your future group leaders. Your pastor will recruit the leaders. The leaders will gather their groups. Your coaches will provide support to get the new groups started and to keep them going for the long term.

CHAPTER 5

EFFECTIVE STRATEGIES FOR RECRUITING LEADERS

Opinions abound on who should lead small groups. Some churches insist all of their group leaders should be members and fairly mature in their faith, while other churches will recruit anyone who is breathing. There is no right or wrong here as long as your church chooses the right option for you.

The biggest factors in choosing a strategy are your church's acceptable level of risk and how quickly you want to connect your congregation into groups. For instance, if I had continued handpicking leaders at New Life in Turlock, it would have taken probably one hundred years to have enough leaders for everyone who wanted to be in a group. Considering our groups only involved 30 percent of our adults after seven years, and the church continued to grow steadily, handpicking leaders simply did not serve our purpose of connecting and discipling our people. By taking greater risks, we reaped greater rewards.

The risk was calculated. Before we changed the requirement for "hosting" a group to "whosoever will," we studied our congregation through the survey I mentioned in chapter three to assess the potential fallout. We wanted to know if they were in a group, when they came to Christ, and how long they had attended our church.

We discovered the average person who attended our church had been a Christian for at least eighteen years and had been a part of the church for at least six years. Then, when we made the general invitation for group "hosts," we understood the bull's-eye was nearly as large as the actual target. The averages were certainly in our favor for recruiting mature leaders for our groups.

After we recruited, we discovered we had very few axe murders or Satanists leading. In fact, there were none. A few problems surfaced like people who were cohabiting but weren't married. There were a few folks who needed to make more progress in their recovery before they led. Others were facing a marital separation or were going through a divorce. These discoveries led to opportunities for a pastoral conversation, and in no way put a black eye on the strategy. Our problems amounted to about 2 percent of all of the leaders we recruited.

Let's face it, most churches will have that number of problems anyway. The question is whether your church will tolerate problems for a good reason, or will just settle for problems for no good reason at all. Most "problems" come from being unaware of how God is working. While a new recruit may not be the right candidate to lead a small group, he or she could certainly receive care and help in an area of great need in his or her life. We never want to give people the impression that we only care about what they can do for the church. People should know we care about them, and are ready to serve whether they fit our agenda or not.

WHO DO YOU RECRUIT?

Who you recruit depends largely on how you will form groups. If your groups will be advertised through the church bulletin, a groups directory, the church's website, a small group "fair," or if the church will be sending people to the groups, then your hosts or leaders need to be well vetted. By promoting the group in any way, the church is essentially endorsing the group. This raises a certain expectation of the quality of the group.

Let's say we rated spiritual maturity on a scale of zero to ten. Zero being someone who is unsaved, and eight or so being Billy Graham. If the group leader is a spiritual three and the people who sign up for the group are fives, sixes, and sevens, then there is a problem. The relatively immature leader will frustrate the more mature group members. Of course, over the years I've seen some very "mature" Christians pitch a fit over the most ridiculous things. Makes you wonder how mature they really are.

Now, if the same spiritual "three" invited his or her friends to the group, who would be invited? Mostly likely the group would include threes, twos, ones, zeros, and possibly those in negative numbers who are far from God. What would have been a problem for a publicly promoted group is actually a good fit for an invitation only scenario.

Let me introduce you to Miranda. Miranda walked up to the small group table one Sunday morning and said she would like to start a group with her friends. She was a little reluctant. Miranda had just been released from prison.

I asked her what she was thinking about as far as forming her group. She said she had some friends and neighbors who might be interested. Several of them were far from God. I handed her the materials and put an experienced group leader in her life to coach her.

Miranda followed every instruction she was given about starting and leading her group. In fact, she was a better new leader than most of our official leaders. I told my pastor after the series had concluded that we really needed to recruit more parolees. They made outstanding group leaders.

If you don't advertise the groups and people are inviting their friends to join, since they are friends, they already know each other. They should have a pretty good idea of what to expect. The person starting the group has already been accepted by the group, so their inexperience at group leadership shouldn't be an obstacle for the group. They are friends. I would still ask if the new leader was struggling with a life-controlling problem or facing a major relationship issue. After all, as their pastor, I want to help.

But if someone is invited to a group by their friend, then later complains that their leader is inexperienced, doesn't know how to lead, or runs a terrible meeting, then my response would be, "Hey, you picked the group. It's your friend. I didn't send you there. So, this is on you, not me." But I have never actually heard a complaint like that. People give a lot of grace to their friends.

So should you recruit leaders for groups you would promote or for groups you wouldn't promote? I would say, "Yes." While groups of friends end up being better groups that tend to last, there will be folks who are new to your church or who are new to the area that may not get invited to a group. Open groups that are advertised are important in making sure no one is left out.

Again, why you are recruiting leaders will greatly determine whom you recruit. Give an option to the potential leaders. Do they want to lead a group open to new members, or do they want to invite their friends and form an invitation-only group? The extroverts, who have never met a stranger, will easily go public with their group. Introverts might choose invitation-only where they are responsible to recruit 100 percent of the group members. They don't want strangers coming to their house! But, they will do the study with their friends.

The more requirements for group leadership, the fewer leaders you will recruit. If you required all of your new leaders to be church members, complete a lengthy leadership training process, or graduate with their Master of Divinity, you limit the number of groups you could launch. You have set the bar too high.

Your level of acceptable risk will greatly determine the reward. If you invite people to do a study with their friends, then you are only limited to people with friends. If you increase the requirements, you lessen the impact.

If you choose to lower the bar, then lessen the risk by forming "unpublished" groups. If the groups don't appear on your church's website, groups listing, or bulletin, you are not implying any kind of official endorsement of the groups. If friends invite friends, you will form good, lasting groups, and if someone gets in a bad group, well, it was their friend's group after all, right?

WHAT ARE YOUR LEADERSHIP REQUIREMENTS?

The comfort level of your leadership team is important. If the pastors, staff and/or elders of the church have determined membership, for instance, is a requirement, then start with your membership list.

This was the case at Oak Cliff Bible Fellowship in Dallas, Texas. The team announced to me on a call one day that membership was required to host a group at their church. My immediate reaction was that we were dead in the water. With this news, I didn't anticipate launching more than fifty new groups.

I asked, "How many members do you have?"

The team replied, "We have around seven thousand members."

What a relief! I thought, "Okay, I can work with that."

Decide on the acceptable number of requirements for group leaders prior to launching groups. Clear this with your pastors, elders, and other decision makers, then make the most of it.

As you read in chapter two, Dr. Evans successfully recruited five hundred new hosts for the *Destiny* series. Some of the folks who responded were not church members, so they were redirected into joining a group. But, all in all, it was a success.

HANDPICKING LEADERS

As you can probably tell at this point, I don't have enough bad things to say about limiting your groups by handpicking leaders. In fact, just because the small group pastor personally selects leaders doesn't mean the group members will have a quality experience or that the leaders are necessarily the cream of the crop.

Now, there are very good reasons to handpick leaders. If a church has never had small groups before, the experience of piloting a few groups with personally selected leaders is a great way to start. While I was intrigued by the experience of others, it took my own experience to solidify my commitment to groups. Over the years, my groups were formed in various ways through lower-risk experiments, which, once proved, opened doors for many groups in both the churches I served as well as those I have coached.

If you serve a smaller church, there is far more at stake for you if you are launching groups for the first time. It would be a good idea to start with leaders you know and trust rather than throw the door wide and caution to the wind. While you don't need as many groups, the margin of error is far slimmer for you. Recruit with care, especially on your first time out.

Once you've had some wins with groups, then you and your congregation will gain confidence in launching groups in other ways. Starting small is a good idea before you decide to go big with groups, whether that means church-wide groups or community-wide groups.

RECRUITING HOST HOMES

I gave a thorough description of the HOST home model in chapter one. The strength of the HOST strategy lies in offering not only an alternative term to "leader," but also a new set of requirements. While "leaders" might need to have teaching or leadership gifts, "hosts" just need to be hospitable, relationally warm, and friendly. You don't need Bible scholars or longtime believers. A host only needs to be friendly to qualify.

This is an effective move for churches stuck at 30 percent or less of their folks in groups, or those frustrated with handpicking leaders like I once was. Instead of the small group pastors and directors attempting to identify all of the qualified group leader candidates, an appeal for people to host groups allows host leaders to self-identify, thus the sheer number of candidates increases dramatically. While there should be some initial training, the real test of the viability of group hosts as full-fledged leaders lies in their ability to gather and keep a group. This next statement may seem a little Darwinian, but if someone has what it takes to gather a group, they will keep the group going. If hosts can't gather the group, then no amount of support will keep their groups together.

A few years ago one of my established leaders brought a potential host to me. My established leader didn't know the other guy very well, but wanted to make the introduction. When I walked into the meeting room, this new gentleman sat at the table with a three-inch binder of material he had downloaded from the internet about the end times. I looked at my established leader and thought, "Really?"

I knew from the get-go this was going to be a disaster. But over the years I have gotten tired of being the bad guy who prevents others from learning from their own pain and mistakes. In fact, it has been a pretty big step for me as a pastor to allow others to make mistakes and to learn from them. I always wanted to rescue them. (And, yes, I'm working on my stuff.)

Our church was weeks away from a new alignment series. I encouraged our Eschatological Web Surfer to put this topic aside in favor of starting a group for the church's next study. He consented. Then, I whispered to the established leader on their way out, "And, you are going to be his coach and attend every meeting, because you started this."

Sure enough, he set up a table at the Small Group Connection event, and had two or three guys sign up for his group. After a few weeks, the group just sort of fell apart. I had seen it coming, but I needed to allow him to have the experience. There was never any mention of an End Times Prophecy small group ever again.

This was an exception. Most of the HOST home groups I've seen start over the years have been successful in varying degrees. People enjoyed getting together with old friends or making new friends. And, the best part is seeing more new groups and new leaders than ever before. For me, the risk of introducing the HOST home was worth the reward of seeing so many people engaged in leading and participating in groups.

The HOST strategy, however, has nearly run its course for churches in general. If you have only handpicked leaders up to this point, then embrace the HOST strategy. It will take you so much further than continuing to handpick leaders ever will. But, many churches have become stuck with the HOST home strategy—even churches with thousands of people in groups.

When our team first met Steve Poe, Lead Pastor of Northview Church in Carmel, Indiana, the church already had 75 percent of their four thousand adults connected into groups. To date, they are probably one of the best examples of the impact of the HOST strategy. In fact, they had taken the HOST strategy to a point I had never heard of by achieving 75 percent in ongoing groups. I've talked to many churches who reach 50 percent this way, but 75 percent was amazing. With Northview's success in groups, connecting the next 25 percent was really a bit of a different animal.

Rather than starting with a blank slate and launching a ton of new small groups with a church-wide video-based series, we had to come up with a solution to help the one-thousand-plus remaining adults say "Yes" to groups when they had been saying "No" for a while.

Pastor Steve had the idea for creating a family series, but didn't really have the bandwidth to write six new talks for the curriculum video. Like many pastors, Steve had years and years of great sermons on family, so the team mined his previous sermons and created scripts for the ten-minute videos we needed for the series curriculum. Once the scripts were drafted, they were passed back over to Steve to make it what he wanted.

With scripts in hand, the church gathered a group of thirty people to participate with Steve in the teaching portion of the shoot. Now, this wasn't just an audience to teach to, it was a group to interact with. This went even one step further—not only did the group offer feedback and their experiences on camera, the setting also provided Steve with a way to model groups for the entire church through the video curriculum.

Once *Family Matters* was completed with a small group video and study guide, we came to the challenge of turning one thousand "Noes" into "Yeses." Rather than recruiting HOST homes where people were either assigned to groups or prospective members chose a group from the church's website, the new strategy took an entirely organic approach.

Every member of Northview Church was invited to gather a group of friends together and grow spiritually. Then, we all waited. Had we reached the saturation point? Could we break the ceiling above 75 percent in groups?

After three weeks of recruiting "hosts" for "groups" without using either of those words, two hundred new groups were started in addition to the three thousand folks who were already in groups. A new series launched shortly after *Family Matters* ended helped to retain the vast majority of new groups.

The HOST strategy is a great tool to break churches out of traditional models of groups, and especially to accelerate leadership recruitment over the handpicking method. Recruiting hosts works extremely well in communities with high turnover like college towns or churches near military bases. The continual churn of church members will keep the HOST strategy viable for many years to come.

But if your church has been using the HOST strategy for a decade, more than likely your groups are stuck, and you need a new strategy. At New Life after we had recruited hosts effectively for eighteen months, on the fifth alignment series I stood in the briefing room after the service all by myself. It was time for something new.

GATHER AND GROW

While the HOST strategy was an innovation for church-wide campaigns back in 2002 and the years that followed, there are certainly some limits. People have become savvy to the change in terminology from "leader" to "host." In fact, while the video-based curriculum provides much of the leadership for the group, there are still leader elements even if the term "host" is used. The jig is up.

The HOST strategy also implies a group of ten to twelve people who are either acquainted or are assembled for the series. This poses a couple of problems for groups. The notion of ten to twelve people gathered for groups eliminates the possibility of hosting a group if a person's house is too small to accommodate such a group. Now, while I don't believe the originators of the HOST strategy ever considered the size or meeting place as rigid criteria, the perception is a problem here.

While group size is an issue for some, the prospect of ten to twelve strangers arriving on one's doorstep is off-putting to others. As one author put it,

When our pastor rose to make the announcement, I suspected we were in for it again. "We're going to be a church of small groups," he told us, like a child pleading for his parents to read from a well-worn book one more time. "A church of small groups instead of a church with groups."

My heart sank. Been there; done that . . . a church of small groups? Sounded like forced relational hell to me.[29]

If more flexibility was applied to the HOST strategy, it could remain viable. It could propel churches to over 100 percent connected into groups. But, then again, everyone is already in a group.

At New Life, as we witnessed the HOST strategy beginning to wane, we knew we were done. Our church was growing, and we still had people to connect. We took the "gift bag" idea I mentioned in chapter one and went a step further.

If we were open to people we did not know very well hosting groups, then why not allow them to gather their friends and do the study on their own? They could invite as many friends as they liked. Some met with three or four friends. One host announced they had twenty-five! Some included only people they knew, while others invited friends of friends of friends.

How groups are formed has much bearing on the likelihood of the group continuing after the series. Groups artificially assembled based on willing souls who live in the same zip code or prefer meeting on a certain day of the week are more prone to failure. Granted, some folks are highly committed to group life, and will stick it out no matter what. Most people will try a group like this for a series, but they are more likely to abandon the group once the series ends.

Groups of friends tend to last longer than groups of strangers. Remember, everyone is already in a group. By having a connection to someone prior to the study's start, the relational bond is strong enough to keep them together. If they've just met, the group may or may not work out.

Those who previously didn't have time for a group really meant groups were not a priority to them. If they are willing to do a study with people they choose rather than people who are chosen for them, suddenly they will find time for doing a study with their friends.

The next time we launched an alignment series, we held our typical Small Group Fair, where hosts met prospective members

EFFECTIVE STRATEGIES FOR RECRUITING LEADERS   93

face-to-face, but we added a component. In fact, we made a road sign. If people wanted to join a group, they followed the arrow pointing right. But, if they wanted to start a group, they followed the arrow pointing left. Guess where the line was? To the left. They wanted to start their own groups rather than join a group.

IDENTIFYING POTENTIAL LEADERS, HOSTS, OR WHATEVER YOU WANT TO CALL THEM

Allow me to repeat: the greatest influencer in your church is the senior pastor. Trying to cast vision and build momentum for groups as a staff pastor wasn't futile, but the results paled in comparison to the results my senior pastor brought to starting groups. After that first invitation for the *Passion of the Christ* groups back in 2004, I have never personally recruited a small group leader again. None of the small group pastors and directors I've coached have either.

When the senior pastor is ready to launch groups, the small group team needs to be ready. While the pastor will make the invitation, the team must have their coaches in place as mentioned in the previous chapter and be ready to handle more new leaders than they're ever imagined.

WHEN YOU INVITE IS MAYBE MORE IMPORTANT THAN THE INVITATION ITSELF

Before you make an invitation to lead or promote a series, you need to give a heads-up to the established discipleship ministries in your church, especially if you lead a legacy church. Over the years, your church has accumulated a variety of ministries. As I mentioned in chapter one, you want to build new groups alongside, not instead of, existing ministries. To make the series mandatory or to force people to leave what they're familiar with to join something unfamiliar to them is just volunteering for unnecessary trouble.

A short conversation with established group leaders, Sunday school teachers, and Bible study leaders will go a long way in diverting hostility. You probably want to visit these ministries and explain the purpose of the series in connecting more people and helping them to grow spiritually. The groups and classes may raise a question about why the church just doesn't do more to promote the ministries that are already active. Be prepared to offer a thoughtful answer.

Sunday school is a dying breed, but it's not dead. Most people are not willing to spend four hours at church on Sunday morning. While classes are great for children on Sunday morning, the logistics of a large percentage of your adults in Sunday school creates an impossible situation. Most churches don't have the educational space for more adult classes on Sunday morning. The numbers just don't work. If space is your problem, do the math ahead of time. Show them how the numbers wouldn't add up.

For most churches, the space issue is also accompanied by a parking issue. In every church I have surveyed in the last three years, parking was perceived as one of the top three obstacles to the church's future growth. If your church needs to turn over the parking lot in a short amount of time on Sunday morning, people staying for classes will impact the parking for sure, which in turn will have a negative impact on the worship service. Most people don't think about parking logistics when they want to add to their classes or even add classes. Most people usually just think about themselves.

But, if the class wants to participate in the study, then they certainly could be promoted along with everyone else. The momentum of the alignment series will be just as beneficial to existing groups and classes as it is to new groups. The key is to invite established ministries into the series, but not force them to participate.

The goal in reaching out to established classes and groups is not to achieve complete agreement. That may be an impossible task. The goal really isn't even to get everyone onboard with the alignment series. The big goal here is to at least keep these folks from opposing where the church is headed in the alignment. After all, people are down on what they're not up on, as they say.

The best seasons of the year for a group launch are the fall, the new year, and Easter, as I've mentioned before. As you build momentum for a series, you want to promote well in advance. Let people know the series is coming. Show short video clips of the making of the series, if you're creating your own video curriculum. If you've purchased a curriculum, then use the preview videos provided by the publisher.

While you want to promote well in advance, you don't want to offer sign-ups too far in advance. If someone agrees to start a group three months ahead of the series, odds are that decision will be a faint memory when the campaign is ready to begin. You don't want to allow people a month or more to get cold feet. When they say, "Yes," it's time to move.

A PTA president advised me once to never hold sign-ups for more than three weeks. The simple reason is everyone waits until the last minute to register. She said to promote well in advance, but only sign up people when you are ready to start. Great advice.

Registering new leaders and groups over a three-week period has another significance—everyone doesn't attend church every Sunday. If registration is only offered for one week, then the church will miss out on two-thirds of their potential leaders.

This two-thirds scenario played out a few years ago with two churches I was working with. The churches were about the same size. One was in New York. The other in Florida. At the end of their recruitment periods, the New York church complained they only had one-third of the result the Florida church saw. I asked the small group pastor how many weeks they had recruited leaders. He told me that while the series was well publicized, they only registered new leaders for one Sunday.

The Florida church, on the other hand, had registered new leaders for three weeks and saw three times the result. In fact, the New York church's numbers matched the Florida church's recruits after their first week as well.

Now, some may be prone to blame this on the cultural differences between Florida and New York. After working with both churches for twelve months, the New York church launched a significant number of groups. And, besides, most people in Florida are from New York anyway.

To capture the most new leaders possible, a longer promotional period followed by a short registration period is key. In addition, registering for three weeks is also a major factor. If the church registers new leaders for more than three weeks, then the invitation becomes "Yada, yada, yada," and everyone waits until the last week to sign up anyway.

I was talking to the gal who cuts my hair about this one day. Why was I talking to her about this? Well, we talk about all kinds of things, and she's a captive audience. She's not a barber, and I don't like having a "stylist," so we'll just call her "Lorraine," since that's her name. Lorraine is retired, but she still has mercy on my hair. She is also a member of Brookwood Church, where I served. As I was spinning the tale of two churches with group launches and the importance of recruiting for three weeks, Lorraine spoke up, "I'll tell you why it's important to recruit for three weeks. That's how Rich and I ended up leading a group." (Lorraine is Italian and grew up in New Jersey. Do you have that picture in your mind?) She spun me around in the chair and started telling me her story, brandishing the comb toward my face for emphasis. (I was looking out of the corner of my eye to locate the scissors. I was safe.)

Lorraine went on, "The first week when our pastor from the stage invited us all to lead groups, I said, 'Nope, there is no way I'm going to do that. No way!'" The comb wagged faster. "Then, the next week, he invited us again. I thought, 'Hmm, maybe I should think about this?' When he invited us the third time, I said, 'That's it, Rich, we're leading a group.' See if the pastor didn't ask three times, I wouldn't be leading."

I would have offered a high five, but I still wasn't sure of where the scissors were located, so we just had some congratulations and a little laughter instead. Then, the haircut resumed.

Some, let's call them "Innovators," will jump in with the first invitation. They are good to go right off the mark. There's a second group, "Early Adopters," who need a little time to think about it. They've been caught flat-footed and are not prepared to respond. When the pastor makes the invitation again the next weekend, they've had a little time to think about it.

If a church is recruiting leaders like this for the first time, not everyone will get onboard during the first group launch. The average church will connect thirty to 50 percent of their adults on the first launch. (Of course, there are some exceptions.) Mostly Innovators and Early Adopters will start groups in the first series. Then there's the "Early Majority" who needs a little more time to see how all of this is going to work. They want to make sure nothing goes terribly wrong or nobody dies from this before they jump in. That's just their nature. We will discuss offering multiple launches, and the research behind this approach, in chapter eight.

HOW TO RECRUIT NEW LEADERS

The most effective way to recruit leaders is during the weekend service, but not among fifteen other announcements for various ministries. The reality with launching groups in the fall or the new year is that other groups and ministries are also competing for airtime in the services. To effectively launch groups in a big way, you have to clear the deck as much as possible and offer a singular message about groups. Now, this isn't forever, but it is for three weeks in a row prior to the group launch.

If a church is casting vision for more than one thing at the same time, then the church is creating di-vision or division. (Thanks to my friend Gilbert Thurston for that one.) There are a lot of reasons not to create division in your churches. Some are biblical!

How does a pastor clear the deck for communications without ticking other people off? Well, that can't be totally avoided, but if a pastor has done his due diligence in preparing existing ministries for what is coming, hopefully there will be less negative fallout from the communication strategy for the group launch. There are a few ways to promote other ministries without directly competing.

If a fall series launches in late September or early October, then with the three weeks prior reserved for recruiting leaders, other ministries can promote during late August or early September before the group leader recruitment is in full swing. The same goes for the new year. Rather than launching a series in the middle of January, run the series between Super Bowl Sunday and Easter (or what's known to liturgical churches as Lent). Promotion for other ministries can happen in late December or early January, and then the pastor can begin recruiting leaders for a February series start-ing in late January.

If it's impossible to avoid promoting other things during the leader recruiting process, then the pastor can utilize airtime no one else has access to—the sermon. If the invitation to lead a group comes in the middle of a pastor's message—whether he's speak-ing on community or it's an aside to another topic—the invitation will stand out to the congregation. It's unusual. The pastor typically doesn't invite people to do things in the middle of the message. This is special. This gets everybody's attention.

In the middle of the sermon, the pastor stops and briefly ex-plains what the church is doing with the upcoming group launch. This is also a great time to show a short video about the series. If the church produced its own curriculum, then the promo video should have as many familiar faces as possible—the pastor, other speakers, the crew, the people who provided lunch, everybody. Then, the pas-tor makes the invitation for people to lead groups.

If the pastor is inviting folks to host a group, then the challenge is for people to open their homes and provide a place for the group to meet for six weeks. If the pastor is promoting the Gather and Grow strategy, then the invitation is to "gather a few friends and do the study together." Essentially the pastor is inviting people to host a group without saying "host" or "group."

The pattern to effectively recruit leaders is simple. First, the pas-tor offers an invitation in the service. Next, the people are given a opportunity to respond right then and there. Then, the new leaders are given a next step.

What if the difference between success and failure lies in the few steps between the sanctuary and the lobby? That's what I wit-nessed a while back. The much-beloved founding pastor of a multi-site megachurch invited his congregation to open their homes and invite their friends to join them for a six-week study the church had produced. The curriculum was awesome. The pastor did the teaching. The topic was relevant. It was a sure thing.

But don't be so sure. At the close of the service, the pastor made an impassioned appeal for his members to take the next step and start their own groups. But, it wasn't just one next step, it was twenty or thirty next steps out to the lobby. That evening a crowd of one thousand adults netted only eighteen new leaders. All of our hearts sank.

The pastor had said the right words. He was presenting the right invitation at the right time. The church was familiar with small groups. Why the poor result?

Over the years, I've seen great messaging become ineffective simply by the distance between the invitation and the response. The best curriculum, the strongest leadership, or even the most carefully crafted appeal can all unravel in a matter of minutes if the wrong step is given in recruiting group leaders. A few simple nuances can net a profound effect.

At that church, we made a quick change. Rather than prospective group leaders responding by signing up in the church lobby after the service, the new next step involved no steps at all. The response was simply to take out a communication card and sign up right there in the service. The cards were collected at the end of the service. The result went from eighteen new leaders to 248 new leaders in less than twenty-four hours. The final result over the next three weeks was 1,100 new groups across all of their campuses.

I am convinced most people only think about church when they are sitting in church. Any efforts to send people to the lobby, or, God forbid, send them home to sign up on a website, simply do not work. By the time well-intended church members hit the threshold on Sunday morning, their stomachs have raced to lunch and their minds have raced to evacuating the premises as soon as possible. The moment has gone.

The closer you connect the invitation to the response, the better the response. If the invitation is made in a service, then collect the response in a service. If the same invitation is made by a video email at midweek, then collect the response in the email. By simply providing a link in the email, you can allow a willing member to click the link and sign up to start a group right on the spot.

In a perfect world, church members would go home, log in to the church's website, and sign up electronically. No fuss. No sign-up cards. No data entry. Simple. That world does not exist. To send someone from the service to the lobby or to their computer to sign up is equal to making no invitation at all. The reverse is also true. To send an email midweek asking for a response the following weekend is just wasted megabytes.

Think like the people who sit in your rows.

- What's available to them in their row?

- Is there a response card, or do you create a card?

- Do they have a pen?

- Who will collect the cards? Are they placed in the offering, collected at the end of the service, or handed to an usher on the way out?

- Maybe pen and paper doesn't cut it. What else do they have? What about their phones? Can they send a text to a designated number (not yours!) or fill out an online survey on their mobile device in the worship service?

- When you send an email invitation, can they fill out a survey or a web form?

Missed opportunities occur when you can't adequately collect the response. These thoughts may seem elementary. They may seem unnecessary. You may feel you are getting a good enough result from how you're collecting responses now. Or are you?

The card, web form, or digital survey the members fill out in the service needs to only ask for a few things: their names, preferred phone numbers, preferred email, and a selection of which briefing they will attend to get more information about the series. We will discuss more about the briefing in the next chapter. While there may be multiple dates for the briefing, only the next two briefing dates should be listed on the card. If the briefing occurs too far in the future, then there will be unnecessary falloff before the new leaders even get started.

If people are responding with a paper card, then the card must be collected during the service. Once the card goes out the door, it probably won't be seen again.

The pastor's invitation over three weekends plus an immediate way to respond is a winning strategy in recruiting new leaders. Most churches will net more new leaders this way than any other.

RECRUITING LEADERS VERSUS RECRUITING MEMBERS

While a church will certainly benefit from the pastor's invitation to group life, it's crucial to avoid clouding the invitation with different requests for groups. Namely, if the pastor has consented to make a group invitation for three weeks in a row, as described above, then the opportunity should be used to recruit leaders, not group members.

Let's face it, if a church has a bunch of people who want to be in groups, they may or may not start groups. But, if there is a leader, then there will be a group.

Use the pastor's willingness to promote groups to ask for leaders. Remember, if you have leaders, you will have groups.

If the message becomes muddied with signing up group members, then you actually handicap your leader recruitment in two ways. First, you truncate the three-week recruitment period by using the second or third week to recruit group members. Second, by changing the focus to group members or trying to recruit leaders and members at the same time, you are competing with your own group values! Now, the person in the pew has to decide, "Do I want to take the uncomfortable path and lead a group, or do I comfortably join a group as a member? Let me pray about that. Hey, I already have an answer, I'm going to choose comfort over discomfort!" Some very good potential leaders are comfortably sitting on a friend's couch and probably won't consider leaving.

Keep leader recruiting front and center. People will get connected into groups, but joining groups doesn't need a big push from the pulpit. You need that muscle to recruit leaders.

It may feel like I just said the same thing five times here, but I cannot overemphasize the significance of this strategic moment. The small group pastor recruits the coaches as discussed in chapter four. The senior pastor recruits the leaders. Then, the leaders gather their groups (more on this in chapter seven).

Recruiting leaders doesn't need to be scary. Decide on your acceptable level of risk, then choose to either enforce or delay the requirements for group leadership. This is a big step for any pastor—to release control in ministry in order to grow the ministry. At least this was a huge challenge to me in the beginning. The points of control any small group pastor or director can retain: the curriculum choice and the coaching relationship. By this, I don't mean some sort of dictatorship. But, the overall direction and teaching in groups should be kept in control.

If your groups are stuck, it's time to start a new strategy to recruit leaders. I've seen churches recruit as many as 30 percent of their adults to lead groups in a single day! What is your God-sized goal for group leadership?

CHAPTER 6

TRAINING

INITIAL TRAINING: THE PURPOSE OF THE BRIEFING

During my early days leading a groups ministry, I tended to overload group leaders with training before they even started anything. What I discovered was that my training was actually detrimental to launching groups in some ways. The more I talked about how to address various problems like people not showing up or people not shutting up, the more reasons I gave the new recruits not to start a group. Who needed to add this much more trouble to their lives?

Don't get me wrong here. All new leaders need training. The question is what to train on, how to deliver the training, and the overall timetable. In this chapter, we will discuss the initial training for small group leaders as they are starting groups and lead their first study. In chapter ten, we will talk about ongoing leader training.

Let's start with the anatomy of new group leader training. To get them started, I like to use a briefing because it contains the word "brief." And, believe me, I've started far more groups that have lasted by briefing them than I ever did through overloaded training on the front end. To effectively train your new recruits, there is some strategy to consider in who to brief, when to brief, and what to brief. The way you handle these next steps will largely determine the success of your group launch.

WHO TO BRIEF

The easy answer is you want to brief everyone. But, the briefing will vary depending on what you recruited leaders for. Granted, all of the group leaders have been recruited to meet with a group of people for a short-term commitment and do a study. What's the determining factor?

The key factor is how the groups are formed. If you recruited leaders or hosts whose groups will be advertised in your church through the bulletin, the website, a Small Group Connection, a Small Group Fair, a groups directory, or if you plan to send prospective members to these groups, then the church is effectively endorsing the groups. Prospective members will expect a quality experience with a good leader.

While your appeal for leaders could have consisted of inviting any breathing person with the ability to run a video, if the groups are going to be advertised, then you'd better get to know those new leaders and fast. More on this in a bit.

If you recruited people to do a study with their friends, it's a completely different situation. You're not advertising the group in any way. You're not sending anyone to the group. The new leaders are simply inviting their friends. The expectations are much different. Their friends should have a pretty good idea of what they are being invited into.

Now, before you begin to lament about all of the different kinds of training meetings you might need to lead depending on how the groups are being formed, here's a little secret: you can train them all at the same briefing. While there will be some additional requirements for the advertised groups, the initial training can definitely be the same.

WHEN TO BRIEF

The new leader briefing should occur in close proximity to when they said, "Yes" to the pastor's invitation to start a group. In fact, add a line to the response card giving them the dates of the next two briefings. Now, they have committed to leading a group and have committed to the next step in starting their group.

Hopefully, you are convinced by now to recruit new leaders in the three weeks prior to the start of the series. (I would say don't try to recruit leaders on holidays, but Dr. Tony Evans did recruit 260 new hosts on Labor Day weekend.) During the three weeks of recruiting, you should plan for new leader briefings to coincide with the invitation to lead a group.

Most churches have found that holding a briefing immediately after each of the worship services is a great way to get these new leaders started. Since briefings by definition are brief, you are only asking people to stay for ten to fifteen minutes at the end of the service. They should be able to stay for the briefing, then get on with the rest of their weekend plans.

Give the children's ministry a heads-up, so children can stay in their classes while their parents attend the briefing. (You will owe your children's ministry staff Starbucks for the next month, however.) This way at the end of the service your senior pastor can invite new leaders to go directly to the briefing, and their kids can stay right where they are. If they pick up their kids first, then the briefing will be over by the time they get there. Remember, it's brief!

The best way to get people to the briefing is for the pastor to say, "Meet me in room such and such right after the service." The pastor comes in, thanks everyone for choosing to lead a group, then turns the meeting over to the small group pastor or director to fill them in on the details. Sprinkling a little senior pastor dust will go a long way in building momentum for the briefing and the upcoming series.

The briefing room should be located in close proximity to the sanctuary. If people have to walk too far to get to the briefing, they may change their minds on the way. Now, I know people should be more committed than that, but it is necessary to eliminate as many distractions and excuses as possible. If there is not an available room nearby, then consider having the briefing in the sanctuary. Ask the new leaders to gather in the front, then begin the briefing as the congregation exits. These may seem like basic points, but eliminating excuses, even your own, is very important in order to keep groups moving forward. And, who knows, someone may overhear the briefing in the sanctuary and decide to start a group even though they didn't sign up yet.

Briefings could also be offered on a weeknight. While it's always a challenge to get folks to come back for a meeting, the reality is even though you will have a lower show up rate, you will definitely have a higher level of commitment from these folks.

For those who absolutely cannot attend a briefing, record your briefing and make the video available online to those who want to lead a group. While the face-to-face meeting is better in that the new leaders meet an experienced leader who will coach them, an online version is certainly better than losing a potential group because the new leader can't attend a briefing in person.

Once you have set the dates, times, and locations of your briefings, experienced leaders who have offered to coach the new leaders should be scheduled according to their availability (see chapter four). You will also need to personally invite some experienced leaders to briefings to fill in any gaps in the schedule. When new leaders meet the experienced leaders face-to-face, the coaching starts off on the right foot. It helps to eliminate the fear of cold calling, and the new leader knows why they are being called and who is calling them.

If possible, pass around a schedule at your Sneak Peek meeting for established leaders and have the experienced leaders willing to coach sign up then. Since these leaders will continue to lead their groups in addition to helping a couple of new leaders, they only need to be present at one or two briefings, since they will only pair up with one or two new leaders. They will help the new leaders starting at the briefing through the end of the series. The weekly phone calls should begin at this point. Remember, the period from when the new leaders say "Yes" to when the groups start is mission critical. You have the potential to lose more groups in this window than at any other point.

To get new leaders to the briefings, reminders are very important. It's important to note here because new leaders and groups will be in flux throughout the recruiting and launching phase. A list of new leaders should be compiled from the response cards that were turned in during each service. Managing this list is a Monday morning project for each week of leader recruiting. If the new leader both signed up and attended a briefing on Sunday, then the mission is accomplished. Otherwise, they will need a reminder for the briefing they signed up for.

A spreadsheet will suffice at this point for recording the new recruits. Once groups have indicated they will move forward into a second series, then you might add them to a church database. At this point, you merely need a simple communication tool like a spreadsheet to send reminders and track who has attended a briefing. We will talk more about record keeping in chapter eleven.

From the list of new leaders, send a reminder about the upcoming briefing. If you are able, a phone call would also be appropriate to thank the new leader for signing up and reminding them to attend the briefing. And, of course, the pastor should also mention the briefing at the end of the service and ask new leaders to "Meet me." They should be well reminded.

At the briefing it's important to have a sign-in sheet at the door as new leaders come into the room. This will give you a list of briefing participants to compare to those who signed up for the briefing. While no one wants a lot of administrative red tape, there are three lists significant to leader recruiting: (1) the Sign Up List from the response cards, (2) the Show Up List from the briefing sign-in sheet, and (3) the Start Up List from the applications the new leaders will turn in at the briefing (more on this later). This will help to close the gaps between Sign Up to Show Up, and then Show Up to Start Up. Anything you can do to encourage new leaders to move forward will be well worth it, especially when you gain a new group you might have lost in the gaps.

If someone misses their chosen briefing, then simply send them an email inviting them to the next briefing. They may have forgotten or something came up and they were unable to attend. If they don't respond to the second reminder, it would be good to have someone call them and see what's going on. They may have gotten cold feet or were discouraged in some other way. While no church will have 100 percent of those who sign up attend a briefing or start a group, you want to make your best effort to get them to a briefing.

If they cannot attend in person, then offer an online option to view the video of the briefing. They will need to be assigned to a coach, which will turn into a bit of cold calling, but if this is the only option, then offer that option.

If, between the email reminder, the senior pastor's reminder at the end of the service, possibly a phone call, and the online option, you cannot get the new leader to a briefing, then you've given it your best. Not every group is meant to be. Move with the movers and put your energy into those groups who are moving forward.

One of the best ways to get prospective leaders to a briefing is by giving them their study materials at the briefing. Over the years, I've learned the hard way that if you set up a table and give a study guide and DVD to everyone who wants one, well, "free" is very popular. You will have absolutely no idea how many groups have started versus how many books and DVDs are on eBay.

By distributing the materials for new leaders at the briefing, you give them an incentive to attend the briefing. If your church is using digital resources rather than physical resources, then provide the access codes and download directions at the briefing.

If you are using physical materials, but they aren't ready for distribution, then give the new leaders who turn in their information sheet a "coupon" to collect their materials later or other instructions on how to obtain them. But, to repeat this one more time, whether you are handing out materials, access codes, or coupons—this needs to take place at the briefing.

WHAT TO BRIEF

New leaders will have a ton of questions about starting their group. Since the briefing is short, you want to cover material in a couple of different ways. I suggest dividing the material between what you will say in the briefing and written material collected in a briefing packet that your new leaders can take home and study on their own time.

You will need to determine what to emphasize live and in person, and what to offer the new leaders in written form that you will refer to, but not discuss, in the briefing. By offering written material, you will give additional details to new leaders who want more information. You will also keep your briefing from getting lost to questions like "How do we handle childcare?" While childcare is an important question, it can certainly derail your briefing. When someone asks about childcare, simply reply, "You can find five or six different ways to handle childcare on page ___ of your new leader packet. Choose one of those." Then, move on! You can find an example of a briefing packet in the appendices.

As a pastor or small group director, you have decent knowledge about what a group might face, but let me caution you here: you don't want to paint too many negative scenarios or problems that might scare away your new recruits. Narrow your presentation at the briefing down to things your new recruits need to know. You may not cover everything they want to know, but between the live instructions you give and the written materials they walk away with, you will have answered most of the questions new leaders have. And, remember, your ace in the hole is the experienced leader who will be coaching them.

You want to keep the briefing focused on four things: the logistics of the study, gathering a group, sharing responsibilities in the group, and pairing up with a coach. Everything else can be made available in printed form.

1. THE LOGISTICS OF THE STUDY

Explaining the logistics of the study should be fairly simple and clear. Again, you don't want to overcomplicate any of the key aspects of the briefing, but you do need to touch on them. It's good to reinforce what you are saying by adding the information to the briefing packet you are handing out and putting up a few Power-Point slides. You don't necessarily need to use blanks for them to fill in. This will slow down your briefing.

In both the packet and the presentation, you will need to go over the dates for the series. Explain how the lessons will connect with the pastor's sermon series, and give the dates on which it begins and ends. The importance of these dates is that you want the group study to keep up with the sermon series, but not get ahead of the sermon series.

If the group has to miss a meeting, then make it up at some point. It's not the end of the world. But if the group study is off from the topic of the weekend service, the group will lose some of the dynamic of studying what the pastor taught on the weekend. More learning takes place by discussing the lesson based on the sermon from that week. An alignment helps with both application and just jogging everyone's memory.

The group also does not want to get ahead of the pastor. If the group discusses the lesson prior to the sermon, it creates an unnatural flow. In fact, it almost seems like the pastor is "cheating" because the group already knows what's coming. Now, that may just sound silly, but there is something to it. You want the pastor to preach the sermon first, then follow with the group lesson, not the other way around.

You will also want to include other key dates such as when the group materials will be available (unless you are distributing them at the briefing), when a Connection event or Small Group Fair will take place (if you're having one), and any other events associated with the series like a serving day or an outreach day in the community.

Every new leader should choose a day of the week and time that works for them. The leader has the privilege here. Over the years, I've seen far too many groups bend over backward to accommodate one person who said if they moved the group from Tuesday night to Thursday night he would attend. Sure enough when Thursday night rolls around, guess who isn't there? Mr. Thursday night. Tell your leaders to make the meeting night work for them.

If the church has a lot of commuters, then weeknights are typically out, since they have to rise at some insane hour to hop in their cars and drive one hundred miles. Friday nights and Sunday nights tend to work well for commuters. If the group meets on Fridays, then they don't have to get up early on Saturday and go to work. Sundays typically work for everyone, because there's not much competing with Sunday afternoon or evening.

Most new leaders will be able to figure out the day and time that works best for them. Let them get creative. I was talking to a pastor in Kentucky who said he has a lot of coal miners in his church whose shifts end at 5:00 a.m. I suggested starting a 5:00 a.m. Waffle House small group. Throw in an all-American breakfast combo, and I'll be there. If your church is in the South, and it's football season, then groups can only meet on Tuesdays and Wednesdays, because those are the only days without football. (I'm being facetious . . . kind of.) While you don't want to make the choice of the day ridiculous, you do want to steer new leaders away from things that will inhibit their group meeting.

As groups are starting, their meetings should be weekly. Weekly meetings help to facilitate new relationships. The group members will tend to remember names and other details better. If the meetings are every other week, then it's harder for group members to get to know each other.

My wife and I started a group several years ago that met every other week. It really took a long time for the group to gel. While we thought every other week meetings would be easier on everyone's schedules, it just wasn't easy on the group. Finally after about nine months we began to feel like a group. The key was that at the nine month point we were doing an alignment series, and our group was meeting weekly.

If you have established groups who meet every other week, then invite them to meet weekly during the series with a promise that they can go back to "normal" after the series is over. Most groups will make a change for a six-week study. If it's absolutely impossible for a group to meet weekly, then make an exception and help them figure out how to do the study every other week.

One year we ran our alignment series in October and November. A group who couldn't (or wouldn't) change from meeting every other week to weekly meetings wanted to do the study. I gave them the materials thirty days in advance (now I'm about to break a rule), and they started the study in September. They did two lessons in September, two in October, and two in November. This worked for them. It didn't start an epidemic (there might have been a threat from me about telling other groups what they were planning). They didn't add new members to their group, but they participated in the study in their own way.

You don't need to cover all of the exceptions at the briefing. In fact, new groups should only have one option: meet weekly. Any exception to that can be discussed outside of the briefing.

You will also need to touch on how the new leaders can prepare for their first meeting. Encourage them to review the first video and the printed lesson. Remind them to pray and ask for God's help. (They will be praying, believe me.) Recommend offering some refreshments for the first meeting. If they feel overwhelmed, then encourage them to invite a friend to bring something to the first meeting. In addition to these simple instructions, you might add a page like "Leading for the First Time" to your briefing packet, which they can take home and read (you can find an example in the appendices).

2. HOW TO GATHER A GROUP

The second of the four topics for your briefing is how to gather a group. Whether the group is open to new members or not, every new leader needs to personally invite people to their group. Even if the church is using a Group Connection event or a Small Group Fair, the key to a successful start is personal invitation.

As I mentioned earlier, you can brief both new leaders who are starting open groups and new leaders starting groups with their friends in the same meeting. The second item you will refer to in the briefing packet is essentially an application. I suggest calling this an Information Sheet, as you will ask your new leaders to provide information about their proposed group. My example, which you can find in the appendices, includes two check boxes at the top for the new leaders to indicate the type of group they are starting.

What kind of group will you be (check one):

☐ Open to Anyone

☐ Invitation Only

"Open to Anyone" signifies they are a typical open group or HOST home group which will be advertised to the congregation.

Like I said before, you will need to get more information on them. If the group is "Invitation Only," which sounds better than "Closed Group," the new leaders are responsible for recruiting 100 percent of their group members. This may result in smaller groups, but it offers a comfortable place for people to start if they are unwilling to start an open group. Let them start where they are comfortable. You can challenge them to get out of their comfort zone later on.

New leaders starting either kind of group can begin recruiting by thinking about people they know who would enjoy or benefit from the study. So, who do they know? Several tools and exercises can help them identify who to invite.

Brett Eastman and Lifetogether popularized the Circles of Life, which is also called the Five F's Exercise. While there are different versions of this, the idea is to think about Friends, Firm or Factory (coworkers), Family, Fellowship (other believers), and Fun (social relationships or acquaintances). Each new leader is to make a list and pray for an opportunity to invite some of these folks to the group. If the new leader is married, then the spouse's list is also a key part of this. Then, once the first person is recruited, take a look at their list as well.

When I was on staff at New Life in California, one Sunday morning, our pastor, David Larson, instructed the congregation to get out their cell phones and turn them on. I thought he had lost his mind for sure. Pastor Dave encouraged everyone to look at their speed dial list and challenged them to give their friends a call after the service and invite them to join their group. Then, he asked everyone to turn off their cell phones and put them away. Sanity was regained.

For the briefing, ask the new leaders to consider their contact list, their Facebook friends, and other social media to start inviting people to their group. While these simple strategies can be effective in forming groups, the key strategy, if you will, is prayer. God has an idea of who should be in the group, so every new leader should ask him who to invite.

If your church chooses to host a Small Group Connection event or Small Group Fair, then include a page in your briefing packet with the details of when and where this will take place. Since only the open groups will participate, don't spend a lot of time discussing the Connection event at the briefing. You can include plenty of instructions in the packet, and communicate to leaders of open groups at a later time. Even if the leader plans to meet prospective group members at a Connection event, encourage them to also invite people they already know. Then people can be added through the Connection event, sign-ups, the website, etc. By inviting people ahead of the Connection event, the group will have a solid relational base to build on as they add more group members at the event. If groups are started in the right place relationally, they are far more likely to continue.

3. SHARED OWNERSHIP

I have already lamented my struggles with the apprentice model, which involves selecting and training one person to lead a group. While there are potential apprentices in every group, often the group leaders have trouble identifying them. The solution is to train the entire group to lead. This is done through rotating responsibilities and sharing the ownership of the group.

Now, while that may sound complicated, it is actually as simple as the leader passing around a sign-up sheet asking the group members to take part in some way. The members could bring refreshments (that's the easiest one to give away). They could host the meeting in their home for one week. They could lead the prayer time or even lead the discussion for a week. By taking part in some aspect of the group meeting not only do the group members gain experience in leading a group, but they also feel more a part of the group. As group members share responsibilities, the group moves from being "your group" to feeling like "our group."

Now, the way this doesn't work is if the leader asks "Would anyone like to . . . ?" The choice being offered is "Do you want to be comfortable and have me do everything, or do you want to become uncomfortable and take on a responsibility?" After much thought and prayer, most group members will choose to remain comfortable and let you do everything. Now, if the invitation goes more like "Everyone in the group needs to sign up for something," then the response tends to be much better. They will sign up if you are serious about them signing up.

In a men's group I led, I would announce on the first week of the study that "Today is the first and only day I am leading the discussion." Our group met in restaurants, so the refreshments and meeting place were covered. The guys would all sign up to lead.

On one particular week, our leader was a guy who was literally half my age. He sat across the table from me and led a study I had written. He did a great job. The only negative was the rest of the group making fun of the questions: "Who wrote that question? That's a terrible question."

I replied, "Hey, I'm sitting right here!" We all had a good laugh.

When group members take responsibility in the group, they will feel more ownership in the group. The leader will enjoy the benefit of having help. And, there is great potential for identifying those who have the ability to possibly lead a group on their own one day.

4. PAIRING NEW LEADERS WITH A "COACH"

The fourth and final topic for the briefing is matching the new leaders with the experienced leaders to coach them. (While I hesitate to call experienced leaders "coaches" at this point, I will use the terms experienced leaders and coaches interchangeably in this section.) I apologize for repeating myself a little in the following paragraphs, but this handoff is crucial, unless you want one hundred new leaders emailing and calling you.

Toward the end of the briefing, announce to the new leaders that you would like to introduce "some very important people who are going to help you get your group started." Remember, these are the folks whose phone calls tend to be returned. Then, ask the experienced leaders to stand.

New and experienced leaders can be matched in a variety of ways, but the best way is if they already know each other (except if they are related). Coach the experienced leaders to take the initiative and approach the new leaders they already know. This introduction is the start of the coaching relationship.

In a church of any size, there are bound to be folks who don't know each other. While it's best to lead with relationship in choosing coaches, you may need to resort to other means. If your church has affinity groups like men's groups, women's groups, singles' groups, neighborhood groups, and so on, then identify experienced leaders by the affinity, and ask the new leaders to go to the coach within their affinity.

Other churches assign coaches by geography. I honestly believe this is the least effective way. If you have to resort to this kind of crowd control, then see if a coach and new leader within the same geographic region might at least know each other first.

Once the experienced leaders and new leaders are matched up, inform the new leaders that the experienced leaders will be calling them weekly from now until the end of the series, and they should politely take or return the calls. Be clear about the experienced leader being the new leader's go-to person with their questions. Whether you are starting dozens of new groups or hundreds, you cannot effectively shepherd all of these new leaders yourself.

On the Information Sheet, there is a place for the new leader to list the name of their coach, so you have a record. It is equally important to make sure the coach and the new leader exchange contact information (cell phone numbers are preferable) before they leave the briefing. Starting on briefing day, the coaching will begin with a "nice to meet you" call within forty-eight hours.

If for some reason there were not enough experienced leaders at the briefing to match with new leaders, then collect the new leaders' information and let them know a coach will be contacting them. This needs to happen in the next twenty-four hours. You may actually have another "crisis" to recruit from, which is not a bad recruiting strategy. Once the coach is assigned to the new leader, then the first call still needs to be placed in the first forty-eight hours after the briefing.

The very last thing at the briefing is to collect all of the Information Sheets from every new leader who is ready to move forward. (Again, you can find a sample Information Sheet in the appendices.)

If the group is invitation-only, then you need the new leader to complete only the contact information and their coach assignment. You don't need the rest of the information.

If the group is open to anyone, then you need more information, such as the story of the new leader's spiritual journey, including when they came to Christ. It would also be good to know how long they have been part of your church. If it's been a short time, then maybe ask what church they attended before. Lastly, you do want to cover the question: Is there anything going on in your life that might harm or embarrass the church or the cause of Christ? As I stated in chapter three, you want to add the specifics related to sexual sin, life-controlling problems, and relationship issues. This is not a litmus test for leadership, but as I stated before, if someone is addicted to drugs or going through a divorce, the person needs to receive care and support before they consider group leadership.

One last word on the Information Sheet. The most troublesome question tends to be what day of the week the group will meet. Some folks will hesitate to turn in their form because they haven't decided on the day. Collect the forms anyway. Once the form leaves the room, it is very unlikely you will see it again. Be gracious here. Some folks won't turn in their forms because they don't want to admit a sin issue in their lives. Others legitimately need to talk to their spouse. Use your wisdom here. If it's only a "day of the week" issue, then collect the form. Otherwise, give them a break. After all, you do have the sign-in sheet to follow up on those who attended the briefing, but did not turn in their Information Sheet.

Once the Information Sheet is turned in, the new leaders are officially (or unofficially) on their way to forming their groups. For invitation-only groups, the only other thing they need is the regular contact with their coaches. The new leaders of the open to anyone groups will need to meet with their coach so the church can get to know them a little better before their groups are advertised to the congregation. If time is short, then you can certainly triage the open group leaders by interviewing the lesser-known new leaders before you start interviewing the charter members of the church. For long-standing church members, you probably don't need to interview them at all unless they indicated something in the last question about harming or embarrassing the church or the cause of Christ.

To sum up the long explanation of a briefing . . .

1. Invite by email and the senior pastor's announcement.

2. Cover: (1) Logistics, (2) Group Formation, (3) Shared Ownership, (4) Coaching Assignments.

3. Collect the Information Sheet.

4. Start forming groups!

WEEKLY TRAINING FOR NEW LEADERS

While the coaching has started, additional training should start as well. Think about things new leaders will need to know while they are forming their groups and during the weeks of the group study.

Who to Invite
How to Invite
When Someone Says "No" to Joining Your Group
Preparing for Your First Group Meeting
Following Up on "No Shows"
A Reminder about the Importance of Shared Ownership
The Disparity between the Sign Up and Show Up Rate
    in New Groups
Keys to an Effective Prayer Time in the Group
Dealing with Overly Talkative Group Members
Recommending the Next Study for the Group

You will certainly come up with other topics on your own, but this is a start.

Training can be delivered in a variety of formats, but certainly not meetings. Since new leaders are starting a weekly group meeting, frequent training meetings might push them over the edge. If you are creating your own curriculum, then you can include your own training in anticipation of what new leaders might need to hear from week to week on a DVD, streaming video, or another format.

While video training on the curriculum has been an effective method, I prefer sending a short, weekly video to new leaders. First, you are pushing the training out to the new leaders every week rather than expecting them to view the DVD training on their own. The email itself is a reminder to watch the training. But, you need to keep it short. Most people will watch an online video if it's less than two minutes, but won't watch for much longer than that.

You also want to design your email to optimize mobile use. Most people will watch your training video on their phones rather than on a computer. Shoot your video in landscape rather than portrait format on a mobile device. Think of the videos you watch on your phone or online. Copy what they look like.

Send a screenshot of a frame of the video instead of just sending a link. Links will get lost in any text you provide. A link by itself will look like a phishing email. By providing the screenshot, your leaders will know there is a video to watch. You will want to design your email to work across various formats, so choose an online video service that works with the majority of devices. You can embed the video URL in the screenshot, but also add something like "Trouble viewing?" with the URL just below the screen shot.

This may seem really picky, but if you take the time to provide training through an online video format, then you want to make sure the training is actually used. You should probably consider an email service where you can check the open rate for a particular video training email.

You don't need to get fancy with the production. The cameras on most phones are more than adequate to capture the video. If you flub, it's fine. You're human. If you need help focusing your thoughts, then use a simple teleprompter app on a tablet. You can run the prompter app and record your video on the same device at the same time.

Again, the key to effective online training is short videos pushed out to your group leaders. Instead of email, you can use a church app or some other means. I'm in favor of whatever works.[30]

By far, your greatest asset in training is the experienced leader in the life of the new leader. Check in with your experienced leaders on a weekly basis to see how it's going and what they are learning from the new leaders. Give the experienced leaders an FAQ for coaching new leaders including information on the topics mentioned earlier in this chapter. Assume calls are being made. If they aren't, then give them a deadline and call them in a couple of days to check. If you have more "coaches" than you can keep up with, then ask your small group team to contact them. In turn, you will need to check in on your team and make sure calls are being made. Remember, only the things that are supervised get done. You are a new parent who has left your newborn with a young babysitter. You need to check in!

Coaching and training don't stop here. We will discuss ongoing training and the leadership track of turning "hosts" into group leaders in chapters nine and ten.

CHAPTER 7

GROUP STRATEGY—CONNECTING PEOPLE INTO GROUPS

Before we dive into the strategies for effectively and ineffectively connecting people into groups, I'm going to spend a little time on the reasons behind these strategies.

If the number of group members at your church doesn't exceed the weekend adult attendance, then you need to shift your thinking. This was a shift I had to make in my own thinking before I was able to move to more effective strategies in the churches I served. In fact, I will take this a little further: if your groups aren't effectively impacting their neighborhoods and your community, then you need to shift your thinking.

Stay with me here. I'll get us to where we need to go.

Once our church in California had caught the vision of rapidly expanding our small groups through church-wide campaigns, self-produced curriculum, and large-scale leader recruitment, it seemed like nothing could stop us from connecting 100 percent or more in groups. Well, nothing, except for people who weren't joining groups.

We invited our congregation to participate in a health assessment based on the five biblical purposes as articulated by Rick Warren in *The Purpose Driven Life* and *The Purpose Driven Church*: Fellowship, Discipleship, Ministry, Evangelism, and Worship. Our members answered a series of questions which were then tabulated to show where our church was strong or weak in each purpose.

Now, in collecting this data, I also wanted to prove to those reluctant to sign up for a group that groups were the fast track for spiritual growth, so I asked the respondents to indicate whether or not they were in a small group.

I separated the results between group members and non-group members. I discovered an interesting result. Group members indicated they were strongest in these purposes (in order): Fellowship, Worship, Discipleship, Ministry, and Evangelism. People who were not in groups rated themselves from strongest to weakest in: Fellowship, Worship, Discipleship, Ministry, and Evangelism.

The results where exactly the same!

I was beside myself. How could people not in a group think they were high in Fellowship when they weren't even in a small group? They didn't even know what true fellowship was! Unbelievable. What were they thinking? So, I sent out a second survey.

I surveyed the people who weren't in groups and asked them what other believers they interacted with on a regular basis. They replied: friends, family, coworkers, neighbors, people they served with at church, customers, and a variety of other relationships. This was when the light bulb went off for me, and I realized everybody was already in a group. I just needed to direct them in doing something intentional about their spiritual growth with that group!

FROM PUBLIC RELATIONSHIPS TO INTIMATE RELATIONSHIPS

Most people already have most of the relationships they need. They are already closely connected with the people who enrich their lives. When they are challenged to join a small group, they might not sense the need, because there isn't a need. (Of course, there are exceptions to the rule. We'll get to that soon.)

An examination of Joseph Myers's book, *The Search to Belong*, reveals four spheres of human relationships: public, social, personal, and intimate. Not all people are connected to each other in the same way. We relate differently to different people. Our relationship with our spouse is much different than our relationship with our dry cleaner. While we might not be best friends with our neighbors, if they fly the same team flag in front of their house that we do, then we have something in common to be friendly about.

Myers writes, "Public belonging occurs when people connect through an outside influence. Fans of a sports team experience a sense of community because they cheer for the same team."[31] When I travel through my second home, the Hartsfield-Jackson International Airport in Atlanta, Georgia, I sometimes run into KU Jayhawk fans. Their apparel gives them away. We will have a great conversation about KU basketball, then go our separate ways for our next flights. We don't even exchange names, but we have something in common and enjoy a friendly conversation. Rock. Chalk. Jayhawk!

The second sphere, social belonging,

> occurs when we share "snapshots" of what it would be like to be in personal space with us. The phrases "first impression" and "best foot forward" refer to this spatial belonging. You belong socially to your favorite bank teller, your pharmacist, or some of the people with whom you work. . . . In social space we provide the information that helps others decide whether they connect with us.[32]

This is my relationship with the folks at my cleaners where I have my shirts done. Once I picked up my shirts to discover one missing. I found out they put eight shirts on a tag. Then, if I have more than eight, the ninth and beyond go on a separate tag. Sometimes the ninth shirt doesn't make it back with the rest. When I brought in more than eight shirts, I would joke about getting their discount, "Bring in nine shirts, get eight back." We would all laugh.

Now, I've never invited the folks at the cleaners over for dinner. I don't see us hanging out. But, I see them on a regular basis and they laugh at my dumb jokes, so they're alright in my book. And, I would never go to another cleaner even if their prices were cheaper.

Personal belonging is the third sphere, in which "we share private (not 'naked') experiences, feelings, and thoughts. We call the people we connect to in this space 'close friends.' They are those who know more about us than an acquaintance would, yet not so much that they feel uncomfortable."[33]

In the most open and vulnerable sphere, what Myers calls "intimate belonging," "we share 'naked' experiences, feelings, and thoughts." Myers notes that "We have very few relationships that are intimate. These people know the 'naked truth' about us and the two of us are not 'ashamed.' "[34]

Myers's perception is that an invitation or urging to join small groups causes people to jump from public relationships—meaning people who attend the same church and might or might not know each other—to intimate relationships in a small group, where they would share the most personal details of their lives.[35] Most groups are not formed by transitioning public relationships into intimate relationships. I am certain that such a premise for forming groups is either bound to fail or is quite short-lived.

First of all, there is no guarantee that folks in small groups will form intimate relationships, or even that they should. When I think of intimate relationships, I think of a very select group of people: my wife, my parents, my children, and my closest friends.

Malcolm Gladwell in *The Tipping Point* says for most of us there are only a dozen people whose deaths would dramatically affect our lives.[36] While we certainly would sense grief at the loss of anyone we knew, not everyone's death impacts us in the same way. Most healthy, functioning folks already have their intimate relationships. Since the limit for most of us is ten to twelve people and the size of a small group is usually ten to twelve people, the likelihood of complete or partial strangers being graduated to my inner circle is quite slim.

"Perhaps, the best we can do with small groups," according to Blair Carlstrom, "is create an environment where close relationships could happen. At our church, we don't even use intimacy to imply 'cozy' because we don't want anyone confused about what we want to accomplish. In fact, we tell people not to expect it in a small group. If we can help set a realistic expectation, then they may have a good experience in a group."[37] According to Carlstrom, pastors should not raise the expectation that any group of members can go from strangers to close friends.

Perhaps, the disclaimer should read: *Results are not typical. Some group members may luck out and develop close friendships over time with much perseverance, but many will experience side effects such as feeling awkward, uncomfortable, or lonely in the crowd, similar to side effects found with sugar pills. Group members should expect much uneasiness regarding their group accompanied by the desire to play hooky on a regular basis.*

Without the equivalent of an online dating service for groups, placing people into groups by preferred meeting day, location, or possibly one item of affinity does not guarantee the formation of biblical community. And for good reason. Since most people already have those ten to twelve spots filled, and since the randomization of group placement does little to guarantee the cultivation of such relationships, perhaps pastors are aiming at the wrong thing in forming small groups. The better fit is to offer an environment for developing personal relationships with the rare possibility of a few becoming intimate relationships over time.

Or, better yet, to invite people to form a group among their current personal relationships.

The other issue raised by Joseph Myers's premise regarding spatial relationships is the starting point: public relationships, which he defines as the commonality of sitting in the same worship space on a regular basis, is an affinity insufficient for intimacy, to say the least. People in churches seated in rows facing the same direction have about as much ability to deepen relationships as moviegoers in a darkened theater. The format is not conducive to developing closer relationships, even if we do turn and shake hands for a few minutes. The odds of joining a group built on public relationships and then expecting to develop lasting relationships seems a bit preposterous. This process of random selection causes few strong groups to evolve and leaves many artifacts along the way.

Yet, some small groups do succeed and thrive over the long term. Are these miraculous occurrences? Or, are these groups created with members who socially travel a shorter distance from departure to destination?

The simplest means of forming new groups that might last really doesn't involve church staff much at all. In addition to the dozen or so intimate relationships a person has, according to Gladwell, most people have about forty personal relationships. A study by MSN Messenger in the United Kingdom found that the average Brit had 396 relationships during his or her lifetime, yet only had thirty-three relationships at any one time.[38] My suspicion is that Americans might have a few more.

While the ten to twelve intimate relationships would be included, the balance would be made up with other friends, neighbors, coworkers, and extended family that we know, though not as well as our intimate circle. We might not know their heart of hearts, but we've spent time together and know quite a bit. We keep close tabs on their lives. And we like them (or else they wouldn't be among our personal relationships).

If small groups are not created to form intimate relationships, but to maximize personal relationships, then the simplest way of forming lasting groups would be to create groups from the forty or so personal relationships we already have. The group is already there. All that a pastor needs to do is recommend a Bible study, draw a circle around them, and call them a group!

Our church in California formed nearly one hundred groups over a twelve-month period. Since then I've seen churches form far more groups like this in a three-week recruitment period. When I first started working with Pastor Troy Jones and New Life Church in Renton, Washington, their congregation of 2,500 adults had about one hundred groups. That's a respectable number of groups for a church that size. But the church desired to connect far more of their congregation and their community into groups.

After two alignment series, one at the start of the new year, and the second after Easter, New Life Church started a total of four hundred new groups. When our partnership with them ended, they were a church of 2,500 adults with five hundred groups. But they're not finished. Pastor Troy has set a goal of one thousand groups. Not one group was formed artificially. Every group was formed by people inviting friends and acquaintances to join them for Bible study.

What we've discovered is that groups of friends far outlast groups of strangers. One person takes the initiative to select ten people or so of their forty personal relationships and they spend time together studying God's word with an easy-to-use video-based group curriculum. This strategy provides both the biblical content and the close relationships to help a group start well and thrive. The emphasis is on application, not teaching. The teaching is delivered via video. The group leader facilitates the discussion on living out what the Bible says.

The potential for creating groups within someone's current personal relationships is much greater than turning public or social relationships into personal relationships. If the average person is capable of maintaining only thirty-three to forty personal relationships at any one time, then to ask someone to accept folks from their public or social relationships into the realm of personal relationships means that we are asking them to essentially replace ten or so personal relationships with relative strangers from their public or social relationships. The person, first of all, might be unwilling to give up any of their current personal relationships and thus never truly bond with the small group. Secondly, we are asking the person to risk ten relationships they can count on with basically the luck of the draw. Who in their right mind would give up their good friends for the sake of another church activity?

Years ago, in his book *A Church for the 21st Century,* Leith Anderson gave an illustration of people being like Lego bricks. "The social structure of churches is made up of people like Legos. They have a limited number of snap on points—few have more than six. After people have been in a church for a couple of years, they are all snapped up. They have all the friends [they need]."[39] I would take this further by saying people who have lived in a community for any length of time are mostly "snapped up" before they enter the doors of the church.

So, think about these relationships: spouse, children, parents, other family, friends, coworkers, sports team, book club, parents of your kids' sports teams or activities, and the list goes on. Most people have all of the dots on their Lego bricks filled. Where do you put a group? Unless they "unsnap" a few of their current friends, which I would not encourage, or unless their current circle of relationships becomes their group, many people don't have the time or capacity for a small group, which are very common excuses for avoiding groups.

Of course, there are exceptions, and we'll discuss them in greater detail at the end of the chapter, but for now consider that a person who has recently started attending the church by moving from another church, from another city, or from the kingdom of darkness probably does not have any personal relationships with people in their new church home. There are other points of transition that influence people's relationships: job changes, moves across town, divorce, life stages, etc. How do they take the step from public relationships at the church to personal relationships?

The easy answer would be to turn their current personal relationships into former friends and adopt new friends from their new church home. But, that's not so easy.

My point is simply this: most people have at least five or six people in their lives that they could invite to do a study together. They don't need to be assigned to a group of strangers and expect instant relationships. They don't need to give up existing relationships to establish new ones. Every believer is called to "Go and make disciples."[40] As pastors equip their people to do the work of the ministry according to Ephesians 4:11–12, let's not make this more complicated than it has to be. Discipleship is not something that we do to other people. Discipleship is what we do with other believers. The people of God, filled with the Spirit of God, interacting with the word of God brings about positive results.

In forming small groups, what are you really asking your people to do?

THE MOST EFFECTIVE METHODS FOR FORMING GROUPS

Over the years, I have both tried and witnessed group formation in labor intensive and highly ineffective ways. Vehicles like websites, sign-up cards, and groups directories prove to be efficient, but on their own are ineffective in forming groups that last. More on these in the next section.

The surest way to get into a group is to start a group. If you start a group, you are in the group. What's more, you can determine who else joins the group by inviting people in your life who wish to participate with you. As I've stated before, depending on the strategies used by the church, forming one's own group could be an advertised HOST home, or it could be an invitation-only group where the leader personally invites all of the members. A sure bet on joining a group is starting a group.

The second-best way to get into a group is by personal invitation. Rather than wishing strangers might become friends through a group experience, remove the guesswork—ask group leaders to invite their friends. This is especially effective in communities with lifelong residents (Baltimore, Detroit, parts of Chicago, and western Pennsylvania come to mind). If the appeal for groups is to gain friends, then they won't join a group for that reason. They already have friends. But, if the appeal is to form a group to grow spiritually, then they can do the study with their friends and fulfill the needs of connection and growth.

Now, in every church there are those who might not be invited to a group. One valuable piece of advice I learned years ago is to "Let the exceptions be the exceptions." Most groups can be formed through personal invitation, but there is a place for the third-best way to form a group: personal introduction.

At New Life in California, we would set up card tables on the church's lawn and conduct a Small Group Fair. Prospective members would meet new leaders and sign up to join the group.

When prospective members meet group leaders, a great dynamic takes place. Old high school classmates are reunited. Coworkers, neighbors, and acquaintances realize they attend the same church. Church members realize there was a group right around the corner from their houses the whole time.

While this sounds a little like speed dating, your members will be grateful to avoid an awkward six-week commitment because they had a thirty-second conversation with someone at a Connection event. On the other hand, when they hit it off with a group leader, they will look forward to what's next. Another upside is that group leaders now know who is coming to their house.

At Brookwood Church, we created an event we called a "sampler" where prospective members could meet the various groups in our church. This was both easy and effective. We arranged groups in our lobby according to affinity and with each group providing food for prospective members to eat. Then, we created a little map so people would know where the different affinities were located in the church lobby.

The sampler turned out to be a great small group open house. Prospective members would sample the food at each table and would meet the group members. In this case, we invited the entire group to participate and not just the leaders. Similar to the Small Group Fair, prospective members would sign up for a specific group at the event. Once they had signed up, they were on their way.

Just to reiterate: the best way to get into a group is to start a group. The second best way is by personal invitation. The third is by personal introduction through a Small Group Connection event like a Fair or Sampler. Over the years, in the two churches where I've served on staff as well as the over 1,500 churches I've coached, I have discovered these three methods of forming groups to be the most effective. Then, there are the assimilation methods I dread. . . .

THE CASE AGAINST WEBSITES, GROUPS DIRECTORIES, AND OTHER SHOTS IN THE DARK

Tools like online group finders and printed small group directories are very helpful at a Small Group Fair or Connection event, especially if they include a mapping feature. They can point people in the right direction for a personal introduction to a group leader, but the tool can only be part of the solution.

When our family was living in southern California, we had the privilege of being part of an awesome church that was well known for their small groups. As I traveled as a church consultant, I was often asked, "So how's your small group going?" I would sheepishly bow my head and reply, "I'm not in a small group right now." I knew that this "do as I say, but not as I do" thing would not stand up for long. So, I decided to join one of the church's bazillion small groups.

I filled out the response card on Sunday morning requesting information on men's groups. I received a letter in the mail directing me to look on the website. I had already been on there. That's partly why I turned in the response card. The website gave me what every small group website gives you: Group Name, Leader Name, Day of the Week, Time of Day, Location, and Current Study. How did I know which group to try? It was a shot in the dark.

Now, I was a bit of an odd duck at the church. Through my consulting work, I knew many of the church staff, but I didn't know many of the members. If a friend had invited me to the church, then they would have shown me the small group ropes, but I was an outsider. I didn't have that connection.

What I began to realize that day was every church has a lot of "outsiders." A job or a warmer climate brought them to the area. They don't have extended family. They like the weekend service, but beyond that they are just at a loss as to where to get started in joining a group.

Some brave souls will roll the dice and contact a group through the web. They believe in the importance of small groups, so they will tough out the awkwardness of the first few meetings to get to the good stuff. But not everyone will do this.

There is a place for the small group website, but honestly, why depend on a programmatic method to form groups that are highly relational? Use relational methods. There is no substitute for a personal invitation or a face-to-face meeting.

I eventually found a men's group at that church. The leader was a former preacher. He talked too much. I went twice, then I stopped going. Eventually, I started a great lunchtime group that has met every Wednesday for years. (It probably was also led by a preacher that talks too much.)

THE CASE AGAINST SIGN-UP CARDS FOR FORMING GROUPS

Churches struggle with the dilemma of connecting a large number of people in a short period of time. When we (pastors and directors) become overwhelmed, the temptation to offer a programmatic solution looms large, aka the sign-up card in the bulletin. While the sign-up card can be a helpful way of recruiting *leaders*, as I described at the end of chapter five, I believe the sign-up card to connect potential *members* to a group is a bad idea.

Sign-up cards create an immediate delay. We live in a culture of immediate access. When we purchase a song on iTunes or a book on Kindle, the download begins immediately. The days of waiting for a package to arrive are quickly disappearing. Don't believe me? Where's the Columbia House CD Club?

When a prospective group member turns in a sign-up card, nothing happens immediately. Most likely, nothing will happen that day or the next day or maybe even the next week. People will wait for the college admissions office, but probably not tolerate the delay in joining a group. The sign-up card creates a delay that you'd rather avoid.

When a church provides a sign-up card as the means for group connections, the prospective group member will expect a solid fit right away. After all, who's a better matchmaker than the church? Now, I know what you're thinking—offer a disclaimer like "the church does not guarantee a perfect match in any group." No thanks. I'd rather just take my chances on my own.

Rather than creating the small groups version of an online dating service, create an environment where groups and prospective members can meet each other face-to-face at a Small Group Connection, Sampler, or Fair like I described earlier in this chapter. People will get a sense, even in thirty seconds, whether a group will be right for them over the next six weeks.

A while back I was working with a church on the opposite coast. The staff had decided to use sign-up cards, so we used sign-up cards. I tried to help a church member who thought he had been neglected, since no one responded to him. From literally three thousand miles away, I was matching possible groups with prospective members. The issue? The group leader had the wrong email address. An "r" in the member's email address was input as a "c" on the spreadsheet they used. Someone had responded to him, but communication failed due to a typo. It's not worth losing a person over a jot or a tittle.

Now, you could say, "Well, if they registered online you might not have this problem." Actually people are just as likely to make typos as they are to have poor penmanship. The point here is that a small error could keep someone from connecting in a significant way.

So, let's say that you've ignored the first three points in this section, and you've collected sign-up cards. You or your assistant or an intern or a dart board has now determined which groups each of these prospective members should try. You or your assistant or your intern sends a list of new members to your group leaders. You would think the group leaders would be excited. Think again.

Everyone hates cold calling, including you. How would you feel if a list of six or seven names arrived in your inbox? You might send an email. You probably wouldn't make a phone call. You might Google the names or check for criminal records. The last thing you want to do is pick up the phone. How do I know this? Because you just pawned off the assignment you didn't want onto your small group leaders. If the pastor of the church won't call these folks, then how could you expect a volunteer group leader to call? No one likes cold calling—not even salespeople.

Let's say that you luck out in connecting sign-up card prospects with group leaders and half of them stick with a group. (I'm a pastor. I am prone to exaggerate. Bear with me.) If half are happy, then the other half are, well, unhappy. So, half of fifty people or one hundred people or one thousand people adds up to a lot of disappointed people. Oh, and who's at fault? You are. You placed them in the group.

When the recently-burned group member has left the group they didn't like, what are the chances that they will try another group? Slim to none. As you extrapolate the sign-up card fiasco over the years, well, a lot of people have a bad taste in their mouths when it comes to your groups.

And, as a concerned citizen, how many trees had to die to print your sign-up cards? (Sorry, after eighteen years in California, I just can't help myself.)

How do I know sign-up cards don't work? I have to confess. I've had a small stack of sign-up cards sit on my desk for a week before. I secretly hoped they would fall into the trash can. I didn't want to follow up on them, so I sent them to my group leaders. My group leaders didn't want to follow up on them either. No one was served very well, and many people were frustrated with the whole process. Sign-up cards for group leaders is a handy way to get a quick response in the service. Sign-up cards for group members creates an administrative nightmare which produces poorly formed groups.

TIMING THE CONNECTION EVENT WITH YOUR SERVICE

After your pastor has done a great job of challenging the congregation to try a group for a six-week series, the next step is providing a convenient and effective way to join a group. They're all dressed up. Where do they go?

When groups are promoted in a service, you want to get a response ASAP. I know what you're thinking: why not use a sign-up card? Putting something in your congregation's hands during the service will make your invitation stronger. That's why it's effective for recruiting leaders. But, a sign-up card is the wrong thing. Instead, put a list of groups in their hands, or a small group FAQ. Now, I know what you're thinking, "Allen, didn't you just say groups directories were bad?" Keep reading. During the service, use the information to get them thinking about their next step after the service.

Then, hold your Small Group Connection event immediately after the service. Allow the prospective members to meet the group leaders in the church lobby. Remember, you'll want the pastor to reinforce the invitation at the end of the service by saying something like "Meet the group leaders in the lobby right now, and sign up to try a group for six weeks." Churches have held these Connection events outdoors, in the lobby, or around the perimeter of the sanctuary. Choose a large, convenient location.

If the logistics of a post-service Connection event aren't possible, then ask your members to come back for a Small Group Connection event that evening or during the coming week. You will have fewer people come back, but you will have a higher level of commitment.

Prospective group members need options: days of the week, time of day, location, affinity. The more options you can make available, the better chance of prospective members sticking. Again, the list or guide they received during the service (or as they entered the Connection event) serves to start them in the right direction. The next step is to meet the leaders in person.

If you're doing a church-wide series, ideally you want all of your groups studying the same thing. It's easier to point people to groups that are all doing the sermon-aligned series. Other types of groups can be featured at different times. At Brookwood Church, we held a Connection event in the fall of the year for the groups doing the church-wide study only. Then, we offered another Connection event to promote all of our groups, the sampler, every January. Some folks may just want to join a group regardless of the study, or maybe they're looking for something specialized like Financial Peace University or a ministry placement study like Network. If your goal is exponential group growth, offer as many options as you possibly can to connect as many people as you possibly can.

Using personal invitation and personal introduction will usually connect two-thirds of a congregation into groups over time. The last third of any congregation is really a bit of a different animal.

EXCEPTIONS TO THE RULE

The delusion of success is that what we need next is more of what we've already experienced. After all, if HOST homes and Turbo Groups and apprentices and church-wide campaigns helped us connect the first 70 percent of our members into groups, then one last push should put us over the top. For those of us who have achieved 71 percent or more, we understand that this simply isn't true. What connected the first 70 percent will not connect the last thirty percent, no matter how attractive the appeal.

I have observed that the last 30 percent fall into one of three categories of people—independent, introverted, or isolated. These folks do not want to fit into anyone's system. They would rather practice personal spiritual disciplines like contemplation than face their greatest fear—your living room. They might have a disability or a disadvantage that keeps them away. A cookie-cutter approach is not the answer to getting them into groups. A great solution for some of these folks is an opportunity to start their own group on their own terms.

Whether it's just a couple of friends who meet for coffee every week, or someone who prefers to lead a group off the grid, they need alternatives to the status quo of forming groups. Let's explore these three categories of folks.

ENLISTING THE INDEPENDENTS

Independent people struggle with our systems. They are smart enough to know that they don't really need one. They don't buck the system so much as they avoid it. These natural leaders look at things much differently than the connected 70 percent.

Our church was launching a church-wide campaign one fall a few years ago. A long-time member called and told me that he had an unofficial small group. I'm never threatened by such an admission. (Secretly, I wished every member had this news to share.) He asked if his group could do the church-wide study. I told him, "Absolutely not," and then I laughed. Then, I asked him why his group was flying under the radar.

"Well, it's like Dean Martin used to say," he started. (Huh?) "The difference between a drunk and an alcoholic is that drunks don't go to all of those meetings." (My apologies to folks in recovery: those meetings are a good thing.) I told him that I only had two meetings a year. He said that might be possible.

Independent folks don't want to fit into a system. They're not rebellious as much as they just dance to the beat of their own drummer. They don't want recognition. They don't want training. They don't want supervision. They just want to get together with friends. Sometimes they'll discuss spiritual things. Other times they'll go to dinner. They are a group. They just don't obsess over structure like most pastors do.

Independents won't attend host briefings or leadership training. It's not that they're above that. It's just against their nature. In my experience, most independents possess a leadership gift already. They are capable of leading. They just need an opportunity. So, how do you get independents involved in groups?

Give them the material with no strings attached. They know how to lead. They know how to gather a group. They just need the materials.

Now, for all of the control freaks who are hyperventilating at this point, consider this: by selecting the curriculum and providing a coach, you have given direction to the group. Most leaders are not working hard to teach heresy or form a cult. They are devoting themselves to vacuuming their living rooms and preparing refreshments.

Starting groups for independents is as simple as putting a table in your church's lobby with a sign that says, "Start Your Own Group." Find out who they are and get their contact information. Give them all of the resources you would give any new leader. Give them access to a coach who can answer their questions at their request. When the six-week study ends, invite them to leadership training. They may or may not attend. That's okay. When they need help, they will come and find you. Independents need a long, invisible leash.

Some pastors object. "Why can't these independent folks honor the authority that God has placed over them by doing it my way?" Whoa. Calm down. That kind of thinking will keep you right at the numbers you currently have. Community is much bigger than your system or even your church.

To attract the independents in the last 30 percent, you must be willing to take a different approach. If you start where people are comfortable, then you can lead them to other things. If you try to drag them toward discomfort, you'll lead them nowhere.

ENGAGING INTROVERTS

Another important group in the last 30 percent is introverts. Like independents, introverts don't fit well in the system that serves the other 70 percent so well. Unlike the independents, they aren't going to form an unofficial group on the sly.

Introverts are not like the other 70 percent of members who have already joined groups. Granted, some introverts joined a group with their spouse, and in the words of Joseph Myers, each week they endure "forced relational hell."[41]

An introvert's greatest fear is knocking on the door of a stranger's house and meeting twelve new people. It's overwhelming. It's enough to make them pull the covers over their heads and call it a night. That doesn't mean introverts are antisocial.

Most introverts have good friends. The difference between an introvert and an extrovert is that introverts just need a few friends while extroverts have never met a stranger. Introverts don't comfortably fit into the usual structure of a small group. They don't do groups of ten or twelve people. They are far more comfortable with one or two. Can three people count as a group? Jesus seemed to think so, "For where two or three gather in my name, there am I with them."[42]

But who said that small groups should be comfortable? Shouldn't we be challenged to grow? Shouldn't we step out of our comfort zones? Down, pastor. Down. Pastors get up and speak before hundreds or thousands on Sundays. Fine. Introverts are back there in the corner. What works for you won't work for them. I am an introvert, and I am in a group. But I'm a small group pastor, so there's a level of professional responsibility that pushes me into groups. That's not true for every introvert. So how do you get introverts connected in groups?

Friends are the key to attracting introverts. Introverts have friends. They probably have better friends than extroverts, in that they've taken time to get to know a couple of friends very well. A pastor's invitation to join small groups probably won't do much to motivate introverts in that direction. It will only reinforce their greatest fear. But if their friend thinks it's a good idea and invites them, there's a much better chance of them going to a group.

The nuance here is that introverts connect in groups by relationship, not by strategy. Don't plan to launch groups where no one has to talk. Instead, encourage group members to think about the people in their life who would enjoy or benefit from the group's next study. A simple exercise of identifying their friends, neighbors, coworkers, and others is a great way for them to start praying about who to invite. You won't connect 100 percent of your introverts this way, but it's a much better way than sending them into a Connection event.

Maybe you need to rethink your group model a bit. What is a group? We usually come up with twelve, since Jesus had twelve disciples, but is twelve the right number? Many small group pastors, like Saddleback's Steve Gladen, advocate groups subgrouping when they exceed eight.[43] Then, there was the seminary class I took that defined a small group as three to thirty people. (What?)

Not every group needs to be the exact same size. Sometimes things that happen with two or three in a group can't happen with eighteen members present. If we had a group of only three people named Peter, James, and John, would we give it the green light? Again, introverts aren't friendless folks. They have good friends. In fact, we might even call good friends a small group. The formula is simple: friends + intention = change. We provide the intention by directing the group's focus, usually by offering small group curriculum. If we make the study available to any person who wants to get together with a group of friends, then we have a better chance of including introverts. We've even announced on a Sunday, "Some of you haven't found a group yet. You might not even like our small groups. Why not get together with your friends and start your own group?" Curriculum sold like hotcakes.

At one event a woman walked up to the "Start Your Own Group" table and said, "Four of us meet together at Starbucks every Thursday morning, could we do the study together?" Absolutely! They were in a group of friends, but they weren't in a "small group." Why not help them do something intentional about their spiritual growth while they were meeting together as a group of friends?

There's also the option of online small groups. As more and more of life is pushed toward the internet, we find ourselves in virtual family reunions and class reunions on Facebook practically on a daily basis. Technology allows us to encourage each other daily even when we're not together.[44] Through online chat and video conference sites, it's possible to connect online for a small group. Whether you're represented by an avatar or your actual video, online small groups offer flexibility and allow members to meet from the comfort of their own homes.

Some object to online small groups, saying that people can pretend to be someone else online and don't have to be themselves. If you've been in small group ministry for very long, you understand that this behavior is not limited to online small groups. Self-disclosure is an issue in both online and off-line groups.

Years ago, Robert Schuller started a church in a drive-in movie theater because people wouldn't attend church if they didn't have nice clothes to wear. He figured if they stayed in their cars at the drive-in, it didn't matter what they wore. Online small groups can also provide a level of comfort that will get introverts into the game. Besides, if the leader asks a tough question, Google is but a click away.

Introverts will join small groups, but most likely they won't sign up to join a group of strangers. By innovating and taking a different approach, connecting introverts into groups or helping introverts start groups will close the gap on the last 30 percent.

INCLUDING THE ISOLATED

People are isolated for a variety of reasons. Sometimes poor health or a disability limits their participation. Parents of special-needs children are often isolated. Rotating shifts or even certain occupations can work against group participation. Connecting isolated folks takes some creativity, but can lead to some great results.

Some barriers are easy to remove. If single moms can't afford to pay for childcare, then figure out a way to cover the costs of childcare for them. In the past, I have given group leaders gift cards to the church bookstore to purchase either childcare vouchers for on-campus childcare or study guides, based on the leader's good judgment of the situation. While the church may not offer free childcare to every group, single moms are really our modern day widows and orphans.[45] If your church lacks means, then enlist volunteers to provide childcare while these moms meet.

Health problems can also greatly limit small group participation. With the aging of our population and the rise of autism and other disorders, this segment of the church body is growing every day.

Our son was born with some special needs. When he was little, we would feed him and put him to bed before the group started. The baby monitor was nearby, so we were always close at hand during the group meeting. While we couldn't allow other group members to host the group in their homes, this was the best solution for us to be involved. This has helped me think about ways to meet the needs of people who are isolated by the conditions of their lives.

If folks can't get to the group, then bring the group to them. Maybe you will need to send someone early to help get their house ready. Maybe the size of the group or the length of the meeting will need to be unusual. It will take some creative problem solving and some extra effort to include the isolated members of a church in groups. In these cases that extra effort is necessary to include them, going that extra mile will mean a great deal to everyone involved. Some jobs make small group participation difficult. If a business or agency runs on rotating shifts and gives varying days off, it's impossible to commit to a specific day of the week for group. At New Life in California, two couples had this exact situation. They started a group with just the four of them. One week they'd meet on Tuesday. The next week they'd meet on Friday. Since there were only two rotating schedules to coordinate and fewer people involved, they could make the changes they needed to without inconveniencing others or missing meetings.

A few occupations add complexity to this kind of problem. For instance, police officers can get an interesting reception in mixed groups. One couple tried several groups, had a number of difficult experiences, and finally gave up. In the first group, someone wanted them to fix a ticket. In another, someone wanted them to intervene for their child who had a brush with the law. These officers needed a group that would give them a level playing field, so they decided to form a group of just first responders. They don't meet to talk shop, but they have a common understanding of life. No one is asking to get a ticket fixed.

One dilemma they faced was rotating shifts, so they chose two nights of the week for the group to meet based on the typical schedules of police officers in the area. While members only went to group once per week, their shift schedules dictated which night they could go.

There are many other groups of isolated folks out there. A church in Hilmar, California, holds a men's group at 4:00 a.m. for dairy workers. They get a Bible study before they milk the cows. I had one leader start a group on a commuter train. Rather than reading the paper on the way to work, they gathered every Tuesday morning to study God's word. (Once they started, word spread and they filled an entire section of the train!) Folks who work swing shift may like a group at midnight when they get off work. Others working the graveyard shift might prefer a group at 7:00 a.m.

Isolated, independent, and introverted folks don't fit neatly into typical small groups. Rather than expecting them to get with the program and join a predetermined group, why not give them permission to create biblical community on their own terms? You will be surprised at the ideas that surface.

At this point, there may be some hand-wringing among small group pastors. I have advocated advertised groups, invitation-only groups, on-campus groups, off-campus groups, then groups for the independent, introverted, and isolated. How many systems are we talking about here?

I only advocate one system. Every leader, regardless of the type of group they start, would receive the same coaching and training. If they are resistant, then they are resistant. Take the good with the bad.

In launching groups, there is a logical sequence, however, in introducing group strategies. First, start with your existing leaders and give them the Sneak Peek as described in chapter four. Then, look at your membership role and think about who else should be leading a group. Personally invite those people to lead a group. The senior pastor then takes the next step by inviting folks who are willing to open their homes to create a HOST group. Lastly, for those who would prefer to gather their friends and grow, especially those in the last 30 percent, present an option for them to start their own group or do the study on their own.

When churches bring in capital campaign companies, their first step is in recruiting large donors who contribute at least 50 percent of the financial goal. This way when the campaign is launched, the pastor can announce that the church is already halfway to their goal. This gives other folks an incentive. Everyone wants to join a winning team. Similar to this thinking, a small group launch is a "human capital" campaign. As the senior pastor, small group pastor/ director, or the small group team enlist influential leaders, the pastor can also announce the progress toward the goal of connecting people into groups.

While you don't necessarily have to use all of these strategies together, the key to involving more people in groups is giving them something to say "Yes" to. If they won't "lead" a group, would they "host" one? If they won't gather with strangers, then would they gather with their friends?

In my experience, multiple strategies are necessary to connect more than 100 percent of a congregation into groups, but only one system is necessary to coach, train, and direct these groups.

Recruiting leaders and connecting people into groups can benefit from new strategies, but more important than strategies is the attitude of those leading the groups ministry. You can form types of groups you never imagined if you give your people permission to form a group on their own terms. Something as simple as making the format or schedule for groups more flexible makes a huge difference. If people have the opportunity to start a group that's out of the norm or even off the books, they will figure out how to make a group work for them.

Many groups ministries are stuck because they've been using the same tired strategies for a long time. While I would never encourage any pastor to wreck what they have, I would clearly encourage them to add a strategy or two or twelve that will appeal to those who are not engaged by the current offerings. It's not their fault. They will do a group. You just have to give them something they can say "Yes" to.

THE STRUCTURE

CHAPTER 8

SUSTAINING GROUPS

The excitement of a church-wide campaign or any large group launch is starting a lot of groups all at once. The fear is what comes next—losing a lot of groups all at once.

Several years ago a small group pastor joined our coaching program. He had gone from having no small groups in his church to actually launching 233 groups for a forty-day church-wide campaign. At the end of the campaign, when it was all said and done, he ended up with three groups. What a heartbreak! This doesn't have to be the case. With a few key changes, more groups can last well beyond a campaign.

The longevity of a group largely depends on three key factors: how the group is formed, how the group is coached, and how the group is led into a next step. While that may sound like a simple formula, it is the result of over twenty years of trial and error in group life.

The formation of groups greatly determines the long-term or even the short-term success of the group. In the last chapter, I elaborated on successful and unsuccessful ways to connect people into groups. I won't rehearse all my group formation philosophy again, but a few things need to be pointed out.

Have you ever gone on a blind date? I have. For my first ten years in ministry, I was single. Believe me, being a single pastor is certainly a predicament. Everybody wants to set you up. They would say, "Poor Pastor Allen. He must be so lonely. I know a nice girl . . ." I went on a few dates because I didn't want to insult the kindhearted people who arranged them. Looking back, I should have considered my own feelings over theirs, but past is past.

Now, I know blind dates have worked out for some. I even know a few people who married their blind dates, but for most people it just doesn't work this way. For me, blind dates were awkward. Even when I did my best to make the most of it, it was just stressful. I spent most of the time praying it would end soon or hoping the Lord would come back.

When we assign people to a group, send them to the church website, or some other task-oriented approach to connecting people into groups, the groups don't tend to last. We've set them up on a blind date with a small group. Why are we surprised when it doesn't work out?

The more relational affinity the group members have going into the group, the better the chance of the group continuing for the long haul. This doesn't mean that every group member needs to know every other group member from the very beginning, but it is important that everyone knows someone going into the group. This is why I emphasize the effectiveness of personal invitation in forming groups.

Over the years, small group pastors have really sold people a bill of goods by promising if they join a group, they will make some of the best friends they ever had. I have actually apologized for grandiose claims like this. If people are thrown into a group because they live in the same zip code, or they need a group on Tuesday night, they might make friends. At least the group will be friendly. And there will be a few people who are tolerated for six weeks during the series. If the new group members are highly committed to the idea of group life, they will make it work. But, most new group members are not highly committed to the idea of group life. They got in because of the pastor's invitation to a short-term commitment.

Groups that last are those who start with some relational basis. Again, the best ways to join a group are by either starting a group, by personal invitation, or by personal introduction. These groups tend to stick. Groups formed through online sign ups, sign-up cards, or group placement by the church tend not to fare as well. Think about it. Being assigned to a small group by someone in the church office is sort of like being set up for a blind date. Meeting in person is so much better when someone decides to join a group. Speed dating is better than blind dating any day.

If the relational piece is in place as the group is formed, the group has satisfied the first key to staying together and moving forward. Groups of friends last longer than groups of strangers.

The second key to group longevity is the involvement of a coach with the new leaders. Don't underestimate this point.

Coaching is not a phone number new leaders can call if they get into trouble. In fact, a method like that functions more like getting called into the principal's office when a problem occurs than confiding in a trusted friend who is willing to help.

Great coaching is built on relationship, not efficiency. Leader training conducted by lecturing classrooms of new leaders is efficient, but it is not effective. Sending bulk emails to group leaders is efficient and informative, but it is also ineffective. If you attempt to coach your leaders through an email distribution list, you aren't coaching them. You're spamming them. The small group hotline often becomes a tool of last resort when it's too late to help.

Coaching is a relationship. As suggested in chapter four, the coaching relationship should start at the new leader briefing where the new coach and the new leaders can meet face-to-face. Coaching is carried out through personal interaction with the new leaders. As trust is built, the new leaders will be willing to confide in the coach about difficulties before there are big problems for the group.

A coach is also the best training tool for a new leader. The coach's experience has equipped them for encouraging and shepherding their leaders. If a larger problem occurs in an area where the coach is not experienced, then the coach can turn to the person supervising him or her. In churches with less than one thousand people in groups, this would be the small group pastor or director. In churches with over one thousand people in groups, this would be the member of the small group team that the coach reports to.

The significance of a coach is in the ability to deliver unique training to each group leader as he or she needs it. New leaders show up with various levels of experience and ability. Cookie-cutter training will work for some, but not for all. By individually coaching new leaders, the training becomes more effective by helping them with specific issues as they occur. It's teaching during teachable moments.

For instance, in the past, I've trained group leaders on how to deal with overly talkative group members before they even started their groups, but the reality was that most of the training went in one ear and out the other. The new leaders didn't need this training until they found themselves with an overly talkative member of the group. When they're in the situation, they need the training (and fast). When they can simply pick up the phone and talk to their coach rather than waiting for the next small group seminar to roll around, the lesson will not be easily forgotten. Coaches give new leaders the training they need right when they need it.

The final key to keep groups moving forward is offering a next step to the new groups. The intention in a six-week trial run is to offer a low-risk introduction to group leadership which will lead to an ongoing group. The reality is most of these new groups intended only to sign up for six weeks and then conclude at the end of their six-week commitment. I don't know where they would get a crazy idea like that. In order to keep groups going forward, they need a next step.

Most new groups do not have a strong opinion of what they want to study next. How many times as a group leader have you presented a selection of curriculum to the group only to hear, "They all look good. Why don't you pick one?" It happens almost every time.

Of course, the other issue here is the fact you invited folks to join a group for six weeks and not for the rest of their lives. For some strange reason, once the six weeks ends, they feel like their commitment is up—because it is.

When we launched groups at our church in California for the first time, we started in the spring. Our fear wasn't just Day Forty-One, but also Days Forty-Two through Ninety-Six. It was a high hurdle over the summer. We gathered the new leaders midway through the spring study and invited them to join our next series, which began on the second Sunday of *October*. Then, we held our breath. It's a long stretch from mid-May to mid-October. October held a big surprise.

When we gathered groups in September of that year to give them a sneak peek at the fall curriculum, 80 percent of the groups who started in the spring were right there ready to join the fall study. You could have knocked me over with a feather. Giving the groups a next step, even a huge step over four months, is key to helping groups sustain. If I hadn't experienced this first hand, honestly, I wouldn't have believed it.

Wendy Nolasco, small group pastor at New Life Center in Bakersfield, California, found a similar result. After successfully launching one hundred groups in the spring, they gave their groups a heads-up on their fall campaign and then said a prayer. When fall came, seventy-five of those one hundred groups continued into the next step Pastor Wendy gave them.

Offering a next step for a fall or New Year's campaign is not quite so daunting. They don't need to wait three months for another study. They can start a new study the following week. Once a group does two back-to-back six-week studies, usually they are good to continue from that point forward.

In offering a next step to new groups, don't give them choices. Offer a single next step. If you send your new group leaders to the internet or the local bookstore, they will get lost in the plethora of selections. In fact, it will take them so long to make a decision, more than likely the group will falter before they can choose their next step.

You want the groups to make one decision: whether or not they will continue. You don't want to add complexity to that decision like what they will study, where they will meet, etc. Keep the decision clear: Will the group continue?

If you started the group with a video-based curriculum, then the next step should involve a video as well. Again, if you invited folks to form groups with the idea that they didn't have to be Bible scholars, because the expert was on the video, they will need that strategy again. Whether the next series aligns with the Sunday sermons or not, a specific next step will take them past Day Forty-One and into a longer group life.

Now, you may ask, "How long can groups continue with video-based curriculum?"

Carl George put it this way, "As long as there are videos."

The key to helping groups move forward is to have them make the decision to continue *before* the current study ends. Don't wait until the last week of the study to make the decision.

After Seacoast Church in Mt. Pleasant, South Carolina, launched groups with their self-produced *Make Room* study a few years ago, they created a second study based on the church's best-selling sermon series called *The DNA of Joy*. While the first study involved creating all new material, the content had already been developed for the second study. It just had to be reworked to fit a small group format. By offering a next step, Seacoast Church saw many of their new groups continue.

This may be the opportunity for a church to produce a video-based curriculum with the theme of "How to Be a Group at Our Church." The group would spend the next six weeks learning what it means to be a group in your church's culture. A curriculum like this could be used for every new group following a church-wide campaign. Since the curriculum is only used with new groups, the issue of repetition disappears. Also, it relieves the production team from producing another series, and it lightens the expense on the church budget in purchasing group kits.

One important clarification here: the follow-up study should be presented as a next step for groups rather than another major church-wide campaign. Most churches can only hope to launch groups two or three times per year in a church-wide campaign. If the pastor makes more pushes for groups than that, then the congregation will develop campaign fatigue. Even though every week the members will participate in a weekend service and the groups will be studying something, congregations don't tolerate constant pushes for forming groups. It becomes white noise after a while.

WHAT IF THE LEADER CAN'T CONTINUE?

There are instances where the new group leader simply can't continue with the group. You could take the guilt route: "If you love Jesus and want to go to heaven . . ." I wouldn't recommend that.

If the leaders legitimately cannot continue, they are probably not considering other possibilities for the group to continue. They think if they can't go on, then the group can't either. But, that's not necessarily true.

When a leader informs you around Day Twenty-Four of your current campaign that they won't be able to continue with the group, have their coach begin to investigate whether another member of the group would like to step up and lead. If the group has been rotating leadership during the study, someone may very easily take over leadership so the group can continue.

So how do you get your leaders to state their intentions around Day Twenty-Four? You ask them. I've used both a survey and a mid-campaign leader meeting to determine who is interested in continuing and who isn't. Before I walk into the huddle, I like to know what to expect. Often I will send the survey first. It serves as what John Maxwell calls the "meeting before the meeting." Then, when you walk into the room, you know who plans to continue and who needs to be given some options for their group to continue.

All in all, Day Forty-One is just the beginning of group life. With the right encouragement and next steps, groups who started to only complete a six-week study can find themselves enjoying quality group life for many studies to come.

AVOIDING DISPOSABLE SMALL GROUPS

Often the sheer number of groups participating in one church-wide campaign after another will give the illusion of progress. After all, if you had thirty groups in your last campaign and have fifty groups now, then haven't you made great gains?

The question here is whether the thirty groups you had before are part of the fifty groups you have now. No church will keep 100 percent of their groups moving forward. Some groups are simply a bad fit for their members and shouldn't continue. They might do more harm than good.

If there is constant turnover in groups, then there is another issue to consider. In evaluating groups, if a significant number are doing one six-week study, and then choosing not to continue, this should be a clear warning sign that something is broken in your groups ministry. Is there a communication problem? Is there a coaching problem? Is there a commitment problem?

While the premise of a church-wide campaign is the offer of a short-term trial run, if a church is not retaining at least 80 percent of the groups from the previous campaign, then something is wrong. Often this is missed because the overall number of groups continues to increase, and the new campaign is regarded as a success. Some believe as long as their numbers are up and to the right, then everything is okay. But often it's not.

Groups should not be disposable. We have a two-year-old in our house. As much as we'd like to make cloth diapers work, disposable diapers are just easier. They're not easy on the environment, but they are easy on the parents. The idea of disposable groups, however, is really quite ludicrous. Here's the bottom line (so to speak): diapers are useful for a brief period of time, but the goal is to potty train our children. If our group ministries stay in diapers, we're all in trouble. Disposable groups don't create disciples. After all, spiritual growth in groups occurs from life on life, not life on curriculum.

While some small group strategies unfortunately produce groups that are short-lived, or there is no system in place to sustain these groups beyond one series, the reality is that the phenomenon of "disposable groups" can be completely avoided if these three keys are in place: effective group formation, dependable coaching relationships, and a next step for the group.

THE GROUP DECISION PROCESS

Part of the reason churches end up with disposable groups is they truncate the decision process for their leaders. The decision to lead a six-week study shouldn't be seen as the group leader's final decision. The first study is a trial run, a warm-up. It's a free test drive on the path to making the decision about becoming a group leader.

Everett Rogers, in his classic book *Diffusion of Innovations*, outlines research done in the 1940s that reveals five distinct phases in the process for accepting and implementing new ideas.[46] The first step is knowledge. At this stage, churches offer information about groups, their benefits, and their need. It's what I call the "mass media" approach to informing the church body about groups.

SUSTAINING GROUPS   155

Whether the information comes from announcements in the service, in the church bulletin, via email, or from pastoral invitation,
church members are informed. Some will make a decision to jump
in based on information alone.

The second step is persuasion. This is not what you think. Sure,
some will decide to try a group because of the pastor's impassioned
plea, but again, these types of announcements fall more in the first
step of knowledge than in the persuasion step. Persuasion is the
communication between group leaders and potential group leaders
about the experience of leading a group. For folks who are more
deliberate in their decision process or are even downright skeptical about new things, the testimony of those who have tried and
succeeded with groups is highly significant. This isn't about right or
wrong. It's a style or preference of decision making. Hearing from
successful leaders, whether face-to-face or through church media,
can be very persuasive for those who are a little slower in making
their decision.

Storytelling about small groups is a great way to reinforce the
benefits of group life to current group leaders and members as well
as those considering a group. Everyone likes to be part of a winning proposition. Celebrate your wins, and you will attract more
group leaders.

By capturing the stories of successful groups on video to show
in worship services or send out by email, you cast vision to others. Maybe even tell the stories of group leaders who were initially
reluctant, but are so glad they gave it a try. By telling the stories of
group leaders who have succeeded, you will not only serve to per-
suade prospective group leaders, but also to reconfirm those who
have led. The experiences of healthy groups casts vision to other
groups about what their groups could be.

My cable company advertises their services over the cable
TV I already subscribe to. Why does the cable company advertise to their own customers? Because customers have other
choices. Customers could switch to satellite or streaming video.
There are other ways to access programming rather than paying
a big bill to the cable company each month. By advertising their
services to their own customers, they reinforce not only the

weaknesses of other delivery systems, but also the advantages of cable. After hearing from the "paid professional," the pastor, and the "satisfied customers," other group leaders, now potential group leaders have what they need to move into the next step.

The third step is the decision. A key part of the decision stage is a trial run. Rogers writes,

> One way to cope with inherent uncertainty about an innovation's consequences is to try out that new idea on a partial basis. Most individuals do not adopt an innovation without first trying it on a probationary basis to determine its usefulness in their own situation. This small scale trial is often an important part of the decision to adopt.[47]

For people who don't have previous experience with groups, participating in a short-term series is part of the decision process about groups overall. But, as I said before, the trial run is part of the decision-making process, not the final decision.

There are some people, like my dad, who purchase cars sight unseen over the internet. (In fact, my dad's first purchase on eBay was a car. I thought he was crazy, but it worked out.) There are a lot of others who still go to a dealer, look at the cars on the lot, and test drive the cars that interest them.

For these kinds of people, the test drive is an important part of the purchasing process. Once the customer gets behind the wheel, their old car will never measure up again. The new car has better features. It's clean. It has the new car smell. How could you possibly walk away from that new car and go back to your old heap?

A pastor friend of mine used to sell cars. At the end of the test drive, he would have the driver pull up to the side of the building where a mirror was affixed for the driver to see himself. My friend would say, "You look good in this car." How could you resist that?

Recruiting group leaders is not like buying a car, except that it is. While much of the decision starts with knowledge and persuasion, there is still a "look before you leap" mentality for most people. The last thing anyone wants to experience is buyer's remorse.

By offering a short-term trial run, potential group leaders can test drive leading a small group. They gather some friends and lead for six weeks or so. It's not for the rest of their lives. If they like it, they may be open to more. If they don't, then they might be open to trying something else. But notice the trial run is only part of the decision, and not final confirmation that a group will move forward. The decision is the third out of five steps. Let this sink in for a minute. While a six-week trial run is part of the decision process, it is not the final decision.

The fourth step is implementation. At this stage, a person chooses to put the new idea to use. They had a good experience in the trial run and want to move forward with the group. This is where the next step curriculum comes in.

By offering the option for a next series, the group leader moves from the decision stage to the implementation stage and is one step closer to becoming an "official" group leader whose group will continue. Their good experience has proven to them that leading a group is something they would like to do.

For some group leaders, the second study will occur immediately after the first study. This is ideal. For others, who may have rearranged their lives to lead for six weeks, but cannot continue immediately, they may delay the next step. They are not closed to leading. It's just a timing issue. They are still open to building on a good experience. They're just not sure when.

This is why new leaders need additional on-ramps to leading groups. For some churches, this means a sequence of studies during a ministry year (September–May), which we will explore for the next few pages. For others this means you might need to offer an annual alignment series. If the new leaders can't continue for this year, then maybe they can try again next year. While this isn't ideal because of the amount of falloff, it is certainly better to have a group leader back a year later than to not have them leading at all.

Another factor which brings higher sustainability with groups is the flexibility to allow the group to customize its experience to make it more suitable to them. Again, Rogers,

A higher degree of reinvention leads to a faster rate of adoption of an innovation. The logic behind this generalization is that innovations that are more flexible and that can be easily reinvented can be fit to a wider range of adopters' conditions. Thus the rate of adoption for these innovations is more rapid.[48]

While I am a huge advocate of weekly groups, some groups can't sustain this pace. An alignment series requires weekly meetings, and this helps group members to get to know each other better, but after the initial six weeks, groups should be able to determine the meeting frequency of their own group. I wouldn't necessarily advertise this, since weekly meetings tend to facilitate better group life, but if a group suggests meeting every other week, I wouldn't oppose it. Other variables may include where a group meets, who leads the discussion, or even who leads the group. If the leader who started the group can't continue, perhaps the group could continue under the leadership of someone else. If the group has been together for a while or if there is a dominant felt need in the group different from the prescribed next study, then, again, flexibility would be beneficial in allowing the group to choose another study to do next.

The beauty of groups is in the ability to customize them. To me the ideal is having a thousand groups studying a thousand different things. While there is a great dynamic in an entire congregation studying the same thing together, continually sacrificing the needs of groups in aligning is simply taking things too far. While a group doing a different study may not be advertised during an alignment series, they certainly shouldn't be prevented from meeting. When the time is right, they should be promoted in another season outside of an alignment.

The willingness to be flexible will go a long way in helping to sustain groups. While aligning group studies with sermons does produce a great dynamic in a church, if this is pressed too far, it ends up becoming a case of throwing the baby out with the bathwater. Groups should be allowed to choose studies that suit them, especially if they have completed two or three recommended studies. Moving forward as a group in the implementation stage may mean the group continues as an unadvertised group. That's okay. As the groups continue to move forward, you always have the opportunity to invite them to become "official" groups.

The fifth step in the decision process is confirmation. Now, we're at the finish line. At the confirmation stage, the goal is to help group leaders solidify their commitment to group life. A key method in confirmation is a leadership track (more on this in chapter nine). In short, leaders are offered the choice of continuing in their current pattern or making their group official by meeting the requirements of group leadership established by the church. This point of decision to enter a leadership track serves as a defining moment for a group leader.

If a group doesn't want to become official, that's okay. Provided the group leader is under the care of a coach and receives the other training you provide, this group should be welcome to continue. But, by remaining unofficial, their groups will not be advertised in any way. For folks who are more independent or introverted anyway, not being advertised will be fine with them.

A few years ago, I worked with Van Dyke Church in Lutz, Florida. Van Dyke is a dynamic, growing United Methodist Church. Before their first church-wide series, only four hundred of their 1,800 adults were in groups. When we launched their *Q&A* series in the fall with Pastor Matthew Hartsfield's teaching on the video, their group participation jumped to one thousand people in groups. But they weren't stopping there.

Their second self-produced curriculum, *Shouting at Jesus*, based on a book by Pastor Matthew, was introduced to the congregation in January of the next year. Again, with the pastor inviting folks to open their homes for a group, group participation took another leap. This time they went from one thousand group members to 1,600 group members. At this point, 89 percent of their weekend adult attendance was connected into groups. There was one more campaign in the works.

On Easter Sunday, Pastor Matthew introduced a third self-produced curriculum, *Masterplan*. When he made the appeal for group leaders this time, the capacity for groups easily topped two thousand group members. Once these groups were offered to the congregation, sure enough, over two thousand people joined groups. At that point, Van Dyke Church had over 110 percent of their weekend adult attendance in groups.

It's easy to launch one six-week campaign and get a bunch of folks engaged in a short-term group. You have the low hanging fruit. All of the Innovators and Early Adopters have jumped in. Things look and feel good. But more often than not these groups appear and disappear like wildflowers—here for a season and then gone.

Pastor Don Wink of Lutheran Church of the Atonement in Barrington, Illinois, led his congregation in a "Year of Transformation." The congregation was challenged to lead groups for a three-part series with starts in the fall, the new year, and after Easter. This congregation of three hundred adults distributed 580 copies of their study guide. That alone was significant, but the most remarkable part of their story is that in the transition between the fall study and the new year's study, they only lost one group. Even with one less group, their overall group participation increased! Folks joined the existing groups for the second installment of the series. This was a remarkable result. The loss of only one group between studies was worth celebrating more than 580 study guides distributed.

The secret is the sequence. By offering a sequence of group studies, especially in the first year of launching or relaunching group life in a church, groups not only form rapidly, but they also continue from study to study. A second church-wide study gives the opportunity for more people to lead and for groups to continue.

As mentioned previously, at least 80 percent of new groups will continue if they are offered something to continue into. If the result is less than 80 percent continuing, then something isn't working. Rather than reinventing the wheel by re-forming groups annually, why not keep the groups you have? Unless there is a significant problem in the group, most people like to continue with the group they're in.

While everyone will go through the decision process mentioned earlier in this chapter, everyone does not decide at the same rate. Folks who are venturesome will jump in at the first announcement, whereas some folks due to their personality type and disposition will wait for others to go first, then will learn from the experience of others before they try a group themselves.

In his research, Rogers categorizes adopters of a new idea in five categories: Innovators (2.5%), Early Adopters (13.5%), Early Majority (34%), Late Majority (34%), and Laggards (16%), the groups we talked about in chapter five. These terms get tossed around and renamed, but the basis of these ideas goes back to 1943.[49]

In working for more than a decade with churches that have used church-wide campaigns like Van Dyke Church, I've seen a church's initial group launch connect more than 16 percent of their congregations. The 16 percent would make up the Innovators and Early Adopters combined. Then, I began to look at these adopter categories differently.

Not only will people join groups during different waves of alignments in a given year, people also choose to lead groups during different waves. If your church is not aligning the group launch with a sermon series, you can create the same effect by promoting group studies with this same pattern. Of course, any group promotion works best if the senior pastor is involved in promoting groups. Bear in mind, there are a lot of variables that will determine the number of groups that start during a first campaign.

If the church offers other options for adult discipleship, such as Sunday school, Adult Bible Fellowships, and other groups or classes, there is a smaller pool of potential group leaders and group members. Some churches will take the tack of shutting down other groups which would compete with an alignment series. From chapter one, you understand I do not take that position.

For most churches, there is still a significant group of people who only attend the weekend service, and are not involved in any kind of group. This is the audience you want to reach with an alignment series. While some folks connected in other groups might forsake their class or on-campus group for an alignment out of loyalty for their senior pastor, most of these folks will return to their groups after the series ends. They simply can't maintain a group meeting in addition to what they are already committed to.

A couple of years ago, I was working with a twenty-five-year-old church in Florida that had established a pattern of offering adult Sunday school, Sunday morning worship services, a Sunday evening service, and a Wednesday night service. While they recognized these established groups were declining and were not the future of their church, how could they shut down a midweek service attended by one thousand people? They didn't.

When the senior pastor announced a church-wide study with a video-based curriculum to his congregation of three thousand adults, 360 adults signed up to lead a group. I had the privilege of training them.

After the leader briefing, a group of church members invited me out to dinner. I happened to sit next to the senior pastor's brother-in-law. He said, "Can I ask you a question?" I consented. He continued, "You know we attend Sunday school and Sunday morning worship, then we come back for the Sunday night service, and then the Wednesday night Bible study."

I said, "Yes, in the church I grew up in, we were taught that was the pathway to heaven." He laughed, but then turned serious.

"Now, we're also supposed to do a small group on top of all of that?" he asked. I knew he was especially loyal to his senior pastor since they were related, but I also knew no one could remain committed to so many things for an extended period of time.

I said, "Well, you'll have to decide if you like a small group enough to continue, and if you can keep up with all of this." He confided he would probably do this one study, then just continue with his Sunday school class and the other worship services he was already involved in. I assured him this was okay.

Not everyone can continue in the group they start or joined in a group launch if they are already committed to a lot of other things. Now, the classes and groups that are waning will not be around forever. Pastors should be patient and more than a little apprehensive in intentionally closing things down. But, over time, options that are declining will eventually disappear. In the meantime, these competing values will have an impact on the number of leaders a church can recruit.

The number of requirements a church places on new group leaders will also determine the number of groups that can start. While I would never encourage a pastor or church to go beyond their acceptable level of risk, the choices of who and how many to invite into group leadership will have an impact on the number of groups being launched. The pastors left scratching their heads because their church started dozens of groups while similar churches started hundreds of groups shouldn't have to think too hard to find the reason for their result.

Other factors affecting leader recruiting and group formation include the pastor's enthusiasm and dedication to recruiting. If the pastor invites people to lead groups in a halfhearted way, then the results will be weak. If the pastor makes a strong invitation, but doesn't provide an immediate next step like a sign-up card for group leaders, then a lot of potential leaders will be lost.

With all of these factors and exceptions in mind, let's examine the anatomy of leader recruitment and group formation through a series of launches. While every church will not achieve identical results, gains of some size should be expected.

In the first campaign, Innovators (2.5%) will step up to lead groups. If you lead a church of one thousand adults, then your Innovators will start around twenty-five groups. Once you add in your Early Adopters (13.5%), that number can climb dramatically. In fact, when New Life, the church I served for fifteen years in California, connected 125 percent of our average adult attendance into groups, we discovered this was possible because 13 percent of our adults were leading groups. While I always thought about the overall number of people connected in groups, the game changer is the percentage of adults leading groups. If a church can recruit 13 percent of their adults to lead, then it's relatively easy to connect over 100 percent of the church's average adult attendance into groups. If a church recruits 20 percent or more to lead, the results are exponential. At New Life we actually went from having 30 percent of our adults in groups to having nearly 40 percent of our adults lead for at least one six-week study. Again, the trial run was part of the decision process. Not every leader decided to continue.

I used to think that in order to launch one hundred groups, you would need one thousand people to join those groups. My thinking has changed. In order to launch one hundred groups, you don't need a thousand people. You need one hundred people to lead the one hundred groups. The leaders will fill the groups.

A second campaign also gives the opportunity for more of your Early Adopters, and even some of the Early Majority, to feel

confident in leading. Not everyone will jump in and lead a group
in the first church-wide campaign (or even join a group for that
matter). Some folks want to sit back and make sure this idea of
launching groups with an alignment will actually work and that
no one died in the process. Once they see the success of the groups
from the first campaign and the concept has been proven to them,
they will be more likely to jump into a second campaign.

While the Early Adopters will embrace a relatively new idea,
the Early Majority are deliberative in their approach. If as a pastor
or director you are getting excited about the ideas in this book, you
are probably an Innovator or an Early Adopter. Remember, you
are one or two steps ahead of the Early Majority, and certainly far
ahead of the skeptical Late Majority and Laggards, who hold to
tradition. Give them a chance to catch up.

A third alignment during the first year will serve to greatly
increase not only the continuation of groups from the first two
alignments, but also the addition of new leaders who were still
holding out. While this sounds like a good deal of work in the first
year, the sequence serves to achieve and retain the results of launching a tremendous number of new groups, and more importantly,
recruiting and keeping a multitude of new group leaders.

While the sequence of alignments works very well in the first
year of launching or relaunching groups, once a church has hit the
mark of 80 to 100 percent of their average weekend attendance in
groups, the number of alignments should be reduced to one or two
alignments per year for their second year and beyond.

If the church persists in offering three or even more alignments
after the first year, the congregation can develop what I call "campaign fatigue." Even though group members will be listening to a
weekend sermon and discussing a lesson in the group, if the sermon and the study are aligned too frequently with multiple group
pushes during the year, the methodology becomes white noise to
the congregation.

This does not mean, however, that churches should avoid
weekly discussion guides for use in their groups. A group discussion of the weekend message is actually very effective in helping
group members apply the biblical principles to their lives. It's the

constant push for leaders and groups after the first year that becomes wearisome.

There are some exceptions, however. Churches that are rapidly
growing or have a high amount of turnover can continue with a series of aligned studies every year until their growth plateaus or their
turnover subsides. If a church is located in a college town or near a
military base, not only is there a constant churn from graduations
and deployments, but there is also an annual influx of freshmen and
reassignments. When these folks start attending your church as their
new church home, they will enjoy the opportunity of joining a group
as well. Some may be at a distance from friends and family, and
want to connect with the members of the church in a group. Others will come to town with their military unit, which gives a great
opportunity to recruit those who've joined your church to take the
study back to their military community. When they are reassigned
or deployed, your small groups will end up all over the world.

OVERCOMING SEASONAL CHALLENGES TO GROUP LAUNCHES

The annual calendar offers some challenges to year-round
groups. Some weeks of the year are ideal for group meetings and
for starting groups. Other times of the year, the focus should move
from group meetings to group life. While groups may not meet as
regularly during Christmas, Easter, or the summer, they continue as
a group with a slightly different focus. This change of pace is often
a very healthy thing for groups.

CHRISTMAS: 'TIS THE SEASON TO DISBAND?

Certain seasonal complexities are futile to combat. In the U.S.
one of the most challenging seasons for groups is between Thanksgiving and New Year's Day. Churches in Canada are blessed to have an
earlier Thanksgiving, so they can launch a fall campaign after Cana-
dian Thanksgiving, then enjoy a great six-week run unencumbered.
Both countries, and a few others, face the same dilemmas around
the Christmas season, since it now begins right around Halloween.

Churches should plan their fall alignment series to end just prior to Thanksgiving. While some churches try to encourage groups to meet the week after Thanksgiving and into December, most people's schedules are far too complex. Between school activities, work parties, family gatherings, and church events, people are pressed for time and stressed out. The plausibility of regular groups meetings on top of this is, well, unreasonable. But, this doesn't mean groups have to stop.

Churches and their groups can roll with the Christmas season. Groups can attend Advent services and other special Christmas services together. Rather than meeting regularly for Bible study, the group could have a Christmas party and invite prospective members who might join them for a January series (or they could just be neighborly and friendly with no agenda).

The Christmas season is a great time for groups to serve together. With additional services and programs at Christmastime, churches certainly could use the extra help. Every community also has needs throughout this season. The group could serve the poor with a nonprofit. They could help with a civic event. Groups could ring a bell for the Salvation Army. A few of our groups did this one year. One group leader decided to sing Christmas carols as he tended his kettle. His singing was so bad that people offered to donate if he would stop singing! The group had a lot of fun at his expense, but they raised a lot of money too.

Group meetings might be difficult during the Christmas season, but group life can continue. Groups need a healthy balance of both anyway. Another dimension of discipleship through serving together or celebrating together is a great change of pace for any group. This is a great opportunity for groups to live out what they've been learning by serving together.

In order for groups to survive the gap between Thanksgiving and New Year's Day, a next step should be offered to groups in the middle of their fall study. I can't overemphasize the importance of groups deciding to continue before the fall series ends. Even if the next series doesn't start until mid-January or after Super Bowl Sunday, if they agree to a next step during the fall study, you won't have to worry about them as much in January.

Speaking of the new year, December is not the time to recruit new leaders for the new year's series. Most people can't even think about the new year until they are actually in it. While you do need at least three weeks to recruit leaders, plan to start your series late in January or, even better, early February, so there is plenty of time to recruit leaders and form groups. Recruiting in December is futile.

THREE CHALLENGES OF AN EASTER LAUNCH

For retaining groups from an Easter launch, there are three big obstacles. They are known as June, July, and August. While I will address the seasonal complexities of groups during the summer in a minute, I want to specifically address some issues related to Easter. A big Easter launch is not the best option for some churches.

For churches in colder climates especially, the spring is a very difficult time to launch groups. Once the sun comes out, people are gone. Competition also comes from kids' baseball games, soccer teams, and other outdoor activities. Now, don't get me wrong. People are doing good things by involving their children in activities. In fact, it's a great way for them to develop relationships with other parents, and maybe even include them in their small group down the line.

I used to teach a Wednesday night Bible study at our church in California. It was a bit of a holdover from years gone by. As soon as the time changed to daylight saving time, that midweek study was a ghost town except for a faithful few. We held on until Memorial Day. Eventually those eighty-five or so people who gathered on Wednesday nights became small group leaders for the most part, so the midweek Bible study ended.

If I just described your church's situation in the spring, then I wouldn't attempt a big Easter launch. I would certainly offer a curriculum as a next step for the groups that started in January or February, but I wouldn't spend the leadership coin on an Easter launch which would produce a mediocre result.

Now, please don't infer that twelve weeks of small group meetings split between the fall and the new year are sufficient for the group members' spiritual development. They're not. Group meetings and group life should go all fifty-two weeks of the year in some form or fashion. My men's group followed a weekly message discussion guide and met for lunch every Wednesday all year long. In its ninth year, the group still follows that pattern.

The significance of groups is helping a bunch of friends or acquaintances find biblical community. They practice the One Anothers of Scripture. They do life together. Life is far more than fifty-two group meetings per year. Doing life together is a 365-day-per-year endeavor. Even in the complexities of springtime weather and the summer months, community should be encouraged to continue, even if meetings don't.

For other churches, Easter could have the biggest potential for launching groups. The beauty of Easter is it's the one Sunday everyone who calls your church "home" will show up. By avoiding an Easter group launch, you could possibly miss the biggest opportunity of the year. So, please pardon me while I speak out of both sides of my mouth here. But, go back and consider Gene Appel's result at Eastside Christian Church that I mentioned in chapter two, when they started 460 groups on Easter Sunday.

Infrequent attenders and people who are more marginally associated with the church tend to have more relational ties outside of the church than they have with people at church. Since they don't attend regularly, they don't know as many church people. If you put a curriculum in the hands of these infrequent attenders and ask them to invite their friends to do a study, then there is huge potential in connecting people who have never darkened the door of your church. If the study is right (see chapter two), then their friends will join a group. This strategy has huge implications for outreach and evangelism! (But please don't call it that. People are scared of evangelism.)

However you handle Easter, the dilemma comes afterward. Now, groups must survive the summer in order to continue.

RETHINK SUMMER

When I was a kid, summer started when school was out just before Memorial Day and ended just after Labor Day, as God intended. We had enough time to actually wonder what we would do with ourselves. Sure, there was a week of church camp and a family vacation in there, but there were weeks and weeks of playing outside and watching old reruns, if you were fortunate enough to have a mom who wasn't hooked on soaps.

Today, summer starts the second week in June and ends about the middle of August. It's about six to eight weeks, if you're lucky.

Many groups automatically decide to break for the summer. It's just what they do. They assume that it's too hard to get together or that their group members are too busy, so why bother gathering as a group? But, when was the last time you rethought your assumptions?

We go into summer making a few assumptions like "Everybody's busy traveling, so we might as well not even try to get together as a group." In a normal year, most families do one big vacation and maybe a few weekend trips. While everyone in your group probably won't take vacation on the same week, they also won't be gone for the entire summer. Before school ends, ask your group about their summer schedules. Who knows? They might be available after all.

In this age of staycations and day trips, people tend to be busier on the weekends than during the week. Few of us could be categorized as the idle rich. Yes, it's summer, but we've got to keep our day jobs. While your group might be headed to the mountains or the beach on the weekends, they're in town Monday through Friday, because of their jobs. They might not be around for church services on Sunday, so your group gathering might be the consistent touch they get during the summer.

Your group doesn't need to meet every week to be spiritual. If your group meets every week, then meet every other week or meet once a month during the summer. The goal is to keep the relational connections up. Ask your group to bring their calendars and see when most of the group will be in town. Even if you can only get together once a month during the summer, do it. I've even seen groups spend vacations together, and go on camping trips. At Brookwood Church in South Carolina, one of our groups even went on a cruise together. They met another couple from Greenville during the cruise, and their new acquaintants ended up joining the group! Later the group leader came to me asking tongue in cheek if their cruise expenses could be considered a tax deductible ministry expense. I told him it was between the group, the Lord, and the IRS! Your group doesn't need to have a Bible study every week to be spiritual. Have a party and invite prospective members. If you live in the South, grill out. If you live in the rest of the world, have a barbecue. Ask everyone to bring something. Invite the neighbors, but be sure to only invite people that you actually like.

Groups can serve together with a local organization. Is there a neighborhood school with projects, but their funds were cut this year? Is there a yard in your neighborhood that needs work? Is there a single mom or an elderly person who could use a hand? Is a member of your group moving?

Change it up with your group. While some groups will meet fifty-two weeks of the year, the frequency of the meetings is not nearly as important as keeping in touch over the summer. You never want to give your group the impression that you only care about them September through May, and not as much during Christmas break. Oh, and on the being spiritual part, we are spiritual beings, so everything we do is spiritual. Our spirituality involves every part of us, not just worship services and Bible studies.

As your group heads into summer, take time to ask what the group would like to do together. Don't assume that everyone is busy and that no one wants to get together. If the leaders need a break, then have them ask other group members to host a party or head up a service project. You're not alone.

EMBRACE SEASONS

Regional events should also be embraced, rather than competed with, in group life. A colleague and I were working with a church in Louisville, Kentucky. As we were shooting their video curriculum and talking about their group launch on the side, my friend asked about what the church members did for their Derby parties. While I knew Louisville was home to the Kentucky Derby, I asked, "Is it really a thing for people to have Derby parties?" The entire group looked at me like I had two heads. Of course, it was a thing.

How can you embrace the regional or seasonal events in your community rather than fight an uphill battle? Is there an opportunity for groups to celebrate with others, then possibly invite them to a group? Is there an opportunity for groups to serve together at an event? People don't need to feel torn between church events and community events. In fact, embracing community events will produce much goodwill toward your groups. Despite seasonal complexities with Christmas, Easter, and the summer, groups started with the three keys of organic formation, coaching, and a next step will continue in at least 80 percent of the cases.

If groups start with high relational connections, they tend to continue on with their "Lego" of friends. If a caring coach is following up with them on a regular basis, then group leaders will continue even when they are tempted to quit. When the next step is introduced in the middle of the current series it gives groups a reason to continue on together. These three keys will ensure groups will not only dramatically multiply during an alignment series, but will continue. The last thing anyone wants to do is work hard to form groups this year only to watch them collapse, and have to do the whole thing over the next year.

CHAPTER 9

CREATE A LEADERSHIP TRACK

The success of your groups relies on the care and development of group leaders. Group leaders in turn focus on the care and development of group members. Recruiting and investing in group leaders will guarantee the success of a church's groups.

Years ago, at New Life in California, I wore many hats. When the church was small, I was responsible for groups, our discipleship process, children's ministry, and even led worship for a time. When our church had grown to a point where we could hire a children's pastor, I explained children's ministry to him as clearly as I could. I said, "There are two parts of children's ministry: recruiting leaders and keeping your leaders happy."

He said, "When do I get to work with kids?"

I replied, "You weren't listening."

The right people, the right curriculum, and the right environment are crucial for an effective and fun children's ministry. Without good leaders, that ship will sink rather quickly.

The same is true of groups. If you have a bunch of people interested in forming a group, you may or may not end up with a group. If you have a leader, you have a group. Once you have the leader, they must be trained, coached, and equipped to succeed. A leadership track is a great start in the leader's success.

NEXT STEPS FOR NEW LEADERS

In the previous chapter, I outlined the Innovation–Decision Process as articulated by Everett Rogers. At this point, new leaders have walked through the first four steps in making a decision: (1) knowledge, (2) persuasion, (3) decision, including the trial run, and (4) implementation, indicated by leading their groups into a second study. The final step involves the group leader taking steps toward official recognition through both training and fulfilling the qualifications of "official groups" at your church.

When you arrived at your acceptable level of risk, as discussed in chapter three, you maybe decided to postpone some of your requirements for group leadership until after the trial run. I think this is a good move. After all, a car salesmen wouldn't require a customer to fill out all of the paperwork before the test drive, would they? You only need a driver's license, not a loan application, to take the car out for a spin.

This is the point, however, when you begin to reintroduce your requirements for group leaders. But, let me caution you here— these steps need to come across as optional and not mandatory. If you require additional steps to lead a group, then more than likely the group will continue to meet. They'll just go underground. Face it, you've already let the cat out of the bag. If the group can get their hands on video-based curriculum, they can continue with or without you. But by making the next steps toward "official" status optional, you have a better chance of keeping the groups in the communication and care loop. Most people aren't stubborn when it comes to pastoral leadership, but insisting on mandatory next steps will even make willing leaders turn stubborn. Believe me, you don't need that kind of grief. Some groups will progress through the next steps quickly. Others will take the steps slowly. A few groups won't take the steps at all. That's the key. Remember, the safety net here is that each group, regardless of how they started, has a coach. As long as the coach is involved, you will know what's going on in the group, especially if things get weird.

What requirements did you lay aside for the trial run that you want to reintroduce now? Maybe you waived the requirement for church membership. Maybe you chose to train new leaders for the trial run only through a brief orientation and the support of a coach. Maybe you opened up group leadership to anyone who was breathing and had friends, and didn't require much of anything. While you laid aside these things to get a bunch of temporary groups started, there does come a time to pick the requirements back up.

Let's say your requirements for group leadership are (1) Salvation, (2) Baptism, (3) Church Membership, (4) Leader Training, and (5) a Coaching Relationship. The coaching relationship should already be established from when they attended their briefing for the trial-run series, so that one is covered. If not, then get it started as soon as possible.

In many churches, salvation and baptism are covered in a Membership Class, so all three of those requirements can be introduced at once. Now, you may have asked about the group leaders' spiritual backgrounds before the groups were started, so you already know if they've received Christ or not. If somehow this was missed, then it will be caught in the Membership Class.

The only other missing requirement is some sort of centralized training about how to be a small group at your church, something more substantial than the New Leaders Briefing described in chapter six. The briefing is for new group leaders to get them started in a six-week trial run of leading a group. The centralized training, which I call Basic Training, is for those who have decided to continue as recognized leaders of an ongoing group at the church.

This centralized training should be no more than two or three hours. Anything more than that will give information overload. If group leaders can't meet on campus, then figure out other ways to offer the training through teleconferences, interactive video, or meetings between group leaders and their coaches. Sample content for what you might include in your Basic Training is included at the end of this chapter.

If you require church membership to attend Basic Training, then you have all of the steps toward leadership covered. (Basic Training requires membership. Membership requires salvation and baptism. They already have a coach.) This would be the place to share the biblical background of groups, the importance of groups, the church's vision for groups, and some how-to's for handling different situations. Underscore your group values like sharing ownership of the groups by asking group members to take on leadership responsibilities. Raise the value of developing other leaders who could lead a group of their own. You probably have other things you would emphasize in your training. Add those items as well.

Again, if group leaders don't choose to take these steps toward "official" status, be patient with them. You don't want to lose or alienate these groups. Just keep inviting them.

The group leaders who don't become official need to understand, however, that the church will not advertise their group in any way, shape, or form. The group will not appear on a group listing, on the church website, or at a Small Group Fair or Connection event. For those in the last 30 percent who are independent, introverted, or isolated, this will probably suit them just fine. They didn't want to be advertised in the first place.

While it is easier for the small group pastor or director to have everyone taking the same steps at the same time in the same system, this is not usually the case with groups. Group leaders start in different places in their spiritual journey. They come with various levels of group experience. While they will benefit by common things like coaching and leader training, everyone does not receive and implement training at the same rate or at the same time.

Every group is in a different place and requires a unique next step. While we can centralize some things like Basic Training and Membership Class, we need to understand the dynamic of the group and what to introduce when.

I remember years ago Brett Eastman told me a story about a group at Saddleback who after a church-wide series were all baptized together, including the leader. This may be the case of some groups. If leaders and their group members are not church members, then challenge the whole group to attend Membership Class together.

NEXT STEPS FOR GROUP MEMBERS

New leaders are not the only ones with next steps. Every group member has a next step as well. Some of these next steps might be articulated by the church, like baptism, serving, and Membership Class. Other next steps happen within the group.

Every group member should have responsibilities in the group. Whether they trade off hosting the group in their home, bringing refreshments, leading the prayer time, or leading the discussion, everyone needs to play a part. By sharing responsibilities, group members feel ownership in the group. It's no longer "your group," but it soon becomes "our group." Taking a turn at serving will also reveal the group members' potential leadership ability.

While I am not a big advocate of recruiting and training an apprentice, I am big on not only coleaders sharing the load, but also the entire group sharing the load. Sometimes people don't realize their leadership potential until they actually try something.

If a group member is reluctant to lead an entire discussion, then ask them to lead a portion of the discussion like the icebreaker or the prayer time. After the meeting, debrief with the group member to see how they felt about leading. The answers will range from "I liked it" to "I never want to do that again." Encourage them in the things that went well, but don't twist their arms if they're not ready to try it again. For those who had a positive experience, then offer them another experience to lead a portion of the study or maybe even the whole thing. These baby steps can lead to some great things.

At New Life, Doug Howard, one of my leaders, paid me the best compliment I have ever received. In addition to leading a group, he was also part of my small group team. After serving for a year or so on the team, he told me, "Thank you, Pastor Allen, for showing me I was the leader I never knew I was." Every group leader has the same opportunity with their members. Start with small temporary assignments, then gradually increase their roles as they are ready to take next steps. If they face setbacks, then back off a little, but keep trying when they are ready.

I'm also not a huge fan of splitting groups, even if it is called "multiplying" in some small group circles. I am a big fan of allowing leaders to keep inviting and keep inviting until their home is beyond capacity. Once the group has subgrouped as far as is reasonable, they will begin to feel the pain and will seriously consider starting a new group out of that group. While I never ask a group to split, I will certainly guide a willing volunteer. If the group leader has been training the whole group to lead, then a group member with leadership experience now will be a great candidate to lead the new group.

NEXT STEPS FOR ALL LEADERS

As I mentioned in the previous chapter, growing and discipling leaders happens in a coaching relationship. While other training will be pushed out via email and video, the core next steps a leader needs are with a coach. But, this isn't all leadership training per se.

Group life is based in discipleship. Every believer is a disciple. Whether they are a brand new Christian or have been a Christian for over forty years like me, all of us must continue to grow. A significant part of spiritual growth is change in our knowledge, attitudes, and behaviors. Don't get stuck on knowledge. It has its place, but how much do we already know that we are not obeying?

As I have said elsewhere in this book, accountability is a tricky thing. While we are called to give an account, love keeps no record of wrongs.[50] Where accountability originates will in large part depend on the depth of the relationship between the leader and the coach. Early on, the leader may seek accountability for something. As the relationship deepens, then it would be appropriate for the coach to call something out in the leader's life (positive or negative). In turn, the leader should do the same for his or her group members.

Another aspect of growing as a leader is coaching other leaders as well as leading a group. The most natural coaching relationship would be coaching a leader who was raised up in the established leader's group. Otherwise, a trial run at leadership, as mentioned in chapter eight, would be a great next step for a leader to give coaching a try.

None of us are "done" this side of heaven. We all have ways to grow. Whether we are forsaking bad habits or starting good ones, there is a place for someone to ask us tough questions and to check in with us—not in a heavy-handed way, but in relationship with a fellow Christian.

SAMPLE CONTENT FOR BASIC TRAINING

Starting with the next section, the remainder of the chapter is content I have used in the past in my Basic Training for new group leaders. This is not the only way. In fact, there are some things particular to how you do groups at your church that you should definitely include. I am giving you an example to get started with. You will notice in this section that I change the voice to me speaking to small group leaders as I would in the actual Basic Training.

Start your training with the reasons behind small groups. Tell stories, or have group leaders tell stories, of the benefits of group life. While these stories should definitely be positive, don't use stories that are over the top. You want the stories to inspire, but not overwhelm.

Also, in your introduction, talk about how groups fit into the vision and values of your church. Often group leaders feel distant from the direction the church is going. This is the time to show them how groups play an integral part in the fulfillment of the church's vision. What goes on in the leaders' living rooms is a significant part of the church overall. Your leaders need to understand this connection.

If it's possible, this would be a great opportunity to have your senior pastor share the vision for groups at the start of the meeting. Most pastors have a lot of demands on their time, however, so you might consider recording your pastor giving a short vision talk about groups, then use the recording to start your Basic Training. Here we go.

Basic Training Introduction: The Biblical Basis for Groups

Scripture speaks of all growth and ministry in the context of relationship. Very few people in the Bible are lone rangers. Moses had Aaron and Hur. While Joseph was rejected by his original small group, his brothers, he was adopted into other groups: the Egyptian royal family, fellow prisoners, the royal family again, then his brothers again. Okay, not the perfect scenario, but one with a purpose. Groups are present throughout Scripture.

God exists in community as Father, Son, and Holy Spirit.[51] While the Trinity is certainly a mystery, God is definitely One and clearly Three. Whether he's like an egg, a tricycle, or an ice cube, we'll let the theologians decide. It's not even a question of whether God could exist only as One and not Three. Scripture reveals God is Three in One. Either by necessity or example, this is who God is. The Trinity itself expresses community.

God created man in his image and, while all of God's creation was deemed "good,"[52] the one thing that was "not good" was man living in isolation.[53] The relationship between man and woman, however, was blessed by God.[54] The ideal for biblically functioning community is individuals in relationship with each other and in relationship with God. The family was the first small group.

The fulfillment of God's purposes of redemption and reconciliation both in the old and new covenants involves a "chosen" people: the people of Israel,[55] the disciples,[56] and the church.[57] While over the centuries revivalists have emphasized the need for a personal relationship with God, this was to overcome the idea that salvation was mediated through the church rather than through Christ himself. A believer's relationship with God is personal, but it's not private.

A friend of mine was sitting on a plane next to a woman as she was grading papers about the Old Testament. He asked, "Do you teach Old Testament?"

She replied, "Well, some people call it that." She was Jewish. My friend explained he was a Christian pastor and was just curious.

The woman said, "Can I ask you a question?" He consented. "Why do you Christians have to be saved? Jews are God's People. We didn't have to do anything to be that. Your Bible says Christians are grafted in, so why all of this worry over being saved?"

Obviously, this woman didn't completely grasp the idea that Christians are made and not born that way, but she did have an interesting observation. At times believers overemphasize our need for acceptance and underemphasize the fact that we belong. There is a key decision to be made in order to become "grafted in," but once we're there, our focus should be in the context of belonging to God's People rather than determining how hard we should work to please God.

God, who lives in community, created a marriage, which produced a family, which through a lot of ups and downs eventually created a People. When the People strayed, God sent his Son to reconcile all people to himself through salvation and to create a new People called the church.

The best example of this type of community is found in the small group. The Bible tells us the church met in temple courts and house to house.[58] The church met in a large public setting, which they did not own, and they met in houses, which they did own. Today, temple courts would be the weekend worship service. Groups would meet "house to house."

The early church followed this spiritual growth plan:

They devoted themselves to the apostles' teaching and to fellowship, to the breaking of bread, and to prayer. Everyone was filled with awe at the many wonders and signs performed by the apostles. All the believers were together and had everything in common. They sold property and possessions to give to anyone who had need. Every day they continued to meet together in the temple courts. They broke bread in their homes and ate together with glad and sincere hearts, praising God and enjoying the favor of all the people. And the Lord added to their number daily those who were being saved.[59]

Some people have touted this passage as the epitome of the church. These verses reflect the ultimate of what every church should strive for. Yet, look at the context. These weren't platitudes, but practices. These are statements of actions, not goals and objectives. Then, there's the timing—this wasn't the church after several hundred years. This was the church on Day One!

The Importance of a Group Agreement

Every person in a group has different expectations for the group, whether they realize it or not. Some folks have been in groups before and long for the good old days of comfortable *koinonia*. Others were oversold on groups: "You'll make your new best friend." Everyone has expectations for the group. The key to successful group life is a thoroughly-discussed and well-articulated group agreement.

The key word is "agreement." An effective group agreement has input from the whole group, and a decision for the group "ground rules" is made together. You are not asking your members to sign a contract that you put together for them. If you impose an agreement on them, you may get compliance, but you won't necessarily get buy-in from the group. Don't wonder why no one is honoring an agreement they didn't help to create.

Forming a group agreement doesn't need to be a lengthy or hectic process. In a relaxed atmosphere, just get everybody's ideas on the table. Decide on the group's values together. What's important to the members? When and where will the group meet? How will the group provide childcare, if it does? What will the group study? How will the studies be chosen? How will the group spend their time together?

While there are a number of great templates out there, the group agreement needs to fit the group. Imposing someone else's agreement just doesn't cut it. Examples can be helpful, but you're not looking for a good document, you're aiming for a great group.

A group agreement puts all of the members on a level playing field. Everyone knows what to expect. They know what's acceptable and what's out of bounds. From basic but important items like when the meeting will start and end, the group will know what to count on. If members need to get back to work after a lunchtime group or put kids to bed on a school night, they will know when it's acceptable to leave.

More importantly, the group agreement ensures things like confidentiality. What's said in the group stays in the group. Broken confidences and gossip are group killers. If the group has a party, what will they be drinking or not drinking? If your group doesn't know if any of its members are in recovery, that's an important conversation to have.

How will the group meeting run? While the meeting doesn't have to be the same every week, the members do need to know what to expect. One group I started met in a restaurant for lunch. If we ordered from a menu, then we ordered, discussed the lesson, ate when the food came, and then prayed together. If it's more of a fast-food place, then we would eat first and ask questions later. Now, while these seem like rather specific details, the reality was that the group members knew what to expect, and the new members quickly understood what was going on.

With a group agreement, everyone knows what is expected of them. Some people are reluctant to join groups because they fear being asked to do something they just aren't comfortable with. Will they have to pray aloud? Will they have to read aloud? What if they don't read very well? The group agreement helps them understand if these things are voluntary or mandatory.

If members have to miss the group, what is their responsibility to the group? Should they call or not worry about it? If it's important that the member informs the group, then put that in your agreement.

As the leader, you shouldn't do everything for your group. It's just not healthy, and it robs others of opportunities to serve in ministry. If your group intends to pass around the responsibilities for leading the discussion, hosting the group, bringing refreshments, leading worship, following up on prayer requests, and whatever else you can give away, your agreement should include the expectation that every member would serve in some way.

Again, what are the values of your group? What is expected of each member? Decide together and from the start of the group inform everyone in the agreement.

Your group agreement will not stand the test of time. Circumstances change. Groups change. While you probably should include things like confidentiality and shared responsibility, things like your meeting day, place, time, study, and so forth will change over time. Group agreements should be reviewed at least once per year to make sure that they're still working for everybody.

Group agreements help when new members join. It's important to review key items in your group agreement when new members join your group. You don't have to recite the entire agreement, but important things like confidentiality, childcare details, and so on should be shared with new members. This doesn't have to be formal. "Just to let you know, our group is like Las Vegas. Whatever is said here stays here," or "We're going to order our food, then get into our discussion. When the food arrives, expect a little silence, then we'll close with prayer needs."

Your group agreement doesn't need to be overly formal. While it's good to have your group agreement written down somewhere, you don't need to have it notarized or have your attorney present. I have seen some groups give their agreement a simple thumbs up. I've seen others sign it like the Declaration of Independence. Do whatever works for your group. Some folks are resistant to words like "covenant," so "group agreement" or "ground rules" would work better for most.

I bought the board game *Sorry* for my family. We read all of the rules, but to limit frustration with my young children, we modified a few of the rules. They don't need the exact number to move their pawn home. That works for us now. Later on, we might need to increase the difficulty of the game. You see, there are the official rules, and then there are the house rules. Your group agreement should be the house rules for your group. The rules may change over time, but the most important thing is that the rules work for the whole group right now.

Sharing Ownership in the Group

In my early days of leading a small group ministry, I felt the future and growth of groups depended solely on the ability of small group leaders to identify, recruit, and train an apprentice leader, who would eventually start a new group. My group leaders had a hard time identifying an apprentice. They looked at their groups and didn't see any leaders. By contrast, I looked at their groups, and recruited their group members for a turbo group, where they spent six weeks with me, then were commissioned to launch a group on their own. I could find potential leaders in the groups, but the leaders couldn't.

I put a lot of pressure on my group leaders to find an apprentice. After all, the overall success of our small group ministry depended on the leaders training an apprentice. Things got pretty ugly. My leaders would pass me in the hall on Sunday morning and say, "I'm working on my apprentice." I wondered whatever happened to saying, "Hello."

After a long season of frustration, I gave up on the "a-word." I announced to my leaders they would no longer need to worry about apprentices. They cheered, hoisted me onto their shoulders, and marched me around the church building until the walls fell down. Okay, they cheered.

Now that "apprentice" was a dirty word in our church, I introduced a new idea—instead of training one person to lead, the group leader needed to train the entire group to lead. The cheering stopped. Well, not really.

I knew there were prospective leaders in every group. The leaders knew what I knew, but they couldn't identify them. What we discovered was the best way to identify potential leaders was to let them try their hand at leadership. Shared leadership ranged from bringing refreshments to hosting the group in different homes to leading the discussion (or part of the discussion). Everyone could do something. Everyone was expected to do something.

Some leaders struggled with this. They would come back and say, "Well, I asked our group members, but no one volunteered."

I asked the leader, "How did you invite them?"

The leader replied, "Well, I asked if anyone would like to." You see, there's the problem. If you ask people if they'd like to, then they have to consider whether they would like to remain comfortable in the group or choose the discomfort of trying something new instead. After much thought and prayer, the group members will choose comfort over discomfort. Are you surprised?

In groups I've led, the invitation goes something like this, "Today is the first and only meeting where I'm going to lead the discussion. I'm passing around the list, and everyone needs to sign up." That works.

By taking turns in leading different aspects of the lesson or the group, group leaders can easily identify who's got the stuff to eventually lead on their own. It's much easier to spot potential group leaders this way. And, of course, by having everyone involved by taking some form of responsibility, the group quickly moves from "your group" to "our group."

Balancing Group Time between Developing Relationships and Completing Lessons

Striking a balance between relationships and Bible study can be challenging in a group meeting. Often we fear groups will go to one of two extremes during their meetings. Either the group would be a bunch of Bible eggheads who care for God's word, but don't really care much for each other, or the group meeting would become a freewheeling discussion that is no more than a pooling of ignorance. There is a balance, but it's not the same for every group.

You need to ask, "Why did your group get together in the first place?" People join small groups for various reasons. They want to get to know other believers. They want a better understanding of God's word. They want to feel that they belong. They need acceptance. They want encouragement and accountability. The pastor told them it was a good idea. While most group meetings involve a Bible study, the group is not a class gathered to learn lessons. There are other settings for that. It's always a good idea to talk to the group about their expectations. How many studies would the group like to do in the course of a year? How many meetings out of the month should focus on a study? How many meetings should focus on group life, serving, worship, outreach, or something else? The group may be on the same page, but you don't know until you've had the conversation and decided things together.

The personalities of your group members will also impact the dynamic in your meetings. Are your group members task-oriented or relationship-oriented? What are you? When you lead the discussion are you attempting to cover all of the questions or are you interested in what everyone has to say? If you tend to be more task-oriented, then your goal is to complete the lesson. If you're more relationship-oriented, then you might be tempted to throw the book out of the window and just let everybody talk.

Rather than resorting to an extreme, reach in the opposite direction. Task-oriented folks should train themselves to encourage personal sharing in the group. Maybe even have a night where folks share their spiritual journey and dispense with the lesson all together. When relationship-oriented folks lead a lesson, they should make sure good progress is made in the lesson; otherwise, they might frustrate some of the group members.

Selecting the right curriculum to facilitate discussion is also important. Some small group studies have as many as thirty questions. This is far too much to attempt to cover in a forty-five- to sixty-minute group discussion. The group leader should prioritize the questions according to their significance to the group and to the discussion. If the group is ten to twelve people who actively participate, you might not need more than five or six good questions for the entire discussion. If your group has ten to twelve people, then you should also consider subgrouping during the discussion, so everyone can get their word in. The goal is to engage your group members, not just to complete a lesson.

Be aware of your group environment. Often God does his best work in the unplanned moments of group life. The leader needs to take cues from the group members as well as the Holy Spirit to determine when to pause the curriculum and allow a group member to share.

If a group member becomes a little teary, it's good to pause and take notice: "Dave, I see that things are a little tender right now. Would you like to talk about it?" He may or may not want to unpack what he's dealing with right then, but he will appreciate your sensitivity. To just continue the lesson without acknowledging what's going on is essentially telling Dave, "I'm not sure what your problem is, but we've got a lesson to finish."

I was leading a group discussion a few years ago. We were several questions into the study when one of the group members began telling a story. Her story had nothing to do with the question that I had just asked. It had nothing to do with the lesson. We all gave her our attention and listened carefully.

I quietly prayed and asked God for direction, "Lord, should I let her continue or do we need to move on?" The rest of the group seemed to be attentive to her story. I didn't feel any gut check about redirecting the discussion. She finished. The group responded. Then, we continued with the discussion.

Later, while the group was sharing dessert, the lady's husband pulled me aside. He said, "I can't believe she told that story tonight. She hasn't talked about that for thirty years." Even though her story was off topic, after thirty years, she was ready to share. The time was right for her. The rest of the group made the timing right for us as well. Can you imagine the damage that might have been done if we had just moved on?

Building relationships and doing Bible study is a balance in any small group. If you're going to err one way or the other, then err toward building relationships. Don't dispense with Bible study, but remember that small groups are life on life. It's not life on curriculum.

Encouraging Group Members to Share Openly

Most leaders realize group life extends beyond well-prepared and well-executed group meetings. While Bible study is an important aspect of a group, if everyone leaves thinking, "Boy, that was good. See you next week!" without sharing what's going on in their lives, something is definitely missing. Let's talk about some ways to help group members open up.

First, set the right expectations. When your group members joined the group, what were they expecting? Were they looking for a sixty-minute inductive Bible study followed by brownies and coffee as thanks for surviving it? Were they looking for a free-flowing discussion of everything that popped into their heads? Did they know what to expect?

Managing expectations is crucial for a successful group. Rather than dictating what the group will be or won't be, it's best to start by discussing what kind of group the members actually want. A simple exercise like having everyone write their top three group expectations on a card, then tabulating the results, will go a long way in getting buy in from the group.

If the group skews toward Bible study, then gradually implement some aspects of care. Start with something simple like asking for prayer requests and closing the meeting with prayer. As the group continues to meet, begin to focus more on application questions rather than Bible exploration questions. Don't get me wrong, the discussion should be based on God's word, but you want to aim for where the rubber meets the road, not the physical and chemical structure of a tire.

As the group leader, you need to set the example. "Speed of the leader, speed of the team," is a common axiom from Bill Hybels, founding pastor of Willow Creek Community Church.[60] The leader sets the pace. If you are open with your life, then others will be open with theirs. If you hold back, so will they.

A few years ago someone gave me an older car. It wasn't perfect, but it was transportation and a gift at that. One night I became frustrated with the dashboard lights. About a third of the lights wouldn't work. Out of my arsenal of mechanical expertise, I pounded my fist of the dash. The change was both immediate and dramatic—I now had no dashboard lights.

Driving in the summer or during the day wasn't a problem. But, anytime I had to drive early in the morning or at night, I had absolutely no idea how fast I was driving. I dreaded the conversation with the first officer who ever pulled me over.

"Sir, do you know how fast you were going?"

"No, officer, I have absolutely no idea. My dashboard lights aren't working." I imagined a scenario with multiple traffic tickets involved.

I was embarrassed by my "repair." While I confessed the problem to my wife, I never mentioned it to anyone else until one day a circle of folks in the office were discussing their cars' various ailments. I chose that moment in the safe circle of used car owners to confess my dashboard issue. A woman turned to me and said, "My husband has the same problem with his car. He uses his GPS to check his speed." What a brilliant idea. I had a GPS. I no longer needed to fly blind at night. I had the knowledge to detect my own speed and avoid a traffic violation.

I never would have learned that work-around if I had never admitted my problem. As Rick Warren says, "Revealing the feeling is the beginning of healing."[61] That kind of self-revelation has to start with the leader.

I shared this story about my lack of dashboard lights when I spoke at a church a while back. The next week, the executive pastor called to say that my message was already making an impact. A man confessed to his men's group that his marriage was on the brink of divorce. He and his wife were separated, and he didn't know what to do. Rather than judge this guy for his situation, his group members rallied around him to support him and his wife through their struggle. My illustration of automotive failure helped him open up about his marital failure.

Group leaders are no better than the group members they lead. You must be careful the leader title doesn't block the way for your own vulnerability. If your group isn't opening up, you need to check your own transparency in the group. Your honesty will encourage theirs.

To balance the need for open sharing in the group and the need to meet group expectations, the group agreement is the ideal place to start. If you've never created a group agreement, you should soon.

The ground rules for your group could include an option where the group can help a member process a life situation, but just for one meeting. Some issues merit more than a casual mention during prayer-request time at the end. If a group member has faced a devastating turn of events like a job loss, marital blow up, issues with children, or other bad news, the group should allow space by putting the Bible study aside and supporting their friend in need.

Even so, you don't want your group to turn into the "crisis of the week." While every group should offer support, there is a difference between a small group, built on relationships formed around a Bible study, and a true support group. If a group member needs dedicated support for marital problems, grief, or a life-controlling issue, then a specific support group may offer better help.

There is no perfect way to organize every small group meeting. Your group can't offer only Bible study at the expense of care, but your group also can't avoid Bible study and only focus on care. As Andy Stanley says, "This is a tension to be managed rather than a problem to be solved."[62]

If you notice a group member getting teary or emotional during the discussion, stop and ask if they want to talk about it. They might or might not. The last impression you want to leave is that the meeting agenda is more important than the group members in the meeting.

Avoiding Rabbit Trails

It's certainly easy for discussions to get off course and maybe never come back to the topic. This is partly the challenge of leading adult learners. Adults already have a lot of information and a lot of experience. Think of the brain as a filing cabinet or a hard drive. When we receive any new information, we open a file in our heads with that label only to discover that there are other things in the file.

Let's say your small group is discussing Daniel and his vegetarian diet from Daniel 1. The group members' brains automatically open their mental folders for "Diet." While they're in there, they remember several diets that they've tried and failed at in the past. "Does anyone remember the grapefruit diet?" "How about South Beach?" "How about the tomato and cabbage stew diet?" And, off they go. Now some have cross-referenced from "diet" to "hunger." They're thinking "I wonder who brought the snack tonight. I hope it's not one of those Atkins dieters who only bring pork rinds . . ." Suddenly your group has traveled a long way from Babylon.

You really can't stop adults from being distracted by their thoughts and experiences. It's just how they're wired.

But, you can prevent this from becoming an epidemic in your group.

If your group is fairly new or if this is a relatively new problem, then the facilitator simply needs to redirect the conversation every time it begins to stray. Going back to the failed diet rabbit trail, the facilitator could simply say, "Boy, we've certainly opened a whole can of worms, haven't we? Let's look at the next question." Or, you could go with a little humor, "Wow, that's a topic for another day."

If your group has been around for a while and has formed this bad habit, it might be time to check in with the group and make sure everyone is okay. You might even be losing group members if this is going unchecked. Simply ask the group if everyone is doing okay. You might even add: "Permission to speak freely." Get the group to come to an agreement about staying on topic and socializing at the end of the meeting.

Sometimes we have to walk a fine line. When someone begins to go off topic, be careful not to cut them off immediately. In fact, you might want to whisper a quick prayer and ask the Holy Spirit to help you discern what's happening. Sometimes people need to share a painful experience or a pressing problem, and they just can't wait until the right point in the agenda. If, as the facilitator, you feel that they should continue, then let them continue. If the person just wants to talk about himself or herself every week, well, that's another problem.

Lastly, if you find that your group likes to spend the first part of the meeting catching up with each other, don't fight it. In fact, you might change your prayer time to the start of the meeting and pray right after everyone has caught up. Then, you can start your study. Remember you are leading a group, not just leading a meeting.

What If I Don't Know All of the Answers?

For a new small group leader, this question ranks right up there with public speaking and an IRS audit. No one likes to get caught off guard. Fear kicks in. What if the leader loses credibility? What if the group doesn't trust the leader? What if they don't come back? Here's some help in navigating this issue in your group.

First, group leaders are facilitators, not Bible teachers. If this was a class and you were the teacher, then you should have all of the answers. Shame on you. Not really. Group life is not a top-down exercise. Group members are the branches, but you are not the vine (John 15). Group leaders are not the hub in the center of the wagon wheel. Your Bible knowledge or lack thereof should not jeopardize the group.

Group life is more like a family. As the group leader, you took the initiative to gather the group. You are responsible for the group, but it's not your responsibility to do everything for the group. As a facilitator, rather than a teacher, your job is to get the discussion started and keep it going. You are not the Bible expert. If your group is using a video-based curriculum, the expert is on the video clip. Your role is to ask the questions and help your group get this teaching to where the rubber meets the road.

Secondly, as leader, you are not the sole person responsible for the spiritual welfare of the group. The group is responsible for each other. While that includes you, care is not limited to you.

When someone asks a question you're not prepared to answer, throw this one out there: "What do the rest of you think?" Now, you've bought a little time. Let the group talk. In the process, you might send up a quick prayer, and who knows, you might end up with a solid answer. If all else fails, Google something on your smartphone.

The best answer is simply "I don't know." You gain credibility when you're honest, but you definitely will lose it if you try to fake it. No one has all of the answers (not that I would mention that to your in-laws). Every pastor and Bible teacher gets stumped once in a while. Just confess that you don't know, do a little research, and talk about it again at the next meeting.

You can even go one better than researching the answer yourself. Ask the person with the question to research it and get back to the group. But, a word of caution—not everything on the internet is true. If you don't believe that, then there's a Nigerian man who has forty million dollars for you. Check your email.

Choosing Curriculum for the Group

Back in the day, good studies were few and far between. Today, the problem is the plethora of choices. Which do you choose? Here are a few resources that might help.

First, start by viewing samples of curriculum online. Online booksellers often offer samples of study guides and sometimes video content. If they don't, then the publisher might offer these samples. A quick review of a sample lesson or video might give you a sense of whether the study would work for your group. Often you can print out a sample lesson for your group to review. At a minimum, point them to the website.

Connect with your coach. Your coach is an experienced small group leader who has led quite a number of studies over the years. Since coaches work with groups that are similar to yours, they will have suggestions based on what other groups have enjoyed. They can also help you in evaluating a study that is outside of the norm for the church.

If your group is based on the weekly sermon, a message discussion guide is a great way to help people take their weekend into their week. A discussion guide gives group members an opportunity to take the truths learned on Sunday morning and apply them to their lives. There is no advance preparation apart from attending the weekend services or viewing them online prior to the group meeting.

Some churches have started creating a short video either prior to the weekend or even in between the weekend services as an introduction to the discussion guide. They use simple technology like a small camera or even a smartphone.

The video is uploaded to an online site, then the link is distributed with the discussion guide. The group simply clicks the link, watches the short video together, then enters into the discussion.

At least once a year, the church will align a message series with a small group study. Like the message discussion guide, this offers an opportunity to discuss and apply the teaching from the weekend services. Usually the small group study will involve video-based curriculum. The video allows the opportunity for multiple members of your group to facilitate a lesson, since the pressure of teaching is relieved by the video.

These are just a few ways to choose a study. There are many more. The key is to find a study that your entire group is interested in. If there's a difference of opinion, then plan out the next two or three studies to incorporate everyone's good ideas.

When to Refer a Group Member for Help

Small groups can meet some of their members' basic emotional needs. Everyone needs to feel that they belong. This is a high value among small groups. The Bible teaches us, "For just as each of us has one body with many members, and these members do not all have the same function, so in Christ we, though many, form one body, and each member belongs to all the others."[63] We all want to be included by others. Our small group is the place where we're always included. We belong.

We also need to feel accepted. Regardless of where we've come from or what we've done, the group is a place where we can come as we are to learn, to connect, and to encourage each other. That doesn't mean that our group will allow us to stay where we are. If there are things going on in our lives that are harmful or damaging to our well-being and our spiritual growth, then it's the group's place to address these things in our lives. Sometimes we are blind to things about ourselves that are very obvious to others. The group should never approach anyone with a judgmental or self-righteous attitude. The rest of the group has their issues too.

Our couples' small group in California was diverse. We had a broad age range. Some couples had small children. Others had teenagers. One couple had grown children. One member enforced the law, while another member gave us the impression that he might be running from the law. It was a mixed bag of folks.

Two of our guys would always end the evening by going out in front of our house for a smoke. The rest of the guys were a little jealous of the fellowship they enjoyed out there. For a brief time, we even considered taking up the habit. Word got out to other small groups that we had a couple of smokers. In fact, a member of another group approached me at church one day and said, "It must be embarrassing that you as a pastor have small group members that smoke in front of your house. What do your neighbors think?"

I said, "I know it's terrible. But, what's even worse is that I've heard that some of our groups are full of gossips." Okay, I didn't actually say that. But, if I had, wouldn't that be awesome?

We have to accept people where they are. Think about it. Where else are we going to accept them? I suppose we could put some prerequisites for being accepted into our group. But, why make it harder to be accepted in our group than it is to be accepted by Jesus himself?

While small groups can meet some important emotional needs for members, groups can't meet all of their emotional needs. And, I'll go ahead and say it, they shouldn't try to meet all of their emotional needs either. While the Bible does tell us to bear one another's burdens,[64] it also tells us that each one should carry his own load.[65]

As a group, we can help people process what's going on in their lives. We can care for them. We can pray for them. We can follow up with them. But we can't allow the needs of one member to dominate the group. If we begin to see this happen, we need to gently recommend other resources to address their issues. At that point a support group or counselor could help them. If someone is struggling in a relationship or with a life-controlling problem, the group can certainly support them in their progress, but the group cannot become his or her "support group."

Now, I didn't say kick them out of your group. In fact, the leader should let them know that they are welcome to stay for Bible study and that the group will gladly support them in their journey. But the work that needs to be done has to happen in another setting.

It's important to know what we can and cannot do in a small group. We can offer teaching from God's word. We can offer group life. We can offer prayer. We can offer acceptance and belonging. We can't offer anything that caters solely to one group member and excludes the others. We can't take on all their problems. We can't meet all of their emotional needs. We can't do for them what only God can. But, we can keep pointing them back to God.

A member of my group was struggling with how to help a friend who had a financial need. He wasn't sure about how much more involved he should be. He had already paid some of this person's bills. I asked him what he felt led to do. He gave one of the most honest answers I've ever heard. He said, "I'm codependent. I feel led to solve all of the problems. That's why I need the group's insights." We helped him figure out where to draw the line.

What is your group carrying for your members? Where might your group be trying to carry the member's whole load as well? How do you know when it's time to ask for help? When things like this come up, I would encourage you to check in with your coach and determine what help is truly helpful.

Group Life Cycle: When Should My Group Break Up?

Small groups aren't meant for eternity, but how do you end it? Do you gather your group members together for an uncomfortable conversation? "It's not you. It's us. Can we just be friends?"

While some groups can last twenty years or more, most groups simply can't run that distance. That's okay. After all, we have friends for a reason, friends for a season, and friends for a lifetime. But, how do you know when your small group has run its course? Here are a couple of key indicators:

1. Your Group Has Lost Its Edge

Group life demonstrates a tension between speaking the truth in love[66] and bearing one another's burdens.[67] The balance lies in correcting each other and understanding each other. When a group starts, a member's weaknesses and failures seem more obvious.

"Why does he do that?"

"Why does she treat them that way?"

But, over time, the group begins to understand why. Rather than saying, "You might have more success with a gentler approach," we find ourselves saying things like,

"He's a little rough around the edges."

"His childhood was a nightmare. We understand."

Deep-seated problems aren't resolved overnight. They take a great deal of work and are often beyond the scope of the group's ministry. This is when you need to refer them to other help. The problem in the group comes when our understanding becomes enabling.

The goal of every group should be to help each other reflect Christ. When a group has been together for a while and loses its edge of truth, it no longer helps anyone fulfill the goal. Iron isn't sharpening iron. It's more like marshmallow sharpening Nerf.

If your group started as a Gensu knife, but has dulled and become a butter knife, then it's time to regroup. If your group can regain its edge, great. If not, then it's time to disperse and form new groups. Don't allow members to join groups together unless they're married to each other.

2. Your Group Has Lost Its Members

Over time every group loses members. It's not a bad group. Life just gets in the way. A group member moves out of town. A new job or family activity conflicts with the group's meeting day. Sooner or later, good group members will leave for good reasons. When my men's group reached its fourth year, we had only two original members. One of them was me.

While there were only two in the "senior class" of my group, we have a couple of juniors, a few sophomores, and a couple of freshmen. If Jamie and I were the only two left in the group, we might have gotten together now and then, but we probably wouldn't meet every week. No one likes to see their good group members go. If you've become close friends, you certainly don't want things to come to an end. If your group is beginning to see the beginning of the end, act now to turn things around. Become a more welcoming and inclusive group. Invite prospective members to attend. Develop your freshman classes. Otherwise, "us four" will eventually become "no more."

When your group gets down to just a few people, it's time to reconsider and rebuild—either by invitation or by forming a new group. Sometimes new members won't stick. Some groups will even allow for gracious on-ramps and off-ramps at the end of a study or the start of a new study. While you certainly want to bend over backward to welcome new group members, and no one likes to see members leave, the time might be right for the established members to start groups of their own or try a new group.

One church asks groups to reconsider their commitment every eighteen months. If the group wants to re-up, then they can. If it's time for the group to end, then at eighteen months they have a graceful way of accomplishing that. No one did anything wrong. There are no hard feelings. Breaking up at eighteen months is just the way they do groups.

LAST THOUGHTS ON BASIC TRAINING

I hope you've found these ideas for your Basic Training helpful. These suggestions are certainly not exhaustive. They are just a few ideas for you to get started. Please feel free to integrate or ignore these thoughts as you construct the Basic Training appropriate for your church.

CHAPTER 10

COACHING AND TRAINING YOUR LEADERS TO SUCCESS

Over the years, I've faced many ups and downs with small group coaching and training. A few times when we launched groups at New Life, we either had no coaches at all or didn't coach and train the leaders very well. Soon the groups burned out. You already read the rest of my coaching journey back in chapter four.

WHAT IS COACHING?

We've already covered the importance of encouraging and supporting new leaders during their first group study in an alignment series. Coaching is one of the three keys for successful, ongoing groups.

By now most small group pastors and directors understand coaches are essential to sustaining and supporting small group leaders. While everyone will agree to the necessity of coaches, most don't know what to do with them, and unfortunately, most coaches don't know what to do period. Beautiful org charts in a lot of churches actually net zero results. If coaching is so significant, then why have so many pastors, including my past self, done coaching so wrong or abandoned it altogether? Let's start with what coaches are not.

COACHES AREN'T ACCOUNTANTS

The problem with most accountability in Christian circles is that it becomes too much like accounting. Unlike Santa Claus, coaches do not relish keeping a naughty or nice list. What's more, group leaders don't appreciate being managed by a supervisor. This doesn't mean we throw caution to the wind and do away with coaching altogether, but we also don't put a cruel task master over small group leaders. After all, "love keeps no record of wrongs," right?[68]

Accountability fails when it's conducted by an accountant: "Your goal was to contact your four absent group members last week, but you only called one person. Now, you need to repent and pledge to do better next week." Yikes! Sounds like they'll be skipping the next meeting with their coach, too.

If the purpose of accountability is to confront leaders with their failures, it's a failure. The nature of accountability can't be merely a ledger recording wins and losses.

Accountability works when it's more like coaching and less like scorekeeping. If the leader only got one call to an absent group member in this week, then the response should be: "Good, you called one. What kept you from calling all four? How did you feel after your call with the first one? How did you feel when you skipped the other calls? How can I help you this next week?" What are the reasons behind the success or failure? What motivates them? What demotivates them? Everybody is motivated by different things.

Group leaders need to know the coach has their best interest at heart. Prayers are significant. Short voice mail messages or texts or tweets can encourage them. But encouragement should be given in appropriate doses, otherwise it can seem like a backhanded rebuke.

Ideally, group leaders should be matched with someone who has a measure of victory in the area they are holding another accountable for. A more experienced leader can bring perspective and encouragement into a coaching relationship with a less experienced leader. But, group leaders can also coach each other. While qualifications are great, someone's presence and attentive listening is most important.

Done the right way, accountability can be a good tool to strengthen group leaders and deepen their relationships with their group members and with God. As long as you keep the "Why" ahead of the "What," your group leaders will be well served with coaching.

COACHES AREN'T MIDDLE MANAGERS, BUREAUCRATS, OR SPIES

Remember Carol, who complained about being my spy in chapter four? At that point, I was still recruiting and training all of the group leaders myself. Carol and the other coaches were sent out to visit the groups and report back what they saw. No wonder she felt that way.

In recruiting coaches, we work hard to select mature, capable people to serve with us. Then, often because we don't have the coaching role figured out ourselves, we tend to micromanage them as if they are neither mature nor capable. I didn't keep many coaches that way.

The key is elevating the role of coaching. When I chose coaches the next time around, I invited capable, mature people to join me in a journey. We met every week for dinner to talk about the direction of our small groups. I committed to never make a decision about our small groups outside of that meeting. We led together.

These folks aren't underachievers who need our constant motivation. These aren't people who are prone to wander and need a steady reminder of direction. If they were, then they shouldn't be coaching groups. If they're not, then they deserve more respect than a place in a little bureaucracy.

Pastors will sometimes default to task-oriented methods because of the sheer number of leaders they are working with. Task-oriented approaches to coaching may seem efficient, but they are usually ineffective. When I joined the staff of Brookwood Church, it was a shift from a church where I had spent fifteen years and saw the church grow from eighty-five people to over 1,500. I knew a lot of people at New Life. I'd been there a long time. Walking into Brookwood Church, I suddenly encountered 6,500 people all at once. I didn't know anybody.

With about 30 percent of Brookwood's adults in groups, I knew that not only would I have to work hard on catching up with the one hundred or so group leaders I already had, but we would also need two hundred to three hundred new groups to reach our goals.

Remember, I was the guy who couldn't manage thirty groups by myself. How was I going to take this on?

Fortunately, my predecessor, David Hardy, left me in good shape. Every current leader had a coach. Every coach had a director who served on the small group team. The relationships were already established. Only the discipleship pastor had changed. While it was important for me to spend a lot of time getting to know group leaders, it was mostly for my understanding of what I'd inherited, because the group leaders already had the relationships they needed.

As we recruited new leaders and launched hundreds of groups at a time, we started by recruiting experienced leaders to coach them (as described in chapter four). With hundreds of new leaders and thousands of new group members, it would be tempting to depend on a programmatic approach. After all, it was impossible to be personal with 6,500 people, so a programmatic response was the only choice, right? Now, while I agree that you can't be personal with 6,500 people, you can be personal with the person standing in front of you.

For the group leaders, that personal interaction came with their coach. For the coaches, they personally interacted with their director, a role we later renamed community leader. The community leaders were my small group team, and we met together once per month, and one-on-one occasionally.

Training and supervising are task-oriented roles. While some aspects of coaching are about supervision and training, coaching has more to do with discipleship than with anything else. While group leaders will certainly grow with their groups, there are some aspects of the leaders' growth that take place outside of the group with their coach.

It's not that coaches hold the keys to spiritual growth. Most believers who've spend any amount of time in church services and reading their Bibles are already responsible for far more biblical commands than they are currently living out. They understand how to treat others, how to succeed in their walk with God, and even what things to avoid. Yet believers become so distracted by the busyness of life and the things of this world, they lose focus on the goal to become like Christ and to build his kingdom.

The true purpose of groups is not about assimilation or connecting people into groups. Remember, people are already in groups. The significance of groups doesn't lie in the total number of group members in a church or even in well-produced curriculum. The goal of small groups is to enlist more people into leadership, because people will take greater responsibility for their own character and growth when they know others are watching them.

Now, don't get me wrong, there is plenty of great learning, support, and growth within a group. Small groups are not merely a utilitarian means to give leaders something to lead. God does great things in small groups, but the greater work is in the leaders themselves.

Think about your own life. I'm assuming if you're reading this book, you are involved in some sort of church leadership. Now, compare your spiritual growth trajectory from before you were leading to now. Outside of your first few months as a new Christian, you have likely grown far more by leading others than you ever did when you weren't leading.

The key to growth is not small groups. The key is leading others, yet still needing to be led. This is where a coach comes in.

"THE ROLE OF THE COACH IS TO REFOCUS THE PLAYER"

My friend and mentor Carl George has drilled this phrase into my psyche. When you think about a coach in sports, he stands at the sidelines and guides his players. If the last play went terribly wrong, his job is to refocus the players on the next play. They can't replay the last play on the field. If a bad play keeps replaying in the players' minds, then the next play will also suffer.

Small group leaders have busy lives and are pulled in many different directions. On a particularly hectic day or in a difficult season, it's easy for leaders to become discouraged and wonder why they ever got into this business in the first place. The relationship between the coach and the group leader is key to maintaining momentum in groups. The coach is not making sure the job gets done. The coach is making sure the player is okay.

GIVE YOUR LEADERS THE SPACE TO SEE WHAT GOD IS DOING

The most valuable function of a coach is giving a small group leader an opportunity to reflect on what God is doing in his or her group. Most would admit to the difficulty of working "in" something and "on" something at the same time. It's nearly impossible. Often group leaders are working so hard in the group, they don't see the big picture of what God is doing.

By setting aside an hour or so once every quarter, a coach can give group leaders the space they need to see what God is doing and to identify what is next. This is as simple as the coach asking the leaders to list the names of their group members, then asking them to talk about what God is doing in each person's life. As the leaders discuss their members, the logical next steps will begin to surface for the leaders. As an example, the conversation with the leader of a men's group may result in next steps like these:

Bob—Hasn't been around for a while. I need to give him a call.

Joe—Struggling at his job. I need to pray for him and give him some encouragement outside of the group.

Steve—Lost his job. I need to check in with him and see if there's any way the group can help.

Tony—Making poor choices. I need to pray for him and for the right timing to have a tough conversation.

Brett—Shows strong leadership potential. I need to give him more responsibilities in the group and eventually invite him to colead with me.

You get the idea. The coach must approach this conversation as a learner, not as an instructor. It would be easy for the coach to quickly diagnose each member and offer next steps, but the next steps determined by the group leader will be the next steps that are actually executed.

To make this work, start with a couple of assumptions. Assumption #1: Group leaders have made themselves available to God, and God is using them in their group. If group leaders are going through a hard time, they may be wondering if God is doing anything at all. They need encouragement. But, some group leaders so naturally use their gifts, they might not even realize how gifted they are. They also need a coach's insight. Assumption #2: Who you are as a coach is more significant than what you could ever say to a group leader. Your relationship with your group leaders is the greatest gift you can offer them. When relationship comes first, tasks get accomplished. Without relationship, leaders easily burn out.

SMALL GROUP PASTORS, GET OUT OF YOUR COACHES' WAY

In the sports world, how many team owners or general managers have made their coaches' lives miserable? Small group pastors and directors, like their coaches, should approach their roles as learners, not drill sergeants. God wants to use your coaches. Unfortunately, the biggest obstacle to effective coaching is often a well-meaning small group pastor.

While you cannot give away the responsibility for the ministry, empowered coaches are effective coaches. Disempowered coaches become burned-out middle managers. Your expectations of your coaches should be clear, reasonable, and accountable. But again, don't approach accountability as an accountant. Give your coaches the benefit of the doubt: "How are your groups doing?" not "Have you followed up on your groups lately?" If your coaching system is in disarray, then you're probably in the way.

WHY SMALL GROUP COACHING FAILS

Almost every small group pastor or director will agree coaching small group leaders is important. Yet many of those pastors would also admit they don't know how to adequately coach their small group leaders. Having tried and failed at various coaching structures many times myself, I have found three key issues in unsuccessful (and eventually successful) coaching.

UNCLEAR EXPECTATIONS

Many coaching structures fail simply because no one knows what a coach is supposed to do. Is the coach an administrator or record keeper? Is the coach a trainer? Is the coach a figurehead so we can say we have a coaching structure? What do we expect our coaches to do?

If we need coaches to train leaders, then why are small group pastors still running centralized training meetings? Do we really need coaches to collect rosters and reports? Don't we live in the twenty-first century? After all, an online database like churchteams. com will solve all of these administrative issues.

We need coaches to do the things we can't do ourselves. If we had, say, two or three small groups, then what would we do with those leaders? We'd call them on a regular basis. We'd get together for a cup of coffee. We would personally encourage them, answer their questions, and pray for them. We would invest in the relationships. Coaches can do this with the leaders they serve. Coaching is based on relationship. If there's no relationship, not much coaching will take place.

Expectations of the coaches should be clear. If they are coaching new leaders, then use the simple job description mentioned in chapter four: (1) a weekly call, (2) an offer of encouragement, (3) answers to their questions, and (4) prayer for the new leader.

The clear expectation for coaching established leaders is a quarterly meeting to hear what God is doing in their groups and give them the space to identify their next steps with each group member.

UNREASONABLE REQUIREMENTS

In addition to expectations being clear, they also need to be reasonable. A friend of mine called me a while back. He was frustrated because many of his coaches were quitting. I asked him what he was asking them to do. He wanted his volunteer coaches to hold a monthly training meeting with their leaders on the church campus. Then, I asked him if he'd ever driven in his city. This was a major metropolitan area. So, think of requiring volunteer coaches to hold monthly training meetings in the middle of one of the ten largest cities in the U.S. It wasn't working, and his coaches were quitting.

Face-to-face meetings are great. If the coach can pull them off with all of their leaders together, that's really great. But most people can't. Fortunately, there are some alternatives.

Why not meet "together" with small group leaders online or on a conference call? Every day I coach small group pastors across the country over the phone or by teleconference. I've met only a few of them in person, but we connect on a weekly basis. We have a relationship, and they have seen success in growing their groups. This works with leaders locally too.

Again, coaching is built on a relationship, so some face time is necessary (the real, in-person version). But maybe the face-to-face meetings are with one or two group leaders and not all of them. Use other means to connect at other times. Don't get me wrong. I am not advocating a simple "like" on Facebook or a bulk email to all of the leaders at once. The connection must be personal to grow the relationship.

What is a reasonable number of leaders for one person to coach? Rather than establishing an arbitrary ratio, consider the coaches' capacity. Some coaches excel with one or two leaders, but the coaching falls apart with three or more leaders. Other coaches can track with a dozen or more group leaders. At New Life, one of our coaches personally connected with twenty-five group leaders on a weekly basis. He was available before and after all three services on Sunday morning, and spoke with almost all of his group leaders every week in addition to calls during the week.

Here's a rule of thumb for coaching: draw the line at the maximum number of leaders' spouses' and children's names the coach can remember. When the coach interacts with the group leaders, part of the "How are you doing?" question will involve asking about each leader's spouse and children. While the coach could use index cards or Evernote, committing these names to memory speaks to the coach's capacity for the number of leaders he or she can serve. This number will vary.

In setting reasonable expectations, the frequency of meetings should also be considered. While I would advocate for weekly calls with new leaders and quarterly meetings with established leaders, in times of crisis, more frequent meetings might be necessary. A reasonable expectation would set a minimum number of meetings, but would also include the necessary expectations, group visits, huddle meetings with multiple group leaders, and other things along those lines.

LACK OF ACCOUNTABILITY

None of us likes to make people uncomfortable. Some of us avoid this discomfort to the point of not asking our coaches if they're coaching. Then, we discover not much coaching is taking place. We shouldn't be surprised.

Only what we supervise gets done, but we shouldn't supervise in a heavy-handed way. There are helpful ways of doing this. Ask about important things. If we don't ask, what's communicated is that coaching is unimportant. Sometimes small group pastors and directors don't ask out of fear of hearing bad news. Reports like the group faltering or the leader stepping down are unwelcome, so the question isn't asked. Denial isn't a leadership strategy. In fact, the expectation of bad reports could become a self-fulfilling prophecy. By asking and hearing the truth, not only could bad situations be corrected, but the small group pastor could also receive a lot of good news.

Check in with coaches. Presuming the best about our coaches both honors and motivates them. Giving them accountability helps them keep their commitment to coaching and eliminates the guilt of not fulfilling their commitment.

Effective, motivated coaches need direction that is clear, reasonable, and accountable. How do I know? A good coach taught me that . . . as he was resigning. Do your coaches know your expectations? Do you know your expectations? Are your requirements reasonable? And, if it's truly important, are you holding them accountable? These three simple words will transform your coaching structure: clear, reasonable, and accountable.

WHEN COACHING IS TRAINING

While there is certainly a place for centralized Basic Training described in the last chapter, the best ongoing training comes from a coach in the moment when group leaders need solutions to their problems.

One day I was talking to a pastor who came from a career in corporate training. As we talked about delivering training to group leaders when they needed it, he said, "You know, considering my background, this is going to sound funny, but the best training comes from the person who is proximate to the group leader when he or she is facing a problem." Rather than creating a seminar on common group issues and rounding everybody up at the church on Tuesday night, a conversation with an experienced leader or coach at the right time produced more meaningful training.

Group leaders are best served when the training meets a current need as they are facing it. Leaders aren't concerned with difficult group members until they have one. Leaders can be trained and prepared to a certain extent, but chances are they won't remember what's given to them if they are not currently facing the problem.

The world of training and education has changed. Online courses are replacing many classes on university campuses. In some fields, crash courses are all someone needs to build a successful career. If centuries-old educational institutions can innovate in how they train and equip the future workforce, then it's time for the church to innovate as well and take advantage of the new tools that are being developed.

Training can be a blog post. In fact, that's how my blog at allenwhite.org got started. I would answer one of my leader's questions each week and send the answer to all of the others.

Training can also appear in your video-based curriculum, if you are developing your own. By adding weekly training to the video, leaders have what they need when they need it as they go through the materials.

Training can be sent by video through an email. Any small group pastor or director with a smartphone, a tablet, or a laptop can record a two-minute video (no longer) and send it out to his or her small group leaders each week. This is even better than training delivered with video-based curriculum, because you can answer timely questions as they are asked rather than anticipating what questions they might ask.

Training tools should be developed for individual leaders through digitally interactive technology. Groups of leaders can be trained online, but meet individually with their coach in person. Mobile devices, social media, and voice mail have made it possible to literally "encourage one another daily."[69] Again, connecting your leaders with the experience of other leaders or coaches at the right time produces more meaningful training. One Sunday morning a group leader who was a former member of my small group came up to me in the church lobby. She was concerned about an overly talkative member of her group and how to handle the situation. I had to laugh to myself because this former overly talkative member of my group was asking her former overly talkative group leader about a problem she was having with an overly talkative person in her current group. Ironic, huh?

In just a few minutes, I gave her a couple of tips on how to handle the situation. She thanked me. After the next meeting, the problem was solved. The overly talkative group member felt insulted and never came back. Okay, that's not true. The group member received the message loud and clear and cooperated from then on.

This group leader didn't need to wait for the next centralized training meeting to come around. She came directly to me. She didn't need to take copious notes from my training; it stuck in her head. Why? Because I gave her the training she needed when she needed it. Those are the lessons that stick.

Rather than conducting meetings, develop relationships. Blogs and training videos are powerful and helpful tools that can supplement what the coaches are doing, but the coach is the primary trainer. Small group pastors and directors should invest their time in training coaches and developing their small group team rather than overshadowing their coaches and micromanaging group leaders.

SPECIAL EVENT TRAINING

In both churches I served, I limited live and in-person training meetings to twice per year. In the fall of each year, all of the group leaders, coaches, and community leaders were gathered for the announcement of the fall church-wide series as well as vision casting for the new ministry year (September through May). Group leaders received the first look at the new curriculum, much like the Sneak Peek mentioned in chapter four. And, of course, established leaders were recruited to walk alongside new leaders for the fall campaign. There was plenty of food and a lot of fun.

The second gathering took place around the second weekend in January—an off-site group leaders' retreat in a location at least two hours out of town. The church paid for a speaker. The group leaders paid for their lodging. Many retreat centers and hotels offered great deals the second week of the year, because after the big New Year's celebrations, they were desperate for occupants.

The best thing I discovered about a leaders' retreat is that it's set apart from the normal pace of life. No one could run home. No one had to leave a Friday evening session to tuck kids into bed. The retreat was fairly distraction free. (Though I didn't confiscate cell phones.)

Leaders would come up to me six months after the retreat and could quote things the retreat speaker had taught us. The teaching stuck. I also asked the retreat participants to record a two-minute video about what they learned on the retreat. This had a few purposes. First, the leaders who couldn't attend received some of the training as well as further reasons to attend the next retreat. Next, by communicating what stuck with them on video, the retreat participants had the principles from the speaker further cemented into their memories. And, lastly, my senior pastor could see that the expense of bringing in a top-notch speaker was justified.

TRAINING IN A NUTSHELL

With training overall, I recommend operating on three levels: (1) a briefing and on-the-job training during the first six-week study for the leaders of new groups, (2) Basic Training for group leaders who choose to continue leading a group, and (3) ongoing training that is decentralized and coach-led. While I recommend two centralized training experiences in the year, centralized training as a whole is not working for most churches anymore. By sending video training by email and using the coaching relationship, training can be more customized to the leader's needs and can be received in a more convenient format.

People don't like meetings. Fortunately, meetings are not the only means of training group leaders. With so many great options to push out training to leaders' electronic devices, to create memorable training through retreats and special events, and, of course, to invest in the relationship between leaders and their coaches, meetings just might become unnecessary in your church.

CHAPTER 11

TRACKING WHAT MATTERS

As human beings, we are prone to measuring things. Whether it's our children's growth as denoted by the marks on the door frame or the number of pounds on our scales, we measure. We keep track. Some measurements are related to success toward our goals. Others are merely taken to satisfy our curiosity. What should we measure when it comes to groups? What's a win?

How do we measure spiritual growth or group health? While believers are complete in Christ,[70] we long for a day of completion.[71] Over the centuries we have used many inadequate measures such as the number of meetings attended, verses memorized, or lessons completed. Do these metrics truly reveal the full story? How much life change is taking place? How do we measure that?

One speaker put it this way, "The problem with people is they are just never done." Every person is in process. Whether we're evaluating group members, group leaders, coaches, the small group team members, or ourselves, there are some hard numbers to consider, but there are also some soft metrics to take into consideration. Numbers tell us part of the story, but not the whole story.

BAD REASONS FOR TAKING GROUP ATTENDANCE

Every once in a while, I run into a senior pastor who insists on weekly attendance numbers from small groups. This is not so much for the purpose of discerning how the groups are doing, and isn't even for the purpose of member care. These pastors hearken back to the day of the old attendance board in the front of the sanctuary. You remember those:

Last Sunday's Attendance: 267

One Year Ago: 263

Sunday School Attendance: 56

Offering: $2,158.23

While megachurches are often accused of being "only about the numbers," it seems like others have a little number envy going on themselves. Here is why this record keeping might be a bad idea.

First, groups are more like families than classes. Let's say you have a family of five. Your son has a late practice so he can't make dinner tonight. Sitting around the dinner table, do you have a family of four or a family of five? You have a family of five, of course. Your son's absence at dinner doesn't mean he no longer belongs to the family.

Groups are built on community around a Bible study. Classes are based on a course of study. If you skip too many classes, then you miss the content—the class is really of no benefit to you. But a group is not a class. Belonging takes precedence over curriculum.

Yes, there are group rosters. And, yes, attendance may vary. But what happens in group life—not only during group meetings—is what causes groups to stand apart. Whether you attend the meeting or not, you're a part of the group.

Years ago, we had a neighbor who attended our church and wanted to join our group. She lived right around the corner, so our group was convenient for her. She also wanted her husband to attend the group. He came once, but it was pretty obvious he didn't want to be there.

They had busy lives, so rather than spending an evening apart with her at group and him at home, she opted to stay home as well, but we kept her on our roster. My wife would check in on her regularly, go for walks with her, and once in a while, she would show up for group.

She wasn't a part of anybody else's group. This was her group, whether she was there or not. Attendance records would report her as "inactive," but we connected with her every week outside of the group meeting. Do you see where record keeping can go a little haywire?

Second, group attendance alone is a poor measure of health. While it's important to know overall how many people are connected to groups, ministries, and classes, numbers should never be an end in themselves. What do those numbers mean? "Well, we have 80 percent in groups, so our small group pastor can keep his job." "We've gone up and down with group attendance. Small groups aren't working in our church." That may be, but are you really getting the information you need?

THERE ARE BETTER METRICS FOR GROUP AND CONGREGATIONAL HEALTH

Whether your groups meet Sunday morning or on a weekday, on campus or in a home, all of the groups should possess key elements to qualify as a group. For some churches groups are defined by size. For others groups must provide care and study, or they have to focus on one of the church's objectives while adding a new objective as well. For instance, if the group primarily serves, then they could also start a Bible study. The meeting place or format is irrelevant as long as the groups achieve the vision of the church, but remember that the temptation to conform all of your groups to a single format should be resisted. So, what does your church value?

HOW MANY LEADERS HAVE YOU DEVELOPED?

Every believer is called to "go and make disciples."[72] There are no exemptions from the Great Commission. How are you empowering and equipping your members to gather a circle, regardless of its size, and follow that call? For many churches, an easy-to-use video-based curriculum is the answer. The person doesn't need to be a "leader" or a Bible scholar. They just need to invite some friends. In fact, if the leader instructions are in every group member's study guide, they can see how easy group leadership really is.

Some churches may ask their group leaders to identify a specific person as their coleader or apprentice. As we've explored in previous chapters, I tend to take things the other way by training the whole group to lead. By sharing responsibilities from bringing refreshments to opening their homes to leading the discussion, all of the group members not only take ownership of the group, but also become leaders in training.

The number of leaders in development or the regular practice of sharing responsibilities in the group are key metrics to keep in mind. An occasional survey of the group which is reinforced by contact with their coaches will show how well others are being trained to lead.

HOW'S THE LOAD OF PASTORAL CARE?

"When numbers go up, care goes down."[73] This is why Saddle-back Church has had a proportionately higher number of people in groups than in weekend attendance year after year.

A church will never be able to hire all of the staff it needs. Mini-church or megachurch, it's the same case for everybody. But there are gifted people sitting in the pews every Sunday. If we encourage them, and they say, "God use me," God uses them. We shouldn't be surprised.

As people care for each other in groups, the need for pastoral care goes down. The members of the body are encouraging and serving one another.

Now, every church culture is a little different. Some church members are well trained in calling the church office for every little thing they need. Others simply feel outright entitled to the attention of their pastoral staff. But when care goes up in groups, phone calls to the church office will go down. What does care look like in your groups?

HOW HAS ASSIMILATION IMPROVED?

When people start attending your church, how easy is it for them to make friends? How are they connecting? Groups are a great place for people to start.

In most churches, everyone can't know everybody, but everybody needs to know somebody. Statistically, that number is around six or seven people. That's all it takes for a person to stick. That sounds like a small group to me!

People who feel the connection and care of the church body outside of the Sunday morning service are more likely to stick around. Our family attends one of the largest churches in the U.S. Our kids were actually invited first and loved it. My oldest son immediately wanted to go to church twice a week!

My wife and I joined a group when our family first started attending—not because we had to—but because we were invited. Here's the interesting thing—even though over five thousand people attended our church campus, we ran into the members and former members of our small group on a regular basis. We could just pick each other out of the crowd. There's something really great about seeing a smiling, familiar face in a large crowd. (Begin *Cheers* theme song . . .)

Other than our small group and our children's teachers, we didn't know anybody else at the church. We'd never met our pastor. We didn't know the staff. But we did know our group, and that's all we really needed.

WHAT'S MORE IMPORTANT, ATTENDANCE OR RELATIONSHIP?

If attendance supersedes relationship, when you lose a member here or there, you just replace them to keep your numbers up. After all, if you're posting numbers on a tote board, a decline is sending a bad message.

If relationship is valued over attendance, people will invest in each other and build into each other's lives. Whether members are present at each meeting or not, they are loved, valued, encouraged, and supported. These are harder things to measure, but are far more meaningful.

A report will measure attendance. A coach will take the temperature of the relationships. Both are needed. There certainly is a softer side to group metrics. Some things are easily measured, while others are not. But there are some things that hard numbers do reveal about the health and progress of groups.

GOOD REASONS TO REPORT GROUP ATTENDANCE

First, group attendance numbers alert you to major shifts in groups. Groups who typically have 80 percent or more of their group members in a meeting on a regular basis are in their sweet spot. Even if their attendance occasionally dips below 50 percent, there really is not much to worry about.

There are two situations where the coaches need to intervene:

If groups have too many members, the coach is needed to help the group navigate the situation. Warm, welcoming groups can't help but grow numerically. The members keep inviting their friends and in a matter of days to weeks, the group can grow well beyond what's comfortable for a group meeting or even the average-size house. Rather than putting a cap on how many new people the group can invite, it's time for a conversation. What's next? Subgrouping.

If the group is subgrouping to smaller groups of eight or less, everybody can get their word in. Subgrouping paves the way for new groups to form. I would not recommend using words like *birth, split, multiply,* or *divide.* These are code for "the small group pastor is only concerned about his or her own success and doesn't truly care about people." (While small group pastors know that's simply not true, the reality is group leaders and members are wise to us.)

The best way to get a group to multiply/divide/birth/split is to allow the size of the group to become a problem for the *group.* When they "feel the pain" of an oversized group, they will be more motivated to relocate some of the subgroups to another house. Coach them toward this decision. Don't dictate this, but guide them into something they will feel good about down the road.

Tracking attendance can certainly help groups who are facing a bit of a crisis in overwhelmingly high attendance numbers. The other attendance trend that should greatly concern small group pastors is when a group rapidly declines in attendance.

For most group leaders, especially new group leaders or hosts, a significant decline in attendance often feels like personal failure, even though it's not. If they started with fourteen and are now sitting in a cavernous living room with four people, they assume it's their fault. They will naturally assume that maybe they're just not cut out for this. But, often that is not true.

These group leaders need to know that 100 percent attendance is not necessarily the goal. The goal is letting God work in the group. Sometimes God can accomplish things with four people in the room that might not have happened with fourteen people there. The leaders must be redirected from thinking they are terrible leaders to asking themselves, "What does God intend to accomplish with only four members present tonight?"

A pastor told me about one of his groups that was just having one of those days. Over the course of the day, one member after another called to report they couldn't make it that night. Finally, the group leader's husband called to say he had to work late. She said, "Well, it doesn't look like anyone is coming tonight anyway."

At seven o'clock sharp, the doorbell rang. The leader already had her feet up prepared for a relaxing evening. She thought, "Who could that be? Everybody cancelled."

She went to the door to discover a couple who had rarely attended the group on the doorstep. She thought about telling them the group was cancelled that night, but instead she invited them in.

In the course of their conversation, she learned the husband had never received Christ as his Savior. The leader explained what it meant to receive Christ. The man was saved that night. You have to wonder what might have happened if the whole group had shown up. My suspicion is things would have been business as usual.

When attendance drops, leaders need to be reassured. They need to be encouraged that this doesn't reflect on them. They need to be aware of what God might be up to.

If attendance drops and *stays* low, that's a different issue. What's going on in the group that might be keeping people away? Are the meetings going too long? Is the leader unprepared? Is someone dominating the discussion and turning this into his or her personal support group? Not only is it time to coach the leader, it's also time to conduct some "exit interviews" with group members who have left. This is not license for whining, but it could certainly give insight into what's going on in the group.

The presence of a narcissist or someone with a major life issue could certainly curtail the group's effectiveness and ultimately its existence. Intervention by a coach is essential to the group's survival. Don't hesitate to act.

If a group fails to report attendance, it either means the group leader is not a detail-driven, task-oriented person, or the group is facing trouble they'd rather not report. If the group leader is not a report-taker, then have them designate someone else in the group to submit the reports. Sometimes the leader's spouse is more diligent with reporting. After all, opposites do attract.

If the group leader has gone silent, then the group coach needs to investigate. Maybe the group has stopped meeting. Maybe their attendance has dropped, and the leader is embarrassed to report. If they miss one week of reporting, it's probably no big deal. But missing multiple weeks should put the group on your team's hot list for follow up.

If a group isn't reporting attendance, and the leader isn't calling anybody back, the group has either failed or gone underground. While we live in a free country and people can gather and study whatever they want, there are some key advantages to staying connected to a coach and a small group system.

Failure to take attendance is certainly only one indicator that a group may have "gone rogue." This is not the time to evoke a strict, controlling approach to group oversight. Coaching is built on relationship. Encourage the leader's coach to work on the personal relationship. In time, this will bring the group and its leader back into the fold.

METHODS FOR TAKING GROUP ATTENDANCE

Back in the day, the Sunday school superintendent left a folder in every classroom. The teacher would check off the attendance and put the folder outside of the door. Attendance was fairly easy to collect. But, collecting attendance from off-campus groups can be a little trickier.

Paper forms are probably not the solution, especially if they need to be mailed or dropped off at the church. Digital solutions are far superior. You can use online survey tools to send a survey to group leaders asking them to list their members by name or just give a total for the week, make any prayer requests, and answer questions about group life. An online database such as ChurchTeams.com, which sends a report reminder after each group meeting, can be a powerful tool. Leaders just need to click a link, fill out their report, click "save," and then they're done. ChurchTeams saves all of the data securely online and sends the report to the group leader's coach, as well as sending out analytics at the end of each month identifying potential trouble spots.

While there are many good reasons to take attendance in groups, there are also some negatives around record keeping. Meaningful metrics are much different than playing a numbers game.

WHEN COUNTING DOESN'T ADD UP

As churches I've coached have loosened the initial requirements for group leadership and have launched hundreds of groups at once, record keeping tends to suffer. While there is a big difference between the trial-run group and an ongoing group, some pastors are reluctant in trying new strategies simply because they don't feel they can easily measure the group data. In fact, I've told pastors outright, "We're going to make a mess, but some wonderful things will come of it." While coaching and communication should be in place with every new leader, I still get that nagging question. . .

"How do you track that?" I don't believe that question was asked about converts at Pentecost, but it's the question that I get from pastors of small groups who need to justify their salary or otherwise guarantee job security. (That's what it's all about, right?) But what if the need to track, control, and direct groups keeps these pastors from a wave of ministry that results in dramatic kingdom proportions?

I know all of the evangelical adages. "Don't we count our money? Are people less significant than cash?" After all, the Shepherd did count his sheep only to discover that one had gone astray. If the counting hadn't taken place, then the sheep might have risked deadly peril. Matthew 18 makes it very clear that one individual sheep matters to God.

At the risk of taking the analogy of the Shepherd too far, let me challenge you on this: the Shepherd counted his sheep, but the Shepherd didn't limit the multiplication of his sheep because it might overwhelm the accounting system. My thought is that if the Shepherd had an overabundance of sheep to the point where the lily-white mass stretched as far as his eye could see, his joy over a prolific flock would far overshadow his compulsion for a spreadsheet. When Acts 2:41 records that about three thousand newly baptized, dripping wet believers were added to the church, I don't think they were rounding up from 2,857. We say that people are not statistics, then we quote the statistics about how many people we're runnin' and how many people we're keepin.'

MEASURE PROGRESS TOWARD STATED GOALS

Don't get me wrong. We should know whether our worship services are effective in building the kingdom. I must admit that I am enamored by some numbers myself. I am amazed at New Life in California. Before we launched our first alignment series only 30 percent of the adults were in groups, but in the next two years about 40 percent of the adults led groups in their homes. That's pretty amazing, going from 30 percent sitting to 40 percent leading! But here's where this breaks down for most folks. I didn't know how many people were in each group. In some cases, I didn't personally know the person who was leading the group. It had gotten out of control—well, out of my control, anyway. If we're ineffective, then certainly no number will save us. If we are effective, then no number will do it justice.

What I have learned is that God's people are capable of much more than I initially gave them credit for. The people in the pews can lead a video-based small group study and refrain from heresy and criticism of the pastoral staff. They're too nervous about getting through the lesson to even think of interjecting theological error.

God's people filled with God's spirit interacting with God's word leads to more great things than bad.

Here's another thing I've learned. A general contractor, a retired school superintendent, a multilevel marketer, and a substance abuse counselor together did a better job of leading our small groups than I could alone. I didn't need to train a multiplicity of new hosts. These four did the training. I didn't need to review applications and interview prospective leaders. These four along with their coaches knew every one of them. They knew what was going on in their leaders' lives and what was going on in their groups. That's better than I ever did sitting them all in neat rows and lecturing them for weeks of training.

We have this need to know numbers, and part of me is curious about why that is, but does a number tell us if our church is healthy? Does a number tell us if a group is growing? Does a number tell us if individual believers are being conformed to the image of Christ? Are these numbers good stewardship or just bragging rights?

While numbers have their place, they only tell part of the story. Statistics certainly should not become any kind of limiting factor in group growth. The measurement is exactly that, a measurement. Are we measuring the right things? Are we measuring with the right tools? Are we actually tracking progress toward the goals that we set for groups? These are questions every small group team should discuss.

WHAT SHOULD WE MEASURE?

If we've established goals for groups, and if group members have established next steps for themselves, then these things should be measured. A goal without accountability is merely wishful thinking.

Attendance records for the reasons stated previously in this chapter can be helpful in identifying situations which require intervention. These stats can also cause a false sense of success. While overall numbers are great, what do those numbers truly represent?

For a healthy, growing groups ministry, we need to pay attention to things like:

1. Leadership development in groups starting with baby steps toward leadership (like leading a portion of the group meeting).

2. The amount of contact between coaches and the leaders they serve, and then contact between the small group pastor or small group team and the coaches they serve.

3. Identified next steps for every person within the group ministry, from the small group pastor to every group member.

4. The percentage of a congregation leading groups as well as the percentage who are prepared to lead. This statistic is more significant than the percentage who are connected in groups.

5. Of course, the one overwhelming statistic that matters more than any other is the number of people who have received Christ in a given year. If this number isn't increasing, then what's the point of the rest of it? Are group members bringing unsaved friends to group or to church? Do group members have unsaved friends? If people aren't crossing over from death to life because of the church, then what is preventing it?

We cannot make people grow, but we can create environments which produce growth. We can set expectations for growth. We can give people permission to create group life that is meaningful to them.

Not every believer progresses at the same rate or even necessarily in the same way, but everyone does have a next step. The next step could be adding a good habit or forsaking a bad habit or a sinful behavior. The next step could be a step toward gift identification or leadership development. The next step could involve a behavior or attitude in a marriage or in parenting. Everyone's next step is different. The importance is not in conforming to a process, but in identifying and taking steps toward individual progress. How can the group, coach, or pastor support the work God is doing in each person's life within the congregation as a whole?

For some people an assessment might help them identify areas of growth in their knowledge, attitudes, or behaviors. Some assessments include potential next steps if someone is lacking in a particular area. For others an assessment is completely counterproductive. It's just one more way of showing the person they don't measure up.

The good news is every believer has the Holy Spirit to guide them into their next steps. They may need some help in how to listen and what to listen for, but the Spirit will show them what's next, especially when it comes to convicting someone of sin. The group, in turn, can provide a prayer partner or someone to support each member as they take next steps. The leader is not responsible to serve every group member in this way. The leader is responsible to make sure everyone has the support he or she needs to succeed.

The problem with metrics is they can become merely a numbers game. We could just be churning through people in groups without growing them. With a little finesse, we can make the numbers tell a wonderful story. By looking at all sides of group life with both hard numbers and personal reports, we can better measure what is happening or not happening in group life.

CHAPTER 12

MY CHALLENGE TO YOU

What would your church look like if 16 percent of your adults were leading groups? Those are your Innovators (2.5%) and Early Adopters (13.5%). They are the easiest ones to recruit. Imagine having more people in ongoing groups than you have in weekend worship attendance. Imagine reaching people in the community who've never attended your church. Imagine engaging mature believers who've passively sat in classes and Bible studies. What would it do for them? Imagine how motivated they would be.

When I served at New Life in California, I led a midweek Bible study for quite a few years. This was a long-held pattern in our church. About eighty-five faithful members joined me on Wednesday night in the sanctuary. I enjoyed teaching. They either enjoyed listening or else felt obligated to be there.

One Wednesday night I looked out at that small crowd gathered for my Bible study. I thought, "What if these eighty-five faithful, knowledgeable folks were leading groups, and we didn't need this midweek Bible study anymore?" Within two years, most of those eighty-five folks were leading or involved in groups. The midweek Bible study became an elective of fifteen or twenty people who met in a classroom. I stayed home on Wednesday nights. The ones who started leading groups were getting far more out of their group than they ever did during my midweek study. (Please note, I didn't end the midweek study to get them involved in groups. Their involvement with groups effectively ended the midweek Bible study.)

To recruit the 16 percent into leadership, we might have to redefine what a group is. Years ago in a seminary class our professor defined a group as "three to thirty people." I thought that was

ridiculous. Three was too small. Thirty was too big. After all, Jesus
had twelve. That must be the ideal number.

Over time, I discovered that twelve is the right number for
some people, but not for everybody. For some folks, twelve is too
large. They would never lead a group like that—but they would do a
study with a handful of their friends. For others twelve is too limiting. They are very hospitable and love including other people. I had
to ask myself, "Why am I handicapping leaders who do a great job
at inviting and including others?" So, I stopped. When the leader
felt the group was too large, then we talked about possibly starting
another group.

Nearly two decades after that seminary class, I now say a group
is three to thirty people meeting together, but it took some time to
catch up with that.

The great thing about groups is they can be flexible. The problem
is often those who lead group ministries want uniformity, not variety. By allowing for some flexibility and giving your people permission to define their own group within certain minimal guidelines,
far more people who may have been eliminated by previous requirements or definitions of groups will be open to group leadership.

For example, a few years ago I worked with a church in middle
Georgia. They invited anyone in their congregation to do a study
with their friends. One lady in their congregation told the pastors
she was able to participate in a group for the very first time. Her two
sons were both autistic, so she was concerned about joining a group
since her boys might distract or upset the other members. She also
saw the same problem with leading a group herself at her house.
But now she was given permission to do a group on her terms. If
she did the study with people who already knew and understood
her boys, then the issue disappeared. She started a group with her
friends once a small barrier to leadership was removed.

Your people will become highly creative in how they do groups
if you give them the opportunity. While some people may give
themselves permission to do a group on their own terms and start
a group outside of your church's ministry, most people are loyal
and will follow what the church dictates. But once they are given
the opportunity to start a group in a more comfortable place, like

doing a study with their friends, they will seize the opportunity and start something.

So, here's the good news. You can do this. Your church is not too large or too small. It's not too old or too new. It's not too traditional or too contemporary. Groups will work in any context. The group leaders are right under your nose. If you are willing to start groups or get your current groups ministry unstuck, I've given you a detailed game plan. Now it's time to execute.

Start by sharing some of these ideas with your leadership team. Senior pastors are very interested in maximizing their teaching gift through developing their own curriculum. As I've said, both your pastor and your congregation will be more interested in groups if the pastor's video teaching is the basis for your curriculum. You don't need to spend tens of thousands of dollars on high-end production. Remember the church of fifty people who created their own curriculum (chapter two)? It can be done! And, again, a home-grown curriculum can be used to launch groups with or without aligning the study to the sermon series.

If your team is not ready to launch something church-wide, then run a pilot. Whether you call it an experiment or a skunkworks, this terminology allows for a little trial and error. Sometimes experiments blow up, but sometimes a pilot will give you the confidence to do more based on a positive experience. Remember, I was your guinea pig. All of these strategies have been tested in both the churches I've served as well as the hundreds I've coached.

While there is risk to inviting "whosoever will" to step out and lead a group, there is also urgency. The time is short. People don't live forever, and as someone said, "Christianity is just one generation away from extinction." We can complain all we want about how culture is changing and becoming less friendly to Christians, but here's the thing: if believers were engaged and empowered to disciple others and reach the lost in groups of their friends, then the culture might not be in the shape it is now. It's not too late, but we need to invest our energy in action, not complaints.

We are in a spiritual battle, yet many of our best soldiers are retiring before they've even experienced active duty. We have allowed our church members to borrow from our spirituality for way too long. We have overcomplicated things to the point that it's difficult for us to discern who's qualified. We've become so codependent on our congregation's need for us that we can't empower others to lead because of our own need to be needed. These are some of the issues I faced in my journey toward empowering others to lead. I don't believe I'm alone.

What if church buildings and tax-deductible contributions disappeared? What if there was no longer budget for high-level production in worship services? What if the church couldn't even pay you? While I am not necessarily against any of these things, if the church was stripped down to the essentials, what would it look like? We actually know.

We find churches that lacked all of these things in the New Testament. Here's what they did.

In Ephesians 4:11–13, we read:

> So Christ himself gave the apostles, the prophets, the evangelists, the pastors and teachers, to equip his people for works of service, so that the body of Christ may be built up until we all reach unity in the faith and in the knowledge of the Son of God and become mature, attaining to the whole measure of the fullness of Christ.

According to Acts 2, at Pentecost, the early church suddenly had new power and about three thousand new Christians in one day. How do you assimilate and disciple a group like that from all over the world?

> They devoted themselves to the apostles' teaching and to fellowship, to the breaking of bread and to prayer. Everyone was filled with awe at the many wonders and signs performed by the apostles. All the believers were together and had everything in common. They sold property and possessions to give to anyone who had need. Every day they continued to meet together in the temple courts. They broke bread in their homes and ate together with glad and sincere hearts, praising God and enjoying the favor of all the people. And the Lord added to their number daily those who were being saved. (2:42–47)

This wasn't the description of the church after decades of training and maturity. This wasn't the ultimate goal of what the church
should be. This was the church on day one. Why have we made
this so complex?

Of course, there is one more essential passage I want to mention here, and that's the church's mission statement, given by Jesus
himself in Matthew 28:18–20:

> Then Jesus came to them and said, "All authority in heaven and
> on earth has been given to me. Therefore go and make disciples
> of all nations, baptizing them in the name of the Father and
> of the Son and of the Holy Spirit, and teaching them to obey
> everything I have commanded you. And surely I am with you
> always, to the very end of the age."

I understand you are already very familiar with these verses, but
here's my question: If the essential functions of the church are
"equipping God's people for works of service" and making disciples,
how are we doing? How many things are we invested in that don't
accomplish this? Are those things worth it? What would give you
and your church a sense of urgency in these matters?

The answer is relatively simple. If your church has no groups,
then start groups. If your church is stuck at 30 percent of your
adults in groups, then it's time to change something. Whether you
create your own curriculum, add a new strategy for recruiting
leaders, or change the way people are connected into groups, one
change could add another 20 percent into groups.

Maybe your church is stuck at two-thirds of your people in
groups. Remember, the last third of any church is a different animal. Give opportunities to your independent folks, your introverts,
and your isolated members by allowing flexibility and by redefining
groups.

In all of this, as the leader of the groups ministry, you have to
major on the majors. If you're an associate pastor or the leader of
the small groups ministry, you don't need to recruit leaders. That's
your senior pastor's job. You don't need to connect people into
groups. The group leaders will invite the group members. Your job

is to build the support network that will keep your leaders going long term. By devoting yourself to the leaders of leaders of leaders in your groups ministry, you are investing yourself in a ministry which could easily reach hundreds or thousands of people.

The only true limitation I ever experienced in the churches I served was in my own thinking. I mean, after all, if you think something's not possible, it isn't. The biggest obstacle I ever had to overcome in growing groups was my small thinking, fear, and need for control. Once God helped me deal with this, things happened in our groups that were beyond what I could ever ask or imagine.

Once the groups ministry began to grow, I had to grow as a leader. Now, some will stop in their tracks right here, thinking, "Well, I need to work on my own leadership development first before I use any of these group strategies." That thinking will keep your groups ministry small forever. Acknowledge, like I did, that you have become the lid to the expansion and impact of your groups. As John Maxwell says, "Leadership ability is the lid that determines a person's level of effectiveness."[74] The good news is you don't have to allow this limitation to limit you. Leadership skills can be acquired, and when you increase your leadership ability in the moments you need to, it will stick with you far longer than if you study leadership in a void.

So imagine you are in a church where every person who walks through the door is already in a group. Some of these groups would meet your definition of a group. Other groups are a Sunday school class or an Adult Bible Fellowship. Quite a few of these groups are "off the books." In fact, they are so unlike your definition of a group that they probably don't even see themselves as a "group."

What do you need to do to lead them? How do you call out the natural group leadership that's already taking place? How do you equip them with easy-to-use resources, an experienced coach, and the right amount of training to get them started?

The task is not so hard. In fact, the hardest work is already done—you've changed your thinking. How do you connect everyone into a group? You don't. Everybody is already in a group.

CHURCH CAMPAIGN EXAMPLES

GROUP LEADER SIGN-UP CARD

☐ Yes! I'd like to host a group during this series

I will attend a 15-minute briefing after the
(Circle One)   8   9:30   11   service on:

☐ Sunday, January 17   ☐ Sunday, January 24

_____

Name (first & last)

_____

Email

_____

Best Phone

NEW HOST INFORMATION SHEET/APPLICATION

My Group is: _____   Coach: _____

☐ Open to New Members   This is either your current small
                                  group leader or the coach you met
☐ Invitation-Only Group   in this briefing today.

Name: _____   Spouse: _____

Address: _____

City: _____   Zip: _____

Home Phone: _____   Cell Phone: _____

Email: _____

GROUP MEETING SPECIFICS

Day of the Week: _____   Time of Day: _____ AM/ PM

Location of Meeting (Subdivision, if applicable): _____

Address: _____

Type of Group: Anybody   Couples   Singles   Women only   Men only

Childcare available: Yes   No

1. How and when did you commit your life to Jesus Christ?

2. How long have you attended Brookwood Church? Where did you attend
church before?

3. Is there anything going on in your life that could potentially harm or embarrass the church?

☐ Current habitual struggles or moral issues (an addiction, cohabitation, a
sexual relationship outside of marriage, or similar) that would bring shame on
the name of Jesus Christ or on Brookwood Church.

☐ Current marital struggles (infidelity, separation, divorce in process, or
similar).

NEW LEADER BRIEFING PACKET

WRESTLING WITH GOD SMALL GROUPS

GETTING STARTED

1. **When**: February 7–March 20

2. **The Groups Will Meet**: weekly

3. **Day of the Week**: whatever day works best for you—hopefully coordinated with what other groups in your area are doing.

4. **Time**: whenever works best for your group. Plan for the meeting to be about 1½ hours, but allowing ½ hour for general "hanging around" afterward.

5. **Length of Commitment**: 8 weeks

6. **Refreshments**: People like to eat, but if your meeting is after dinner, they won't eat too much. Provide some snacks and refreshments for your group. You should plan on doing this yourself the first week, then invite your group members to sign up for the following weeks.

BETWEEN NOW AND FEBRUARY 8

1. Make a list of prospective members (use "Five Circles of Life" or a cell phone contact list). Pray the list. Recruit as many as you can. Most groups will start large, and then thin out. If you only have 2–3, read Matthew 18:20.

How People Can Join Your Group

a. Personal Invitation (Five Circles of Life)—who would enjoy or benefit from this study?

b. Church website (make sure your group is listed!)

c. Small Group Connection (1/31)

2. **Cohost:** You need a cohost, because you will need a break! Think of someone (who you like) and invite them to join you as the cohost. There may be someone who signs up who can fit this role. Don't do this alone!

3. **Childcare:** The easier the childcare, the easier it is for people to join your group. Consider some childcare options. Does someone from the church live nearby? Do you know a member of the youth group or someone else who could help? Don't stress on this one—PRAY!

4. **Group Format & Curriculum:** The group discussion will be directed by the DVD. You might want to watch the video ahead of time to prepare yourself, but the video will do most of the work for you.

a. The video will include a small group lifter by Allen White, Bible teaching by Perry Duggar, and some extras.

b. Follow the instructions in the study guide. Start with the "Connect" section, view the DVD, then continue with the discussion questions.

c. If you ever feel like the video is getting in the way of the group's discussion, then turn off the DVD and just ask the questions from the book.

5. **Keeping It on Track**

a. It's easy to chase rabbit trails, so if you feel like your group is starting on a subject outside of the curriculum, just say something like … "well, that's going to open a whole other can of worms, let's go to the next question" or "well guys, that's going to be a whole new (day, show, discussion), let's get back to today's discussion." Don't interrupt people. When you find the opportunity, get it back on track.

b. If the discussion turns to criticism, please ask the critical person to go and speak directly to the person responsible . . . they would love to talk with them about their concern.

c. If something comes up that you don't know how to answer or deal with, just be honest. "I'm not sure about that one. Can I get back to you next week?"

HOST SUPPORT

1. All of the new hosts will have a coach to answer your questions and help you start your group. Your coach will call you regularly and see how you're doing. Most importantly, your coach and their small group will be praying for you.

   a. If you are currently in a small group, then your coach can be your small group leader.

   b. If you're not in a small group, then you'll meet a coach today who will help you get your group started.

2. If there is any issue that you and your coach or community leader can't resolve together, you can call me anytime: Office xxx-xxx-xxxx; email: xxxx@xxxx.xxx

REPORTING YOUR GROUP'S PROGRESS

1. Check in with your coach at least once per week. Let them know how many folks you had and what is happening in your group. Also, let them know of prayer needs or any situation that the pastors and staff might need to know about: sickness, new baby, financial need, major life transition, or similar.

2. I would also like to know what's happening in your group: decisions for Christ, answers to prayer, life changes. Let me know: email me or jot me a note.

WRESTLING WITH GOD TIMELINE

Now & Jan 31	Begin recruiting for your group using the Five Circles of Life.
Jan 31	Small Group Connection
Feb 7	*Wrestling with God* begins
	Last chance sign-ups
Week of Feb 28	Mid-campaign Host Meeting with Your Coach

CHILDCARE OPTIONS

OPTIONS 1–4 COULD CALL FOR THE CHILDREN TO MEET AT A DIFFERENT LOCATION FROM THE GROUP

1. Recruit someone to do children's ministry while your group is meeting.

2. Hire a babysitter. Have each member pitch in.

   NOTE: *Be generous to your sitter. You want them back. If you cheat them, word will spread! The rule of thumb among small groups has been $5 per family.*

3. Allow older children to supervise younger children.

4. Have group members trade off in watching the children.

5. Allow the children to take part in the group. Offer topics and activities where everyone can participate.

6. Have each member arrange for their own childcare.

   NOTE: *The harder it is for new members to arrange childcare, the less likely it is that they will join.*

SMALL GROUP CONNECTION

SUNDAY, JANUARY 31

WHAT TO HAVE AT YOUR TABLE

1. Yourself or a group representative after all three services on Sunday, January 31.

2. A sign with your group: Location, Day of the Week, and Group Type (Couples, Singles, Men, etc.).

3. An information sheet with your name, address, and phone number, the date your group will start, and directions to your meeting place.

4. Registration form to sign up group members.

INSTRUCTIONS

1. List all group members.

2. Do not put your names on the form. They're already there!

3. Leave a copy with People Connect after the Connection.

4. Pick up your small group curriculum when you drop off your form.

LEADING FOR THE FIRST TIME

As a new group leader, there are a few things to think about as you go into your first meeting. In fact, there may be too many things to think about. Focus on the basics and you will have a great first meeting.

PREPARE

As the leader of this group, you don't have to be the expert. If you're using video-based curriculum, there's your expert, so let the video teaching lead the way. Otherwise, just follow along with the instructions in your study guide. Before the meeting it's a good idea to review the video and the discussion questions yourself. The videos are only seven or eight minutes long. Then just read through the questions.

If you find your group doesn't have time to complete the entire discussion guide, that's okay. Prioritize the questions for the time you have available. As you get to know the group, choose questions that are appropriate for the group. If your group has been together for a while, or if your group members are well beyond the basics, then maybe skip the first question and go for the second question, which might be more of an accountability question regarding what they committed to do in the previous meeting.

PRAY FOR YOUR GROUP

If you feel anxious, or even inadequate, about leading the group, that is perfectly normal, especially if you are leading for the first time. The Bible says, "Do not be anxious about anything, but in every situation, by prayer and petition, with thanksgiving, present your requests to God. And the peace of God, which transcends all understanding, will guard your hearts and your minds in Christ Jesus" (Phil. 4:6–7, NIV). So how often should you pray? Pray every time you feel anxious. God will give you peace.

The video and discussion guide are pretty easy to use. It's practically a no-brainer. But just because the curriculum is easy to use doesn't mean you should go into the meeting "cold" spiritually. Commit the meeting to God. Invite his presence into your meeting, then watch him work.

GUIDING THE DISCUSSION—NOT A TEACHER, MORE OF A REFEREE

While everyone should have a chance to share their thoughts and experiences, as the leader your job is to facilitate a discussion, not to teach a class. You want to make sure everyone gets their word in. You also want to make sure no one dominates the discussion. If someone tends to jump in on every question, politely say, "Now, on this next question let's hear from a few of you who haven't had a chance to share." If the person dominating the meeting continues to do this, then you might need to talk to them outside of the group meeting.

You as the leader prepared ahead of time for the lesson, but don't count on all of the group members preparing ahead for this meeting. Remember, they are assigned two extensive lessons in the workbook each week. When you ask the discussion questions, it may take the group members a couple of seconds to put their thoughts together. That's okay. Don't feel that as the leader you need to fill the silence. Let them think a minute.

PRAYING TOGETHER AS A GROUP

Habits are hard to break and sometimes hard to start. Changing attitudes and behaviors requires more than just willpower. It requires God's power. At the end of every meeting subgroup into groups of three to four people, so everyone can talk about their needs, and then pray together. In a large group, some people won't share, and it will take a much longer time, so subgrouping is necessary.

Also, limit the prayer requests to what is personally affecting the group member. Now, they may be concerned about Aunt Gertrude's big toe or something they read about on the internet, but this really isn't the place to discuss that. As much as you can, keep the focus of the prayer time on the changes group members need to make related to the subject of the lesson.

ASK FOR VOLUNTEERS

Don't lead the group alone. Just because you are the designated leader, you do not need to do everything for the group. In fact, delegate as much as you possibly can: the refreshments, the home you meet in, and even leading the discussion. If you do this right, you might only need to lead for the first session, and others will lead for the rest.

As group members become more involved in the leadership, they will feel a stronger sense of ownership in the group. Pretty soon the group will go from being "your group" to being "our group."

RECOMMENDED READING

Cole, Neil. *Organic Church: Growing Faith Where Life Happens.* San Francisco: Jossey-Bass, 2005.

Comisky, Joel. *How to Be a GREAT Cell Group Coach.* Houston: Cell Group Resources, 2001.

Donahue, Bill, and Russ Robinson. *Building a Life-Changing Small Group Ministry.* Grand Rapids: Zondervan, 2012.

George, Carl F. *Nine Keys to Effective Small Group Leadership.* Taylors, SC: Metachurch.com, 2007.

George, Carl. *Prepare Your Church for the Future.* Grand Rapids: Revell, 1992.

Gladen, Steve. *Small Groups with Purpose: How to Create Healthy Communities.* Grand Rapids: Baker, 2011.

Gladwell, Malcolm. *The Tipping Point.* New York: Back Bay Books, 2002.

Mosley, Eddie. *Connecting in Communities: Understanding the Dynamics of Small Groups.* Colorado Springs: NavPress, 2011.

Myers, Joseph R.. *The Search to Belong: Rethinking Intimacy, Community, and Small Groups.* Grand Rapids: Zondervan, 2003.

Stetzer, Ed, and Eric Geiger. *Transformational Groups: Creating a New Scorecard for Groups.* Nashville: B&H Publishing Group, 2014.

Zempel, Heather. *Community Is Messy: The Perils and Promise of Small Group Ministry.* Downers Grove, IL: InterVarsity, 2012.

ABOUT THE AUTHOR

Allen White has devoted more than twenty-five years to helping people find Christ, make meaningful connections, grow in their faith, and find fulfillment in ministry. He has successfully launched hundreds of groups at two churches as the Associate Pastor: New Life Christian Center in Turlock, California (fifteen years), and Brookwood Church in Simpsonville, South Carolina (four years). Additionally, in his work with Brett Eastman and Lifetogether, Allen has coached hundreds of churches of all sizes and denominations over the last ten years. In his coaching, Allen has seen thousands of groups launched with tens of thousands of people connected. It has been a great privilege and a wild ride.

A sought-after speaker, Allen has taught workshops for local churches as well as speaking at the Purpose Driven Church Conference at Saddleback Church, the BASS Church Workers Convention, the Willow Creek Association—Canada, and many others.

Allen has a B.A. in Biblical Studies and Missions and an M.Div. in Christian Education. Most of what he has learned has come through the school of hard knocks: many lessons have been learned through trying new things, failing, and trying again.

Allen, his wife Tiffany, and their four children live in the Greenville, South Carolina, area.

For more information about Allen's ministry, visit allenwhite.org.

NOTES

1. Rick Warren, *The Purpose Driven Church* (Grand Rapids: Zondervan, 1995), 326.

2. Warren, *Purpose Driven Church*, 378.

3. Steve Gladen, *Small Groups with Purpose: How to Create Healthy Communities* (Grand Rapids: Baker, 2011), 160.

4. Carl F. George, *Prepare Your Church for the Future* (Grand Rapids: Revell, 1992), 170.

5. Michael C. Mack, *The Synergy Church: A Strategy for Integrating Small Groups and Sunday School* (Grand Rapids: Baker, 1996), 182.

6. Exodus 18:6, 14–18.

7. Exodus 18:21.

8. Exodus 18:21–23.

9. Steve Rudd, "The Exodus Route," *The Interactive Bible*, http://www.bible.ca/archeology/bible-archeology-exodus-route-population-of-jews-hebrews.htm.

10. Exodus 18:23–27.

11. Peter Drucker, *Peter Drucker on the Profession of Management* (Boston: Harvard Business Review Publishing, 1998), 27.

12. The ministry application of Drucker's principles was introduced to me by Carl George. Carl, in turn, was relating some thoughts brought into the church growth movement by Bob Logan.

13. Jim Collins, *Built to Last* (New York: Harper Collins, 2011), 43ff.

14. Brett Eastman, "The Power and Potential of Small Groups," *Enrichment Journal* (Winter 2008), http://enrichmentjournal.ag.org/200801/200801_090_SmallGroups.cfm.

15. Matthew 19:26.

16. John Ortberg, *If You Want to Walk on Water, You've Got to Get Out of the Boat* (Grand Rapids: Zondervan, 2002).

17. Walter Martin, *The Kingdom of the Cults* (Minneapolis: Bethany, 1985), 307.

18. Robert Wuthnow, *Sharing the Journey: Support Groups and America's Quest for Community* (New York: The Free Press, 1994), 229.

19. Wuthnow, *Sharing the Journey*, 229.

20. Wuthnow, *Sharing the Journey*, 229.

21. Ed Stetzer and Eric Geiger, *Transformational Groups: Creating a New Scorecard for Groups* (Nashville: B&H Publishing Group, 2014), 45.

22. Wuthnow, *Sharing the Journey*, 229.

23. Wuthnow, *Sharing the Journey*, 320.

24. Stetzer and Geiger, *Transformational Groups*, 45.

25. Wuthnow, *Sharing the Journey*, 229.

26. Gladen, *Small Groups with Purpose*, 55–56.

27. Andy Stanley, *The Principle of the Path* (Nashville: Nelson, 2008), 14.

28. John 10:10.

29. Joseph R. Myers, *The Search to Belong: Rethinking Intimacy, Community, and Small Groups* (Grand Rapids: Zondervan, 2003), 9–10.

30. If you find a unique solution and would like to share what is working in your congregation, I would be delighted to hear from you. Send me an email at allen@allenwhite.org.

31. Myers, *The Search to Belong*, 142.

32. Myers, *The Search to Belong*, 142–43.

33. Myers, *The Search to Belong*, 143.

34. Myers, *The Search to Belong*, 143.

35. Myers, *The Search to Belong*, 62–72.

36. Malcolm Gladwell, *The Tipping Point* (New York: Back Bay Books, 2002), 176–77.

37. Blair Carlstrom, "Small Groups May be Overrated," *Church Executive*, February 2005, http://webpages.charter.net/allensbooks/Article%20Archives/Small%20groups%20may%20be%20overrated%20by%20Blair%20Carlstrom.htm.

38. Robin Yapp, "Friends Who Last a Lifetime," *The Daily Mail*, http://www.dailymail.co.uk/femail/article-202987/Friends-lifetime.html.

39. Leith Anderson, *The Church for the 21st Century* (Minneapolis: Bethany, 1992), 136.

40. Matthew 28:19.

41. Myers, *The Search to Belong*, 10.

42. Matthew 18:20.

43. Steve Gladen, *Leading Small Groups with Purpose: Everything You Need to Lead a Healthy Group* (Grand Rapids: Baker, 2012), 159–61.

44. Hebrews 3:13.

45. James 1:27.

46. Everett M. Rogers, *Diffusion of Innovations, Fifth Edition* (New York: Free Press, 2003), 168–218.

47. Rogers, *Diffusion of Innovations*, 177.

48. Rogers, *Diffusion of Innovations*, 183.

49. Rogers, *Diffusion of Innovations*, 282–86.

50. 1 Corinthians 13:5.

51. Matthew 28:19.

52. Genesis 1:4–31.

53. Genesis 2:18.

54. Genesis 1:28.

55. Deuteronomy 7:6.

56. John 6:70.

57. Colossians 3:12; 1 Peter 2:9.

58. Acts 5:42.

59. Acts 2:42–47.

60. Bill Hybels, *Axiom: Powerful Leadership Proverbs* (Grand Rapids: Zondervan, 2008), 94.

61. Rick Warren, *The Purpose Driven Life: What On Earth Am I Here For?* (Grand Rapids: Zondervan, 2002), 213.

62. Andy Stanley, *Managing Tension*, Andy Stanley Leadership Podcast, n.d., http://www.stitcher.com/podcast/andy-stanley-leadership-podcast/e /managing-tension-37211513.

63. Romans 12:4–5.

64. Galatians 6:2.

65. Galatians 6:5.

66. Ephesians 4:15.

67. Galatians 6:2.

68. 1 Corinthians 13:5.

69. Hebrews 3:13.

70. Colossians 2:10.

71. Philippians 1:6.

72. Matthew 28:19–20.

73. Steve Gladen, "Session 2" in *Leadership Training One* (Trabuco Canyon, CA: Small Group Leadership Training Kit, n.d.).

74. John Maxwell, *The 21 Irrefutable Laws of Leadership* (Nashville: Thomas Nelson, 2007), 1.